ELEMENTS OF METAPHYSICS

Samaṃ sarveshu bhûteshu tishṭhantaṃ parameçvaram,
Vinaçyatsu avinaçyantam yaḥ paçyati, sa paçyati !
Samaṃ paçyan hi sarvatra samavasthitam îçvaram
Na hinasti âtmanâ âtmânaṃ. Tatô yâti parâṃ gatim.

Qui videt, ut cunctis animantibus insidet idem
  Rex et, dum pereunt, haud perit—ille videt !
Nocet enim, sese dum cernit in omnibus ipsum,
  Ipse nocere sibi: quo via summa patet.

                    Çrî-Bhagavad-Gîtâsu, xiii. 27, 28.

THE ELEMENTS

OF

METAPHYSICS

BEING A GUIDE FOR LECTURES AND PRIVATE USE

BY

Dr. PAUL DEUSSEN

PROFESSOR ORDINARIUS OF PHILOSOPHY AT THE UNIVERSITY OF KIEL, GERMANY

TRANSLATED FROM THE SECOND GERMAN EDITION
WITH THE PERSONAL COLLABORATION OF THE AUTHOR

By C. M. DUFF

WITH AN APPENDIX, CONTAINING THE AUTHOR'S ADDRESS BEFORE
THE BOMBAY BRANCH OF THE ROYAL ASIATIC SOCIETY

ON THE PHILOSOPHY OF THE VEDÂNTA

IN ITS RELATIONS TO OCCIDENTAL METAPHYSICS

REPRINTED FROM THE ORIGINAL EDITION, BOMBAY 1893

London

MACMILLAN AND CO.

AND NEW YORK

1894

All rights reserved

PREFACE TO THE FIRST EDITION
(1877)

THE nature of things — as it reveals itself to the searching eye, immeasurable around, and unfathomable within, us — is one and at harmony with itself. Therefore truth also, as the reflection of that which is in the mirror of the human mind, must be for all times and countries one and the same; and whatever the great teachers of mankind in ancient and modern time have gathered from the immediate contemplation of nature and revealed in the form either of religion or philosophy, that must (apart from errors, which as a rule touch only what is specific and incidental) be essentially concordant, however varied may be the outward hues and forms it has received from the civilisations and traditions of different ages. If, therefore, we but succeed in gaining the point of view from which the essence of things is dissolved without residuum in understanding, we may expect that, regarded from this point, all revelations of the past also will inwardly harmonise and be reconciled.

This STANDPOINT OF THE RECONCILIATION OF ALL CONTRADICTIONS has been attained in the main, we believe, by mankind in the Idealism founded by Kant and wrought out to perfection by his disciple Schopenhauer. For the truth of this Idealism is the more indubitably confirmed, the more deeply we penetrate into it, by the threefold harmony which we meet in it,—harmony with itself, harmony with nature, and harmony with the thoughts of the wisest of all times. Moreover it is the Kantian distinction between phenomena and the thing-in-itself, and this distinction alone, which makes it possible to give full freedom of action to the natural sciences in their tendency to complete materialism, and yet, by way of the most convincing proofs, to attain to a philosophical view of things in which all essential saving truths of religion are obtained from the mere analysis of the facts of inner experience, and which will in course of time be acknowledged for what it actually is—a regenerated and purified Christianity, constructed on an indisputably scientific foundation.

From the above standpoint and with the closest possible adherence to the thoughts of those immortal teachers, though without in any respect renouncing independence of judgment, the present book aims at separating the imperishable substance of this teaching from its temporal and individual husk, and at exhibiting it, for use in school and life, as systematically, clearly, and shortly as the profundity of the subject will allow. At the same time it seeks to point out the inner harmony of this doctrine with the most important thought-systems of the past, in particular with the Brahmavidyâ of the Indians, with Plato's doctrine of Ideas, and with the theology of Christianity. The justification of the historical views on which these parallels are based, must be reserved for another occasion.

The book, having originated in connection with lectures and being in the first instance intended for these, is adapted to the horizon of students; hence its encyclopædic character; hence also the interspersed quotations, which are meant to incite to the study of the original languages, without which a full understanding of Indian, Biblical, and Greek metaphysics is scarcely possible. Apart from these the work contains nothing but what might be accessible, by a little effort of thought, to every educated mind, more especially after the whole has been read through a second time, when, what has hitherto been obscure will become perfectly clear, and indeed the whole will first appear in its true light. The table of contents, forming a series of questions on all the chief points of philosophy, is designed to facilitate repetition and meditation, which should be unremittingly practised.

P. D.

The first edition appeared 1877, the second, with a few additions, 1890. The appendix, "On the Philosophy of the Vedânta in its relations to Occidental Metaphysics," reprinted here from the original edition (Bombay, 1893) in order to elucidate the parallels of Indian Philosophy scattered through the work, is in the main an abstract of the author's larger book: "Das System des Vedânta, nach den Brahma-sûtra's des Bâdarâyaṇa und dem Commentare des Çañkara über dieselben, als ein Compendium der Dogmatik des Brahmanismus vom Standpunkte des Çañkara aus" (Leipzig, 1883).

CONTENTS

PRELIMINARY REMARKS

PHYSICS AND METAPHYSICS 1
    Two standpoints (§ 1). Common source (§ 2).
    Method and result of the physical method (§ 3).
    Method and result of the metaphysical method (§ 4).
    Synopsis of all the general sciences (§ 5).
    Historical (§ 6).

A. THE EMPIRICAL STANDPOINT

SYSTEM OF PHYSICS

1. ON SPACE 7
    Its infinity (§ 7). Everything in space (§ 8).

2. ON TIME 7
    Its infinity (§ 9). Everything in time (§ 10).

3. ON MATTER 8
    Everything is material; two proofs (§ 11).
    Matter is uncreatable and indestructible (§ 12).
    The world is either infinitely great or infinitely small (§ 13).

4. ON CAUSALITY 9
    Persistence and change (§ 14). The law of causality (§ 15).

	PAGE

Cause and causal constituents (§ 16).
Arguing from effect to cause, from cause to effect; hypothesis and experiment (§ 17).
Two corollaries of the law of causality (§ 18).
The net of causality is without beginning and end (§ 19).
Three forms of causation: cause, irritation, motive (§ 20).

5. ON NATURAL FORCES 12
Laws of nature *a priori* and *a posteriori* (§ 21).
Groups of phenomena and natural forces (§ 22).
Empirically speaking, natural forces do not exist (§ 23).
Causality is no bridge between force-manifestations and force (§ 24).
Threefold object of the empirical sciences in the region of nature and history (§ 25).

6. MATERIALISM AS THE CONSEQUENCE OF THE EMPIRICAL VIEW OF THINGS 14
Everything, also the intellect, is modification of matter (§ 26).
Complete dependence of thinking on the brain (§ 27).
Rejection of spiritualism (§ 28).

7. COMFORTLESSNESS OF THE EMPIRICAL VIEW OF NATURE . 16
The right and the wrong of materialism (§§ 29, 30).

B. THE TRANSCENDENTAL STANDPOINT

SYSTEM OF METAPHYSICS

THE SYSTEM OF METAPHYSICS

PART I. THE THEORY OF UNDERSTANDING

1. PRELIMINARY SURVEY 18
Perceptual and abstract representations: Understanding and Reason (§§ 31-33).

CONTENTS

	PAGE
Difference between human and animal Understanding (§ 34).	
Physiological organ of the Understanding and of the Reason (§ 35).	
Significance and danger of rational knowledge for metaphysics (§ 36).	

2. THE PROBLEM OF PERCEPTUAL KNOWLEDGE . . . 21

    How is perception by the senses possible? (§ 37).

3. THE WORLD IS MY REPRESENTATION 22

    The one indubitable truth.
    The Cartesian form of it (§ 38).
    Significance of this truth (§ 39).
    Repugnance to it (§ 40).

4. WHETHER THINGS IN THEMSELVES ARE THE SAME AS I REPRESENT THEM? 24

    Voices from Indian, Greek, and Christian antiquity denying this (§ 41).

5. ELEMENTS OF REPRESENTATION *A PRIORI* AND *A POSTERIORI* 25

    No subject without an object, no object without a subject (§ 42).
    The immediate and the mediate object (§ 43).
    To what the data of *a posteriori* knowledge are restricted (§§ 44, 45).

6. CLUES TO THE DISCRIMINATION OF THE *A PRIORI* ELEMENTS IN REPRESENTATIONS 27

    The six criteria of the *a priori* elements (§ 46).

7. THE *A PRIORI* ELEMENTS ARE: TIME, SPACE, AND CAUSALITY 30

    Witnesses from Indian, Platonic, and Biblical metaphysics (§ 47).

		PAGE
8.	SPACE IS AN *A PRIORI* FORM OF PERCEPTION	32

  Explanation of this truth (§ 48).
  Six proofs: *ex antecessione* (§ 49), *ex adhaesione* (§ 50), *e necessitate* (§ 51), *e mathematicis* (§ 52), *e continuitate* (§ 53), *ex infinitate* (§ 54).

| 9. | TIME IS AN *A PRIORI* FORM OF PERCEPTION | 35 |

  Explanation of this truth (§ 55).
  Six proofs: *ex antecessione* (§ 56), *ex adhaesione* (§ 57), *e necessitate* (§ 58), *e mathematicis* (§ 59), *e continuitate* (§ 60), *ex infinitate* (§ 61).

| 10. | CAUSALITY IS AN *A PRIORI* FORM OF PERCEPTION | 39 |

  Explanation of this truth (§ 62).
  Six proofs: *ex antecessione* (§ 63), *ex adhaesione* (§ 64), *e necessitate*, Hume and Kant (§ 65), *e mathematicis* (§ 66), *e continuitate* (§ 67), *ex infinitate* (§ 68).

| 11. | THE EMPIRICAL AND THE TRANSCENDENTAL STANDPOINTS | 46 |

  Recapitulation of the above (§ 69).
  Three possible standpoints as regards it (§ 70): the empirical (§ 71), the transcendent (§ 72), and the transcendental (§ 73).

| 12. | TRANSCENDENTAL ANALYSIS OF EMPIRICAL REALITY | 51 |

  Origin of perception through the threefold reaction of the Understanding (§§ 74, 75).
  The nature of empirical reality (§ 76). The fundamental doctrine of Idealism (§ 77).
  Sense-perception impossible without the Understanding (§§ 78, 79).

| 13. | ON THE IMMEDIATE AND MEDIATE APPLICATION OF THE UNDERSTANDING | 56 |

  The faculty of immediate (receptive) and that of mediate (spontaneous) reaction is one and the same (§§ 80, 81).

	PAGE
14. WHETHER THERE ARE INNATE IDEAS?	58

    No innate ideas, but only three innate functions of the brain (§§ 82, 83).

15. THE THEORY OF DREAMING	59

    System of the conscious will. Its action in a waking state, in sleep (§ 84).
    Origin of dreams (§ 85).

16. TRANSCENDENTAL ANALYSIS OF MATTER	62

    Decomposition of bodies into force and space (§ 86).
    Matter as the objective correlative of the Understanding; Plato's view (§§ 87, 88).

17. THE DOUBLE WORLD OF THE HALF-PHILOSOPHERS	64

    The evasion of Ideal-Realism (§§ 89, 90). Its inadmissibility (§ 91).

18. KANT AND THE PHILOSOPHY AFTER HIM	66

    Kantism before Kant; Kant's fundamental dogma (§ 92).
    Division of all philosophers present and future into four classes (§§ 93, 94).

APPENDIX TO THE FIRST PART OF METAPHYSICS

REASON AND ITS CONTENT

19. SURVEY	68

    The Content of Reason (§ 95). Concepts and words (§§ 96-98).

20. ORIGIN AND NATURE OF CONCEPTS	70

    The property of nature on which depends the possibility of forming concepts (§ 99).
    Example of the ascent from percepts to specific concepts (§§ 100-102), from specific to generic (§ 103). Categories (§ 104). Pyramids of the system of concepts (§ 105).

21. ON COMBINATIONS OF CONCEPTS 74

 Judgments (§ 106). Synthetic judgments *a priori* (§ 107). The nature of the proposition (§ 108); of the conclusion (§ 109); of the proof (§ 110).
 Source of all concepts and judgments (§ 111). Misconception of this (§ 112).

22. WHETHER THE REASON IS A PARTICULAR PHYSIOLOGICAL ORGAN? 79

 The organ of perceiving and thinking is one and the same. Four reasons (§§ 113-115).
 Unity of function in understanding and judgment. Memory (§ 116).

23. RETROSPECTIVE VIEW OF THE HUMAN MIND IN GENERAL   83

 The intellect is physical, not metaphysical (§ 117).
 Organisation of the intellectual faculties (§ 118).

24. MAN AND BRUTE 84

 Difference between animal and human understanding (§§ 119, 120).
 All superiority of man due to it (§§ 121-124).
 Value of abstract knowledge in practical life; its limits (§ 125).

25. ON THE NATURE AND ORIGIN OF LANGUAGE . . . 88

 Twofold task of language. Derivation from it of three classes of language (§§ 126-128).
 A hypothesis as to the origin of language (§§ 129, 130).
 The instinct of speech (§ 131).

THE SYSTEM OF METAPHYSICS

PART II. THE METAPHYSICS OF NATURE

1. THE PROBLEM 93

 Fundamental question of all philosophy; its meaning (§ 132).

Fundamental error of all philosophy previous to Kant
(§§ 133, 134).
Identity of force, principle, and thing-in-itself (§§ 135, 136).
How Kant closed to us the inner being of nature, and how Schopenhauer found the key to it (§§ 137-140).

2. NATURE, VIEWED FROM THE STANDPOINT OF PURE INTELLECT, THAT IS, FROM WITHOUT . . . 98

Gradual obscuration of nature in proportion as one passes from the *a priori* to the *a posteriori* in it; sudden light (§§ 141-145).

3. THE WAY INTO THE INTERIOR OF NATURE . . . 103

The intellect in face of external and of internal experience (§§ 146, 147).
Inner identity of bodily movement, volition, Will (§ 148).
Inner identity of body and Will. What is Will? (§ 149).

4. CONSCIOUS AND UNCONSCIOUS WILL . . . 107

Two kinds of organic functions (§ 150).
Both are manifestations of the same force; three reasons (§ 151).
Identity of vital force, soul, Will (§ 152).
Man his own work (§ 153).

5. ON THE SOUL AND ITS RELATION TO THE BODY . . 112

The soul is not intellect, but Will; five reasons (§ 154).
The immortality of the soul proved (§§ 155-157).
The marvel of the organism explained (§ 158).

6. THE WILL IN NATURE 116

The ego from without, representation; from within, Will (§ 159).
Extension of this truth to other men (§ 160).
The Will as brute (§ 161).
Two fundamental impulses of all organic beings (§ 162).
Nature of sleep (§ 163).
Nature of instinct, its occurrence in nature (§ 164).

The principle of vegetable life is an unconscious willing (§ 165).
Differences between organic and inorganic forces derived from the principles of the phenomenal world (§ 166).

7. TRANSCENDENT REFLECTIONS ON WILL AS THE THING-IN-ITSELF 125
Three determinations of Will as thing-in-itself (§§ 167, 168).
Preliminary remark on the affirmation and denial of the Will (§ 169).

8. MYTHICAL REPRESENTATION OF THE WORLD-PROCESS . 129
An attempt to portray in the forms of our intellect what in its nature transcends these (§§ 170-174).

9. GOD AND WORLD 132
The metaphysical truth as one and the same for all (§ 175).
Outlines of Indian metaphysics (§ 176).
Development of the Biblical view of things (§ 177).
Chief points of Greek metaphysics up to the time of Plato (§ 178).

10. THE WILL AND THE IDEAS OF PLATO 140
The Ideas as the adaptation of the Will to the forms of the phenomenal world (§§ 179-181).
Contradictory character and inadequacy of the Ideas (§ 182).

11. THE OBJECTIFICATION OF THE WILL IN NATURE BY MEANS OF THE IDEAS 144
Enumeration of the physical, chemical, and organic forces (§ 183).
The Will and the Brahman of the Indians (§ 184).
Relation of the physical and chemical forces to matter. Generation of inorganic bodies. On the atomic theory (§§ 185-187).
Organic forces; their difference from the inorganic.

Two fundamental impulses of all organic beings; why?
First origin of organisms.
The Right and the Wrong of Darwinism.
Three grades of organisms (§§ 188-190).

12. ON THE TELEOLOGICAL VIEW OF NATURE AND ITS LIMITS . . 156

Adaptation, internal, external; whence? (§§ 191, 192).
Struggle of individuals; moral and æsthetic consequences (§§ 193, 194).

THE SYSTEM OF METAPHYSICS

PART III. THE METAPHYSICS OF THE BEAUTIFUL

1. HISTORICAL 161

   On the inner nature of Platonism.
   Plato's attitude towards art (§ 195).
   Aristotle's view as to the aim and action of art (§ 196).
   Kant's definition of the feeling for the beautiful (§ 197).

2. THE ÆSTHETIC PHENOMENON CONSIDERED FROM THE EMPIRICAL STANDPOINT 167

   A disinterested delight is empirically inexplicable (§§ 198, 199).

3. INDIVIDUAL AND ÆSTHETIC CONTEMPLATION . . . 169

   Two standpoints of thinking, two of perceiving (§§ 200, 201).
   Æsthetic mode of contemplation: the change which it occasions in the subject (§ 202), and in the object (§§ 203, 204).

4. SUBJECTIVE CONDITIONS OF THE ÆSTHETIC PHENOMENON 173

   Escape from self, how possible by increase of Understanding (§§ 205, 206).
   Second way thither (§ 207); Indian voices (§ 208).
   Not willing, but individual willing, vanishes (§ 209).

	PAGE
5. OBJECTIVE CONDITIONS OF THE ÆSTHETIC PHENOMENON	177

    Escape from self through the nature of objects (§§ 210-212).

    How explicable (§ 213).

    Change in the object when contemplated (§ 214).

    Origin of art (§ 215).

6. ON THE BEAUTIFUL AND THE SUBLIME 183

    Definition of beauty (§ 216).

    One-sidedness of our view of nature (§ 217).

    The sublime as key to the beautiful.

    Two kinds of the sublime.

    Two contrasts to it (§ 218).

7. ON THE BEAUTIFUL IN NATURE 188

    Three subjective aids to the contemplation of nature (§ 219).

    Beauty of inorganic nature (§§ 220, 221).

    Beauty of organisms (§ 222).

    Grace (§ 223).

    Beauty of artificial products, wherein consisting (§ 224).

8. SOME REMARKS ON THE BEAUTIFUL IN ART . . . 194

    On the inner nature of art. Spurious and genuine art (§ 225).

    ARCHITECTURE: Symmetry, adaptation; which Ideas are the object of architecture. Classic and Gothic architecture (§ 226).

    Imitating and interpreting arts (§ 227).

    Chief object of art (§ 228).

    The beautiful and the characteristic (§ 229).

    SCULPTURE: Significance. Advantages. Limits. Tendency (§ 230).

    PAINTING: Restriction and freedom. Its strength, wherein consisting (§ 231).

    External and internal significance; historical painting (§ 232).

POETRY: Material. Artifices. Allegory. Metre and rhyme (§ 233).
    Chief subject of poetry. The idealisation of reality.
    Poetry more philosophical than history (§ 234).
    The lyric. The epic. The drama. Tragedy and comedy (§ 235).

MUSIC: its subject. Direct nature of its language.
    Significance of melody, rhythm, harmony. Music and text (§ 236).
    Parting glance at art: how far one may find in it, in spite of its speaking only of this world, the promise of another (§ 237).

THE SYSTEM OF METAPHYSICS

PART IV. THE METAPHYSICS OF MORALITY

1. PRELIMINARY 221
    Twofold standpoint of thinking, perceiving, acting (§§ 238-242).
    Whether morality is a special kind of knowledge (§ 243).
    Order of procedure: Immortality, freedom, affirmation and denial (§ 244).

2. ON THE IMMORTALITY OF THE SOUL 229
    Kant's idealism and the immortality of the soul stand and fall together (§§ 245-247).
    Life is assured to the Will and the present assured to life (§ 248).
    Indestructibility without continuance conceived as transmigration of the soul.
    Half-mythical conception of the continuance of the individuality (§§ 249, 250).

3. ON THE FREEDOM OF THE WILL 236
    The question of the freedom of the Will as a prelude to the Kantian philosophy (§ 251).
    Necessity, chance, freedom (§§ 252, 253).

Physical determinism, metaphysical freedom of the Will (§§ 254, 255).
Three great transcendental truths (§ 256).
Identity of the metaphysical and the moral dualism (§ 257).

4. THE PAGAN AND THE CHRISTIAN STANDPOINTS, OR THE AFFIRMATION AND THE DENIAL OF THE WILL TO LIFE. 244

Exoteric and esoteric Christianity (§ 258).
Why must theology inevitably be founded on Kant (§ 259).
The deeds of morality are miracles (§ 260).
Division of all human actions into four classes (§ 261).

5. EGOISM AS THE GENERAL AND NECESSARY PHENOMENAL FORM OF THE AFFIRMATION OF THE WILL TO LIFE . 250

Proof of this truth; two important conclusions (§ 262).
All nature lies under the curse of egoism (§ 263).
Derivation of malice from egoism (§ 264).
Seeming egoism of moral actions (§ 265).

6. THE EGOISM OF AFFIRMATION AS THE SOURCE OF THE BAD 255

Moral illustration of the fundamental impulses, nourishment and generation (§ 266).
Restriction of the concepts wrong, right, and duty (§ 267).
The sphere of egoism (§ 268); in man threefold (§ 269).
Wrong: three kinds. How far conventional? Two means (§ 270).
The root of badness; testimony of Holy Scripture (§ 271).

7. THE EGOISM OF AFFIRMATION AS THE SOURCE OF EVIL . 265

Suffering is not the cause of denial (§ 272).
Existence is empty, hopeless, aimless, without peace (§ 273).
Three kinds of suffering according to the Sâñkhya System (§ 274).
Outlook over experience; a consoling voice (§ 275).

		PAGE

8. TEMPORAL MEASURES AGAINST THE BADNESS AND EVIL SPRINGING FROM EGOISM 273

    Concept of right (§ 276); of the state, threefold task of it (§ 277).

    Education: two aims, limits (§ 278). Politeness (§ 279).

9. LEGALITY AND MORALITY 278

    Worthlessness of good works (§ 280).

    Form of this doctrine in *Biblical* and *Indian* theology (§ 281).

    Four fundamental truths of Christian teaching and our own; how far moral improvement is independent of ourselves, and how far it is yet our own work (§ 282).

10. ON THE NATURE OF THE DENIAL OF THE WILL TO LIFE 286

    Why the nature of morality is called denial (§ 283).

    Proof that the essence of every moral action is an act of denial of the Will to life (§§ 284, 285).

11. THE TWO WAYS TO DENIAL 291

    Two ways; common characteristics, differences (§ 286).

    The peculiar way in which the inconceivable deeds of denial clothe themselves in the forms of our knowledge (§§ 287, 288).

        1. THE WAY OF VIRTUE (§ 289).

    First step: *Justice.* Two kinds (§ 290).

    Second step: *Love.* Three kinds (§ 291).

    Third step: *Asceticism.* When only genuine? Its derivation from compassion.

    The real significance of asceticism.

    On the Christian doctrine of salvation (§ 292).

        2. THE WAY OF SUFFERING. Suffering as an element of affirmation.

    Suffering in the light of denial (§ 293).

    On the ultimate root of morality (§ 294).

    On suicide: proof that it is affirmation (§ 295).

    The significance of death (§ 296).

	PAGE
12. ON THE PRINCIPLE OF DENIAL	311

Freedom, faith, knowledge, as principles of denial (§ 297).

How the principle of denial may be aptly named, and what it is in its innermost nature. A glance at the Biblical conception (§ 298).

Twofold trace of the divine in experience (§ 299).

CONCLUSION (§ 300) 317

APPENDIX

ON THE PHILOSOPHY OF THE VEDÂNTA IN ITS RELATIONS TO OCCIDENTAL METAPHYSICS

Introduction	323
I. Theology, the doctrine of God or of the philosophical principle	326
II. Kosmology, the doctrine of the world	328
III. Psychology, the doctrine of the soul	332
IV. Eschatology, the doctrine of the last things, the things after death	334

PRELIMINARY REMARKS

PHYSICS AND METAPHYSICS

§ 1. There are two standpoints, and two only, from which we can investigate the nature of things: the empirical and the transcendental.

We are restricted to the empirical standpoint so long as we regard things in the form in which they appear to us, that is, as they are reflected in human consciousness; the result is **physics** (in its broader or ancient sense). From the transcendental standpoint we try to discover what things are in themselves, that is independent of, and apart from, our consciousness, in which they are represented; the result is **metaphysics**.

§ 2. All our knowledge begins with *perception*, which is partly external, partly internal.

Out of both these is built up that sum total of our representations of things which we call *experience*. The empirical and the transcendental methods both proceed from experience, but they do so in different directions.

§ 3. The **empirical or physical method** takes the entire material of experience as given, and by investigating and systematically arranging it, arrives at a **system of physics** which embraces all sciences, whether they have their source in outer or inner experience.

All that we know through outer experience is body, that is, matter in time and space. The relations of time and space are investigated by **mathematics**, whilst the pursuit of matter in its transformations is the object of the **natural sciences,** which, as morphology (mineralogy, botany, zoology), deal with the forms of matter, as ætiology (physics, chemistry, physiology) with its changes and their causes. The science of inner experience is **psychology** (in the empirical sense). As it has for its subject the entire phenomena of inner perception, and accordingly embraces the whole domain of knowing, feeling, and willing, we may include under it logic (with grammar), æsthetics, and ethics, whilst side by side with these, as instances of the same, we may place the history of sciences, arts, and peoples.

§ 4. The **transcendental or metaphysical method** proceeds from the fact that the sum total of experience and of the empirical knowledge derived from it which forms the system of physics, is in reality neither more nor less than a series of representations in our consciousness. Accordingly its fundamental question has at all times been, what are things **in themselves** ($αὐτὰ\ καθ'\ αὐτά$, *âtman*), that is, apart from the form which they assume in our mind? To ascertain this, we have first to analyse the experience filling our intellect, and decide what part of it is **a priori**, that is, inherent in ourselves previous to all perception whether external or internal, and therefore belonging to the innate functions of the intellect itself; and what part we appropriate **a posteriori**, that is, by means of internal and external perception, and consequently have to regard as partaking of the nature of things in themselves. The results obtained by this method, together with their bearing on nature, art, and the action of man, form a **system of metaphysics**, which, supplementing the system of physics, gives us the utmost attainable interpretations of the nature of ourselves and the world.

Remark.—The term philosophy, the meaning of which has in course of time undergone considerable change and is even to-day disputed, denotes in its most limited sense metaphysics; in a wider sense metaphysics together with the sciences of inner experience, which are closely related to it; in its widest sense the general results of all sciences from the most universal point of view.

§ 5. Synopsis of all the General Sciences.

```
                              View of Things
              ┌──────────────────────────┴──────────────────────────┐
       Dependent on the intellect:                  Independent of the :
              Physics                                    Metaphysi
                                                   1. Theory of the under
                                                   2. Metaphysics of natur
                                                   3. Metaphysics of art.
                                                   4. Metaphysics of moral
       ┌──────────┴──────────┐                     ┌──────┴──────┐
    Outer experience :                              Inner experience :
                                                         │
                                                     Psychology
                                              ┌──────────┼──────────┐
 ┌────────┴────────┐                        Logic      Æsthetics    Ethics
 Time and space :   Material world :      (History of  (History of  (History of
   Mathematics      Natural Sciences      the Sciences)  the Arts)  Peoples)
Geometry, Arithmetic        │
                      ┌─────┴─────┐
                  Morphology   Ætiology
                      │           │
  rganic :       Organic :     Changes
  ralogy        Botany, Zoology    │
  logy          Anatomy       ┌────┼────┐
                         Non-essential: Essential: Organic:
                            Physics   Chemistry  Physiology
                           Astronomy              ┌────┴────┐
                                               of plants  of animals
```

§ 6. Historical.—Religion and Philosophy are the two forms in which from time immemorial metaphysics has manifested itself, bringing to light, especially in the Indian, Greek, and Christian world, an abundance of imperishable truths. Until, however, a century ago, there was no clear understanding of the difference between physical and metaphysical knowledge, and as metaphysics attempted to vindicate its truths from the empirical standpoint natural to man, these necessarily assumed a more or less allegorical form and fell into seeming contradiction with each other and with the physical sciences.

At last came **Kant** (1724-1804) and by his "Critique of Pure Reason" laid the foundations of thoroughly scientific metaphysics. On this basis **Schopenhauer** (1788-1860) has reared a metaphysical structure without equal, which, though it may in course of time be modified in details through the never-ending progress of the empirical sciences, will yet, as a whole, at no future time become antiquated, but must remain an inalienable possession of mankind.

If, guided by this doctrine, we seek to penetrate into the inner meaning of the various systems, religious and philosophical, we shall come to the conviction that the essential differences between natural science, philosophy, and religion originate after all in a misunderstanding which can be removed, and which will give way to a mutual recognition of their right of existence.

A. THE EMPIRICAL STANDPOINT

SYSTEM OF PHYSICS

I. On Space

§ 7. Proposition.— Space is infinite in every direction.

Demonstration.—If it were not so, it would have a limit. This would be either a body or a void, therefore again in both cases space. (Compare the instance of the javelin in *Lucretius, de natura rerum*, i. 968-983.)

§ 8. Corollary.—Whatever exists, exists necessarily in space; otherwise it would be nowhere and consequently not at all.

II. On Time

§ 9. Proposition.—Time is infinite in both directions.

Demonstration.—If it were not so, it would have a beginning or an end. Both would be points of time ("now"), would have as such a before and an after, and would consequently be within time and not outside of it.

§ 10. Corollary.—Whatever happens, happens necessarily in time; otherwise it would happen at no time, and consequently not at all.

III. On Matter

§ 11. Proposition.—In space and time exists nothing but matter alone.

Demonstration.—(1) That which operates in space and time we call matter. To exist is to operate in space and time. Consequently all that exists is material. (2) We call possible that which can be represented by us as existing. Only material objects can be represented by us as existing. Consequently there can be nothing but material objects.

§ 12. Proposition.—Matter is uncreatable and indestructible.

This is proved not so much from the experiments of scientists, for, even if it were possible to pursue matter, scale in hand, in its transformations, such experiments would only demonstrate that until now we have not succeeded either in augmenting or diminishing the quantity of matter. The proof of our assertion lies rather, apart from all perception (a priori), in the fact that it is impossible to imagine the creation or the annihilation of matter. And that which is not possible, cannot, in fact, really be at all.

§ 13. The quantity of matter in the world is either unlimited and consequently infinitely great, corresponding to infinite space, or limited, and then, compared with infinite space, infinitely small.

IV. On Causality

§ 14. Substance persists, but it perpetually changes its qualities, forms, and conditions (πάντα ῥεῖ). All these changes, without exception, are governed by the following law.

§ 15. The law of Causality.—Every change in matter is called effect and takes place only after another change, called cause, has preceded it, from which the effect regularly and inevitably, that is necessarily, follows.

§ 16. Inasmuch as an effect is only possible through some foregoing change (called cause) happening under a particular condition of things, which condition itself is but a result of changes, we include, in a wider sense, this condition together with the intervening change under the head of cause, and distinguish in it the different causal constituents or conditions. The sequence of these may in many cases vary.

§ 17. The same cause has always the same effect, while on the contrary the same effect may arise from different causes. Hence follows, that arguing from effect to cause is problematical, while arguing from cause to effect is certain. The former is the way of hypothesis, the latter that of experiment.

§ 18. Immediate corollaries of the law of causality are: (1) the law of inertia, for, where there is no cause, there can be no effect; (2) the law of the persistence of substance, for the law of causality applies only to conditions of matter but not to the substratum of all conditions, forms, and qualities.

§ 19. As space (§ 7) and time (§ 9) are without limits, so also the net of causality is necessarily without beginning or end.

Demonstration.—(a) If it were not without beginning, we should have to assume a first state of things. In order that this state might develop, a change would have to occur in it or to it, which change would itself again be the effect of a foregoing change, etc.

Remark.—This is the rock on which splits the cosmological argument, which confounds the metaphysical principle of salvation (God) with the physical principle of creation.

(b) The chain of causality is without end, inasmuch as no change can take place at any time without proceeding as an effect from its sufficient cause.

§ 20. There are three forms of causation, one general and two specific, since an effect may proceed from a cause in its narrower sense, from irritation or from motive.

1. All changes except the organic proceed from causes in the narrower sense. Increase of the cause here always produces increase of the effect. The causal agent undergoes a change equal to that which it communicates to the effect (equality of action and reaction).

2. Irritation (or stimulus) is the form of causation governing the changes in vegetable life (plants and the vegetable part of animal life). In order to operate, this form requires contact and duration, frequently intussusception. By augmentation of the cause here the effect often turns into its contrary (over-irritation).

3. Motives (determinants) produce all changes in the life of animals and men, so far as these changes belong to the domain of the animal functions, that is, all voluntary movements. The

cause in this form requires neither immediate contact nor a more than momentary duration. As the intellect of the brute is limited to perceptual representations, its action is throughout confined to perceptible and immediately present motives. The action of man, on the other hand, can proceed from abstract representations, acting as motives, in consequence of which his deeds are often enigmatical and inscrutable, but never free from that necessity with which the law of causality sways all that is finite (empirical determinism).

V. On Natural Forces

§ 21. The laws of space and time, the ascertainment of which belongs to the province of mathematics, and the law of causality are, as we shall show later, laws of nature *a priori*. On the other hand, there are natural laws gained from perception by induction and so *a posteriori*, which are nothing more than an expression reduced to rule for the invariable manifestation of the forces of nature.

§ 22. All that we learn and know by the study of nature are phenomena (that is states and changes of matter) in space and time, linked together by the chain of causality. All natural phenomena are divided into groups, each of which is formed by a series of phenomena bearing a common character, and therefore declaring themselves as varied manifestations of an inner unity.

This inner unity is termed force, natural force, an expression borrowed from the observation of our inner self (instances: Gravity, Impenetrability, Electricity, Crystallisation, and all Species of plants and animals). Every state in nature is a tension of conflicting forces, every change is a temporary subjugation of certain forces by others, which, by the aid of causality, have become the stronger ($\pi\acute{o}\lambda\epsilon\mu o\varsigma\ \pi\alpha\tau\grave{\eta}\rho\ \pi\acute{\alpha}\nu\tau\omega\nu$—instances: a building, a chemical union, the human body in the states of health, disease and death).

§ 23. To nature as a whole belong all manifestations of natural forces, but not the forces themselves. Empirically speaking they do not exist at all, and while the scientist cannot get rid of them, and yet will never be able to explain anything but their manifestations, he indicates the necessity of a method which supplements his own and belongs to the province of metaphysics.

§ 24. Thus every event, whether cause or effect, is the manifestation of a force, and the law of causality merely declares that no manifestation of force can take place without another manifestation of force preceding it as cause.

It is therefore inaccurate and reprehensible to speak of a force itself as the cause of a particular effect (as for instance in speaking of gravity as the cause of falling).

§ 25. The object of the empirical sciences is therefore threefold:—

1. The determining and describing of phenomena.
2. The ascertaining of their particular causes.
3. The determining of the forces manifested in them.

This is the task not only of the scientist but also of the historian, in so far as he has (1) to investigate and relate facts; (2) to find out the motive of each action; and (3) to portray the human characters which by motives are manifested in these actions.

VI. Materialism as the Consequence of the Empirical View of Things

§ 26. Since from the empirical standpoint nothing exists but matter in its various states (§§ 11. 14), all that exists must be conceived as modification of matter. To this the human intellect is no exception, the more so, as the study of it is inseparable from that of the brute intellect. Now the intellect of the brute is an organ rendered extremely sensitive by the accumulation of nervous matter, which in consequence of the external irritation of its offshoots, the senses, produces a reaction, from which, as we shall see later, the perception of the outer world arises. The function of this organ is called Understanding. Now the human intellect is nothing more than an augmentation of that of the brute to such a degree of intellectual clearness, that we are able to decompose our perceptions into their elements, and to retain these in a changed order, whence arises, as we shall show hereafter, the apparatus of the Reason with its concepts and judgments.

§ 27. It is the object of anatomy and physiology not so much to demonstrate the materiality of all intellectual processes (which is a truth *a priori*) as to establish it in single cases. If these sciences, owing to the inaccessibility of the thinking organ, have hitherto only partially succeeded in doing this, they nevertheless have at command a series of facts which place beyond question the absolute dependence of thinking on the brain. Such facts are the symptoms observable in childhood and old age, in abnormal development or malformation of the brain (mikrokephali, cretins), in cerebral affections through external injuries or internal morbid influences, causing insanity. In this last case the brain may occasionally have periods of release (*lucida intervalla*), and it may even happen that, in consequence of general exhaustion at the approach of death, the morbid tendencies disappear and the brain resumes for a short time its normal functions (Don Quijote).

§ 28. The philosophical spiritualism or doctrine of the dualism of man (established by Descartes, modified, transformed, combated by his successors and finally refuted by Kant, though even now prevalent as a popular opinion), according to which there are two substances, an extended and a thinking, blended in man as soul and body and separated by death, is a fundamental error, equally unsupported by experience, comprehensibility, and proof, and bars the way to any genuine philosophical view.

Remark.—Kant's refutations are based chiefly on the fact that existence is only the general form of objects, under which, therefore, we cannot comprehend that which in all our representations is the subject only, without ever becoming the object.

VII. Comfortlessness of the Empirical View of Nature

§ 29. So surely as materialism scorns all that is highest and deepest in philosophy and religion, so surely as its results in the sphere of art are flat and vulgar, in that of morality hopeless, desolate, and perverting, so sure is it that, from the empirical standpoint, it is the only true and consistent view of things, and so the "ideal" at which the empirical sciences aim, and to which in time they will more and more attain. It is therefore lost labour to endeavour to refute materialism. But we may well ask if it is not possible to supplement it by a higher view of things, which removes it without, however, contradicting it.

§ 30. Heavy lies on our heart the burden of a world in which for God, freedom, and immortality there is no place. Thanks therefore, in all future time, to those men who succeeded in unhinging this whole empirical world, after having found the δός μοι ποῦ στῶ in our own intellect.

However strictly the empirical sciences deal with matters of fact, they yet, according to their nature, overlook one fact which of all facts is the first and the most certain. Of this we have now to treat.

B. THE TRANSCENDENTAL STANDPOINT

SYSTEM OF METAPHYSICS

The System of Metaphysics

PART I

THE THEORY OF UNDERSTANDING

I. Preliminary Survey

§ 31. The theory of understanding is properly a part of psychology, and as such deals with the origin, essence, and connection of all our representations. These fall into two classes, as being partly primary, partly derivative. The first are called (by denominatio *a potiori*) " anschauliche," that is, perceptual, the latter abstract representations.

§ 32. The faculty of **perceptual representations** is **Understanding** (νοῦς, *mens*, *Verstand*, *entendement*); the science of which might be called **noetics**. It has to show how the mind, by means of its innate functions, after external irritation acting on its offshoots, the senses, (1) produces perceptual representations, and (2) establishes the connection between them.

§ 33. The faculty of **abstract representations** is **Reason** (λόγος, *ratio, Vernunft, raison*). The science which teaches how reason manufactures the materials supplied to it by perception into concepts, and then combines these as judgments and conclusions, is **logic.** The operating with concepts is called thinking. The external vibrations of the air by which we communicate our thoughts to each other, are the words of language, heard also by the brute, but comprehended only by man (hence the German word Vernunft, from vernehmen, to comprehend).

§ 34. The faculty of Understanding is common to us with the brutes. No animal is without Understanding, although those (lowest in the scale) in which the nervous matter is not yet centralised into a brain, have only a very faint trace of it. Starting from these, the Understanding increases gradually with the development of the brain, till it reaches its perfection in man. At this its highest point, the functions of the Understanding attain a degree of penetration which not only suffices, as in the case of the brutes, to produce the perception of the outside world, but is at the same time capable of pursuing the spatial, temporal, and causal connection of the latter to its farthest ramifications.

The only faculty which distinguishes man from the brute, is Reason. Simple as are its functions, they are yet sufficient to explain all the grandeur and beauty which distinguishes human life from that of the lower animals.

§ 35. The same organ which, viewed from within or psychologically, appears as Understanding, manifests itself, when considered from without or physiologically, as brain (represented in the lowest animals by knots or rings of nerves). This stretches out, as it were, its feelers, terminating in the organs of sense, towards external objects.

Reason, on the other hand, as it seems, is not a separate physiological organ. We regard it rather (for reasons to be given later) merely as a particular application, peculiar to man, of that uniform faculty of reaction which we call Understanding or brain.

§ 36. Reason, as will be shown later, receives its entire content from perception, and its activity is restricted to giving to the materials supplied as perceptual knowledge such a form as shall make them easier of survey and so more convenient to handle. In reality, therefore, reason teaches us nothing new, and it is a condition of all true progress, whether in physics or metaphysics, that, before all, we go back from abstract representations to the perceptual world underlying them. And so metaphysics might indeed relegate the study of reason and its abstract contents to logic, and abstain from all inquiry in this sphere, had not the insufficient knowledge of this very faculty and its bearing been the source, both in times ancient and modern, of the most grievous errors in the province of metaphysics. To guard against these, we shall, by way of appendix, take into consideration reason and its abstract representations. At present, however, let us set aside this secondary faculty of knowledge and turn to the world of perceptual representations, which alone are original and embrace all that is real. In this sphere lies the difficult problem the solution of which will remain the starting-point and the basis of all scientific metaphysics.

II. The Problem of Perceptual Knowledge

§ 37. How is it possible to perceive by the senses objects of the external world?

The empirical explanation, according to which objects, either directly or indirectly, by means of rays of light, waves of sound, etc., affect the nerves and through them the brain, would perhaps suffice, if the fact to be explained were my having, whilst perceiving, certain specific sensations within my organism. But in normal perception this is generally not the case. It is not subjective impressions which enter into my consciousness, for I perceive directly and without being aware of a medium, the objects and incidents lying outside of me themselves. In seeing, for instance, I do not perceive the inverted likeness of the object on the retina, but I see the thing itself and yet outside of me. It is not rays of light, not subjective reflections which enter into my consciousness, but the objects themselves directly, which yet are distant from me. This is the fact, and it involves a contradiction.—

No empirical explanation can remove it.

III. The World is my Representation

§ 38. If, to escape from this perplexity, I ask what part of all my knowledge is in reality absolutely and incontestably certain, it is best to begin, as did Descartes, by doubting everything. If now I not only doubt all theory and tradition, but even raise the question, if this world which visibly and palpably surrounds me, really exists, if it is not perhaps a mere dream of my imagination, an illusive phantom of my senses,—there is one truth which I cannot doubt ; it is : **The world is my representation.**

Descartes went too far when he by his famous " *Cogito, ergo sum* " restricted (as it seems) that which is indubitably certain to abstract representations. For, that the world, whatever it be in itself, is given me as a series of perceptual representations, is a primary fact of which I can never get rid, and which therefore also I cannot seriously doubt.

§ 39. To this fact alone however is restricted all indubitable certitude, and our ripeness for the philosophical view of things depends upon our being able to arrive by self-reflection at a real and sincere understanding of the great truth: this whole material world, extended in time and space, is, as such, known to me only through my intellect. Now my intellect, according to its nature, can never furnish me with anything but representations. Consequently this whole world and with it my own body, in so far as I regard it through my intellect, that is, as corporeal in time and space, is nothing more than my representation.

§ 40. Though this truth is irrefutable, we yet feel a strong repugnance to it. This repugnance will increase when we consider that even the most painful injuries to our own bodies are, for our intellect, nothing more than representations, just as much as are the pains and injuries with which we see others tormented. If our relation towards external objects were that of pure bodiless intelligences, the above truth would not offend us in the least. The whole world would pass before us as a series of empty, meaningless phantoms, resembling the apparitions of a dream in which we are spectators only, not actors. But here the case is different. For our relation to the world is twofold, on the one hand mediate, so far as we perceive the world through the medium of our intellect, on the other hand immediate, so far as we are ourselves, in virtue of our corporeal existence, a part of it. What we and the things of this world are in the latter sense, will be taken into consideration later on. At present this question does not concern us, as we have now to analyse the world as material in space and time; for in this form the world is known to us only through our intellect and is consequently only our representation.

IV. Whether Things in themselves are the same as I represent them?

§ 41. The world is my representation. As such it is, in the first place, only the form in which things appear to me. Now the question is, whether things in themselves are the same as I represent them, namely, material in space and time, or if they exist in this form merely for my intellect, which perhaps, by its nature, is not able to reveal the real and true essence of things?

The former is maintained by materialism, the latter is preached to us by certain mysterious voices of the past. Indian sages teach that the root, out of which springs the varied world, is ignorance (*avidyâ*), nay, they conceive this whole world as an illusive phantom (*mâyâ*). Greek philosophers (Parmenides, Plato, etc.) accuse the senses of deceiving us, whilst Christianity teaches that from the moral depravity of mankind comes a darkening of the intellect ($\dot{\epsilon}\sigma\kappa o\tau\iota\sigma\mu\acute{\epsilon}\nu o\iota$ $\tau\hat{\eta}$ $\delta\iota a\nu o\acute{\iota}\dot{q}$ $\ddot{o}\nu\tau\epsilon s$, Eph. iv. 18; one should read in particular 1 Cor. ii.). In all these fanciful sayings is expressed the conviction that things in themselves are other than they appear to us.

An analysis of our intellectual faculties can alone give us the means of deciding this question.

V. Elements of Representation a priori and a posteriori

§ 42. Every representation contains as such two supplementary halves, a representing subject and a represented object. These two make with the representation not three (as a sneering epigram of Schiller has it) but one. No representation is without a subject, none without an object. Now nothing exists for me but representations (§ 39), therefore also no subject without an object, no object without a subject — a truth which Plato (Theaetet. p. 160 AB) has already expressed in his way.

§ 43. All objects of my subject are such either immediately or mediately. As immediate objects I can never have anything else but affections of my ego, that is, sensations within me (represented physiologically as certain specific irritations of the sensory nerves extended in the organs of sense). All other objects, the whole external world and even my own body, as far as I regard it from without, are known to me only as mediate objects: it is only through the medium of those nerve-irritations that I come in contact with them.

§ 44. Thus all data by which I attain to a knowledge of the external world, are restricted to these affections of the nerves which are given as immediate objects. They are the only thing which comes to my intellect from without, that is independent of itself. Consequently all else, all that distinguishes wide-spreading nature with its immeasurable riches from those scanty affections of the nerves, must come from within, that is, must originate in my intellect itself.

§ 45. If we compare the perceptual world which is our representation, to a textile fabric in which subjective and objective threads intersect as warp and woof, then all that is objective, independent of myself, given *a posteriori*, is limited to those affections of the nerves and may be compared to the thin, isolated threads of the shuttle. The warp, on the contrary, which is previously, that is *a priori*, stretched out to receive little by little these interweaving threads and work them into a fabric, is the natural, innate forms of the subject, the totality of which forms just that which we call Understanding or brain.

VI. Clues to the Discrimination of the a priori Elements in Representations

§ 46. The task of metaphysics consists in finding out what things are in themselves, that is, independent of our intellect (§ 4). We must, therefore, first of all, deduct from things that which our intellect contributes to them, namely those forms which inhere in it originally, that is *a priori*, and in which it ranges all materials furnished from without so as to weave them into experience. The following six criteria may serve to distinguish these *a priori* elements of knowledge or innate functions of the Understanding from those which come to it *a posteriori* or through perception. They are to us what reagents are to the chemist.

They may also be regarded as six magnets, by means of which we extract the iron of our *a priori* knowledge from the mixed ore of experience.

1. Whatever is necessary to transform perception, given as affection, into perceptual representation, and consequently precedes all experience as a condition of its possibility, cannot originate in experience but only within ourselves (*argumentum ex antecessione*).

2. Whatever comes to the intellect from without, has the character of contingency, it might be otherwise, or it might even not be at all; that is, I can imagine it as non-existent. Now, in my representations there are certain elements which cannot be thought away like everything else, from which it follows that they do not belong to that which exists independently of myself, but must adhere to the intellect itself (*argumentum ex adhaesione*).

3. For the same reason all data given from without merely suffice to state what is there, but not that something is necessarily so and not otherwise. Perception has no tongue for the word necessity, consequently all determinations of things, with which is associated the consciousness of necessity, must originate, not in perception, but within myself (*argumentum e necessitate*).

4. From this it follows that sciences the

doctrines of which have apodictic certainty, cannot have obtained it from perception, and that consequently that part of the perceptual world to which they refer must belong to the elements originally inherent in my intellect (*argumentum e mathematicis*).

5. Perception can only furnish me with sensations. These are, as such, isolated and fragmentary, for, difficult as it is to grasp at first, the materials of sensation given from without contain only the sensations themselves, but not any connection between them, for such a connection is merely the link between the different sensations and therefore not itself sensation. Consequently that faculty which makes of the variety of perception a unity and so creates coherence between my representations, must belong to me *a priori*. Therefore whatever serves to establish the continuity of nature, belongs to the innate functions of my intellect (*argumentum e continuitate*).

6. Perception can never embrace infinity. If, now, I find in my representations of things elements of which I am conscious as being infinite, it follows with certainty, that I have not taken them from perception, but must possess them as forms of my intellect, wherefore, however far I proceed in representing, I can never get beyond them, in which precisely consists their infinity (*argumentum ex infinitate*).

VII. The a priori Elements are: Time, Space, and Causality

§ 47. Three constituent elements of the surrounding perceptual world, neither more nor less, are proved by these six touchstones to be forms belonging originally to our intellect, in which we range the material of perception, to transform it into representations. These, therefore, must be withdrawn from nature in order to retain as remainder things in themselves. They are:—

1. **Space,**
2. **Time,**
3. **Causality.**

That it is these three which distinguish the surrounding phenomenal world from that of being-in-itself (an-sich-Seiend), is **the fundamental truth of all metaphysics**, therefore it appears again and again, pronounced at least indirectly and as inference, in all the various stages of metaphysical development, as the following instances will show.

In the Vedânta, the most profound metaphysical system of India, the thing-in-itself appears as the *Brahman*, of which it is said, that it is not split by time and space (*deça-kâla-anavacchinna*) and that it is free from all change (*sarva-vikriyâ-rahita*). (Çañkara ad *Bṛihad-âraṇyaka-upanishad*, i. 3,₁₁ p. 79,₁.

—ad *Brahma-sûtrâṇi*, i. 1,4 p. 64,7.) Now where there is no change, there is also no causality.

The exemption from causality of things-in-themselves is also the fundamental dogma of Plato's philosophy. Again and again he recurs to the distinction between the phenomenal world, ruled by causality, which he calls "the Becoming and Perishing, but never really Being" (γιγνόμενον καὶ ἀπολλύμενον, ὄντως δὲ οὐδέποτε ὄν, Tim. 28 A), and Being-in-itself, to which he denies, in the strongest terms, all change (μονοειδὲς ὂν αὐτὸ καθ' αὑτό, ὡσαύτως κατὰ ταὐτὰ ἔχει καὶ οὐδέποτε οὐδαμῇ οὐδαμῶς ἀλλοίωσιν οὐδεμίαν ἐνδέχεται, Phaedon, 78 D). Like causality, he also restricts to the phenomenal world, and expressly excludes from Being-in-itself, Space (πρὸς ὃ δὴ καὶ ὀνειροπολοῦμεν βλέποντες καί φαμεν ἀναγκαῖον, εἶναί που τὸ ὂν ἅπαν ἔν τινι τόπῳ καὶ κατέχον χώραν τινά, Tim. 52 B) and Time (ταῦτα δὲ πάντα μέρη χρόνου, καὶ τό τ' ἦν τό τ' ἔσται χρόνου γεγονότα εἴδη, ἃ δὴ φέροντες λανθάνομεν ἐπὶ τὴν ἀΐδιον οὐσίαν οὐκ ὀρθῶς, Tim. 37 E).

Biblical metaphysics conceives Being-in-itself as a personality, but retracts the limitation implied in this idea, when it maintains as attributes of God (1) eternity, that is, timelessness (mê‘ôlâm ‘ad-‘ôlâm attâh êl, Psalm xc. 2); (2) omnipresence, that is, spacelessness (et-haschschâmajim v°et-hâârez ªnî mâle' n°um-j°hôvâh, Jerem. xxiii. 24); (3) immutability, that is, exemption from causality (hêmmâh [heaven and earth] jôbêdû v'attäh ta'ªmod, Psalm cii. 27).

As dreaming is opposed to waking, so these witnesses of the past are opposed to the arguments for the a-priority of Time, Space, and Causality, which Kant first established, and Schopenhauer has freed from false additions and completed. For both is reserved, as reward, the veneration of many future ages.

If, however, we try in the following to establish these proofs, in part more completely and systematically, in part more comprehensibly than has been done by these immortal teachers, we commit no act of impiety: for here as everywhere we have the right to look at things with our own eyes.

VIII. Space is an a priori form of Perception

§ 48. Space is that constituent element of the perceptual world by means of which all objects are determined in position towards each other. It is, as such, not something independent of myself, but an *a priori* form of perceiving.

First Proof: *ex antecessione*

§ 49. I have the representation of space. This representation must come either from experience or from myself. Now it cannot be drawn from experience, because every experience presupposes it, for what makes experience is my referring certain sensations to something outside of me and their diversity to different places outside of each other. This presupposes, in every experience, the representation of space. Consequently it must spring not from experience, but from my intellect itself.

Second Proof: *ex adhaesione*

§ 50. In my representation of the outer world I can think away everything except space. I cannot imagine that there is no space, whilst I can easily imagine that there are no objects in space. I can, for instance, think away everything in the universe but not the space which fills it, for to think away space is absolutely impossible. Hence follows that space belongs not to the represented objects, but to my representing faculty, for from this and this alone I can make no abstraction when I am representing.

Third Proof: *e necessitate*

§ 51. All particular determinations of space are necessary and whatever contradicts them is impossible. It is necessary, in order to reach a thing, to traverse all parts of space which separate me from it; it is impossible to be nowhere, or in two places at the same time, etc. Every one feels that the certainty of this and similar determinations is of quite a different kind from that which comes to us through often-repeated experience. For experience can only tell me that until now something has never been otherwise than so and so; but not that something is necessarily so and not otherwise. Hence space, the determinations of which are throughout necessary, cannot originate in experience, but must come from myself.

Fourth Proof: *e mathematicis*

§ 52. Geometry pronounces all its propositions apodictically, that is, with the consciousness of necessity. This is the reason why this science knows properly neither controversies nor hypotheses, with which the empirical sciences teem in all departments. Hence follows with certainty, that the dogmas of geometry cannot be gathered from perception, that consequently the subject of this science is not empirical. Now the subject of geometry is space, and it is only in order to investigate the laws of space that geometry imagines its points, lines, surfaces, and bodies. For in these the nature of space is manifested in the same way, as the nature of characters which the dramatist wishes to depict, is revealed in the actions which he invents for the purpose. Space therefore is an *a priori* representation.

Fifth Proof: *e continuitate*

§ 53. Every external perception (whether of a body or of its image on the retina of the eye) consists of an infinite multitude of parts which, as mere affections of my ego, have no relation whatever to each other but only a relation to me. That, therefore, which links these into a connected perception, must lie not without, but within me. Now the tie which connects the infinite multitude of external affections (whether given by one sense or by several) into the unity of external perception, is space. Consequently space must lie within, not without me.

Sixth Proof: *ex infinitate*

§ 54. Space is (as shown, § 7) infinite. I know with the utmost certainty, that beyond all solar systems, in regions where no telescope can penetrate, no experience reach, space still continues. From experience I cannot know this. It follows, therefore, that I know it *a priori*.

IX. Time is an a priori form of Perception

§ 55. Time is that constituent element of the perceptual world by means of which all conditions and changes, whether belonging to outer or inner experience, are determined in their sequence to each other. As such, it does not exist independently of me but is a representation *a priori*.

First Proof: *ex antecessione*

§ 56. The representation of time cannot be obtained from experience, because every experience, in order to be made, presupposes time. For to make an experience, it is necessary to have certain sensations either simultaneously or successively. Now this simultaneity, this succession, does not belong to the sensations as such; consequently it belongs to me and is just that which constitutes the nature of time.

Second Proof: *ex adhaesione*

§ 57. Let us suppose the world were to stand still, all motion being checked, all change suspended. There would indeed, in consequence of the stoppage of all clocks, as well as that of the great world clock (the earth revolving round the sun), be no means of measuring time. But time itself would continue its course undisturbed, and one moment follow ceaselessly on another as before. If in this way I were to extinguish all inner and outer perception (which is nothing but a kind of change), there would still remain to me the representation of (absolutely empty) time, and this would be extinguished only with my intellect itself; from which follows with certainty, that time does not belong to the things existing independently of me, but to my own intellectual faculties, to which it adheres as their indispensable form.

Third Proof: *e necessitate*

§ 58. All particular determinations of time are necessary, and whatever contradicts them is impossible. It is necessary, for instance, in order to reach any period of the future, to live through exactly the amount of time which separates it from the present, neither more nor less. It is impossible to recall any single moment of the past, the certainty of this and similar determinations can never be attained through experience, however universal and invariable it may be. One may doubt, for example, whether Plato's birth took place according to Apollodorus in B.C. 427, or according to Athenæus in B.C. 429; but if any one were to maintain that both authors were right, and that Plato was born twice successively, we should not be likely to observe that such a case had never occurred and was therefore extremely improbable, but we should simply declare such a person deranged, an expression signifying that something in the mechanism of his head must have become displaced, which would, in the present case, be the cerebral function of time.

Fourth Proof: *e mathematicis*

§ 59. The axioms of arithmetic (the generalised form of which is algebra) have, like those of geometry, apodictic certainty. The subject of this science cannot therefore spring from experience. Now as geometry is the science of space, so is arithmetic the science of time, as will be clear from the following. All arithmetic, with its most complicated formulæ and operations, may be regarded as a methodically abridged counting (hence the name ἀριθμητική, that is, art of counting). In counting, I abstract from everything except from time. For counting consists in the repeated marking of unity, for which I employ each time a different conventional term (one, two, three, etc.), merely to know how often I have marked unity. Now all repetition depends on succession, and in succession alone consists the nature of time. So all counting, and consequently arithmetic is the science of time; and from the apodicticity of arithmetical propositions follows the a-priority of time.

Fifth Proof: *e continuitate*

§ 60. Every perception is only possible through my being affected either outwardly or inwardly for a certain period of time. This period, however short it may be, consists of an infinite number of parts which are filled by an infinite multitude of corresponding affections in the subject (whether the object affecting me is at rest or in motion). All these affections of my ego have, as such, no relation to each other, but only a relation to me. The thread, therefore, on which they are strung together to the unity of perception, is not in the affections themselves, that is outside of me, but only within me. This thread, on which I string all affections coming to me from without as from within, is time. It must consequently be given *a priori* as a condition of the synthesis of perceptions.

Sixth Proof: *ex infinitate*

§ 61. Time is (according to § 9) infinite in both directions. I know with certainty that in the most hoary past, to which no knowledge reaches, in the most distant future, which no prophet's eye can pierce, time was and will be. From experience I cannot know it; it follows therefore, without contradiction, that I know it independently of experience, that is, *a priori*.

X. Causality is an a priori form of Perception

§ 62. As space is the order of things according to their position, time the order of things according to their sequence, so causality is the order of things according to their action. Now as every single place and every single period of time is empirically determined, while, on the other hand, space and time themselves, as the general possibility of the empirical occupation of time and space, are *a priori* representations, so also is each single effect empirically determined, but causality, as the general possibility of action, precedes them *a priori*. It is the net which binds together, in the way laid down by the law of causality (§ 15), all effects, that is, all force manifestations (§ 24), and connects them, in various ways, as effects of preceding and causes of succeeding force manifestations.

As such, causality is in no way an abstract concept, but, like space and time, a constituent element of the totality of empirical reality; though we are not able to isolate it (for the purpose of considering it separately) so completely from effects, as we may isolate space from bodies and time from events. That causality, however, is an integral part of the perceptual world, becomes clear if we represent it as filling space and persisting in time, for then it appears as that which remains after all manifestations of force have been separated from things, and which, in contrast to force, is called matter or substance. This, however, can only be explained later on (Chap. XVI.). Here we have merely to prove that causality, like time and space, is an *a priori* faculty of our understanding.

First Proof: *ex antecessione*

§ 63. The relation in the perceptual world of every effect to its preceding cause, which we call causality (that is, the being-caused), cannot be learned from experience but must belong *a priori* to our understanding as an innate faculty, compelling us to regard each manifestation of force as an effect and to refer it immediately and unreflectingly to its cause. This surprising and important truth of the a priority of causality follows with perfect certainty from the fact that every experience, in order to be made, presupposes an application of causality. All namely, that can come to me from without, is (as has been shown in § 44) affections of my sensory nerves, and I should never get beyond these, never attain to a perception of the outside world, if I did not bear within me *a priori* the means of conceiving these affections as effects and of passing from them to something else, namely to their causes, which I project as bodies in space (likewise given *a priori*). This impossibility of explaining, without the aid of causality, the genesis of the perception of the external world, shows clearly and incontestably that causality itself can not be gathered from the impressions of the external world, but must belong *a priori* to the intellect.

Corollary.—It is exactly the same, as will become clear hereafter, whether I say: no sensation can be conceived as body without the help of causality; or, no force can affect me except through the medium of matter.

Second Proof: *ex adhaesione*

§ 64. Causality in itself is not representable (§ 62); it becomes so, when, after its union with space and time, it is called matter. Now, since the proof *ex adhaesione* is based on the inextinguishable nature of certain elements of knowledge (§ 46_2), it is applicable only to objectively perceived causality, that is, to matter. It can only, therefore, like everything in the present chapter which presupposes the identity of causality and matter, be fully understood after studying the theory of matter (Chap. XVI.). Matter has the peculiarity of being at the same time contingent and necessary. I can certainly think away matter (which with space and time is impossible), but I cannot imagine existing matter as non-existent. On this depends its uncreatability and indestructibility which (as already remarked in § 12) is a truth *a priori*, previous to all experience. The impossibility, namely, of imagining either the creation or annihilation of matter proves that I cannot sever my intellectual faculties from its existence, from which follows, that it has not, like the forces borne by it, an existence independent of my intellect, but inheres in the latter as an original form of perception.

Third Proof: *e necessitate*

§ 65. All determinations of causality (enumerated §§ 14-20) have the character of necessity; whatever contradicts these determinations is impossible. We may often, for instance, doubt to what cause a particular effect is to be referred, but, that it must have some cause, we are all firmly convinced. As little, therefore, as a judge would believe an accused, who, called upon to prove an alibi, should maintain that, at the moment in question, he had been nowhere, just as little would he, when a crime has been committed, allow the possibility of this effect being without a cause. If the law of causality were an *a posteriori* law of nature (§ 21), our experience, however general, could not guarantee that it might not occasionally admit of an exception.

That experience carries with it no necessity was a truth of which *David Hume* was as much convinced as *Kant*. But compare the conclusions which the two drew from the same premisses.

Hume argued:—
Experience has no necessity.
The law of causality springs from experience.
Therefore it has no necessity.

Kant argued:—

Experience has no necessity.
The law of causality has necessity.
Therefore it does not spring from experience.

Fourth Proof: *e mathematicis*

§ 66. Besides geometry and arithmetic, there is still a third science the propositions of which have apodictic certainty. It forms that element of the natural sciences which remains, when we eliminate all *a posteriori* laws of nature, these being merely the expression for the invariable operating of the forces of nature (§ 21), and which Kant, in his "Metaphysische Anfangsgründe der Naturwissenschaft," subjected to a separate inquiry. If we take away from our knowledge whatever has been gained empirically by induction, there remains no real action, but only the general possibility of action (that is, causality), which, viewed as filling space and persisting in time, constitutes matter (as will be proved further on). The science of matter at rest and in motion has apodictic certainty; consequently its subject is given to us not empirically, but *a priori*.

Fifth Proof: *e continuitate*

§ 67. If the affections, to which all perception is restricted, are not even capable of giving me any coherence in time and space, still less are they capable of communicating the connection often so remote between cause and effect. If therefore this connection cannot be drawn from perception, it follows, that it is furnished by my mind, which, in the same way as it projects bodies in space and events in time, arranges all perceived force manifestations as causes and effects in its *a priori* form of causality. This, of course, does not exclude the fact that, in making this arrangement, it is guided in all particulars by former experience.

Sixth Proof: *ex infinitate*

§ 68. The net of causality is (as shown, § 19) without beginning or end, that is, it is infinite in time. Whether it is also infinite in space, we do not know, because we are ignorant as to whether the store of matter, to which all effects and consequently all applications of causality are confined (§ 13), is limited or unlimited. So much, however, we know positively, that in the most distant star, in the earliest past as in the latest future, there can never be an effect without a cause. No experience reaches to these times and regions; it follows, therefore, that we know it independently of experience, that is, *a priori*.

Corollary.—From this proof also (as from § 64)

may be deduced the axiom, that matter, which is causality objectively perceived, can never be created and never annihilated.

XI. The Empirical and the Transcendental Standpoint.

§ 69. Recapitulation.—The result of our inquiries so far may be summed up as follows:—

1. The world is a purely material structure, which, interwoven by causality, exists in infinite space, through infinite time (§§ 7-30).
2. This same material world is through and through merely a representation of my intellect, and its materiality is only the form in which things appear to me (§§ 38-40).
3. In itself, that is, independently of my intellect, there exists nothing but that which we have called sensations or affections of the ego (§§ 42-45). These are, as regards their real nature, absolutely unknown to us; for though physiology, in which the intellect appears as brain, recognises its affections as irritations of the sensory nerves, in so doing, it already regards these as they appear to us, but not as they are in themselves.
4. Three constituent elements of the external world, forming the very framework of nature,

namely, time, space, and the causal nexus, are, as we have shown by three times six proofs, the innate forms the totality of which constitutes the essence of the intellect. They are, physiologically speaking, cerebral functions, and consequently not something existing independently of my mind (appearing as brain).

No one can think of evading the conclusions which we shall presently draw from these facts, so long as he has not succeeded in refuting the whole series of proofs brought forward by us. That this should ever happen, that any one should succeed in undermining singly each of the six proofs adduced for the a priority of time, space, and causality, and thereby overthrow the whole structure resting on them, is, in our estimation, for ever impossible. That there will be, however, hereafter as before, those who fancy they have refuted what they have never really understood, is not only possible but highly probable.

§ 70. Regarding the facts established by us, three standpoints are possible: the empirical, which ignores them; the transcendent, which defies them; and the transcendental, which utilises them.

§ 71. **The empirical standpoint** is that on which all men stand by nature, and on which most stand all their life long. It is that which is alone valid for all sciences save metaphysics, and for all practical life, with the exception of purely moral, that is, self-denying deeds, which for that very reason, as will be shown later, bear a supernatural character and are opposed to all actions natural to man. From this standpoint no notice is taken of the facts resulting from the analysis of intellect, for it has to deal only with things as they exist for us, and not as they may be in themselves. Whether the wonderful consistency we meet everywhere in nature, and on which we confidently build our plans, rests on an objective order of things or on subjective laws of the intellect, is of no consequence to practical life and to the empirical sciences serving it. For, though time, space, and causality are only innate forms of the intellect, they yet govern all that is earthly with inexorable necessity, as if they were eternal determinations of things themselves, because (1) the intellect is everywhere identical, and (2) is inseparable from existence. (1) On the one hand, namely, the intellectual faculties in all living beings differ only in energy, that is, in degree, but, as regards their real nature, they are everywhere the same, so that all minds must produce from the same affections essentially the same representations, just as the digestive organs in all men draw from the same food essentially the same materials for the building up of the body.

(2) On the other hand, the intellect is the ever-present pre-requisite of existence; it is, as the Indians call it, "the witness" (*sâkshin*), which accompanies the whole changeful drama of life from birth to death as its indispensable condition, and there is (as follows from § 42) as little a world without intellect as an intellect without world. Let it not be objected that many revolutions of our planet must have taken place, before living and intelligent beings could come into existence, for all these preceding world periods of which geology tells, are neither more nor less than the most immediate present, merely the form in which things appear to our space-and-time-bound mind; in reality there is no time, and so no past, present, or future.

§ 72. **The transcendent standpoint** transcends, as its name implies, the limits of knowledge attainable by experience. For, whatever we have learned through the accumulated experience of ages, and whatever may yet be added to it, is like a small island on the immeasurable ocean. Unsatisfied in its longings and conscious of a higher origin, the human mind has at all times sought to pass the boundaries of knowledge, which have been fixed once for all by the nature of our intellectual faculties, and, for the sake of purity of moral action, have been fixed wisely. But already a thoroughgoing empirical view of nature, the outlines of which have been sketched in the "System of Physics," cuts off the way to all such attempts to fly beyond the atmosphere of experience. For, however far on all sides we would penetrate infinity, we remain for ever in the desolate cage of empirical reality. Kant, in his "Critique of Pure Reason," undertook on a large scale such a relegation and confinement of transcending reason to the limits of experience. Yet in so doing he appears to us like Saul, the son of Kish, who, being sent out by his father (*David Hume*) to seek the asses, found a royal crown. For Kant, in analysing the intellectual faculties, to discover their bearing, came through this inquiry, directed against transcending reason and therefore transcendental, to the greatest discovery ever made in any department of science, the discovery of the *a priori* forms of the intellect, which is and will be for ever the basis of all scientific metaphysics.

§ 73. **The transcendental standpoint,** the name of which we owe to the memory of Kant, does not presume, as does the transcendent, to pass beyond the limits of experience, but contents itself with understanding thoroughly the world as it is given to us. For this purpose it investigates it, in taking away from things everywhere that which is imposed on them only by the forms of our intellect. To

Kant's unexampled acumen is due the discovery of these forms; Schopenhauer's immeasurably wide and profound genius was called to make this discovery fruitful by spreading its light from the centre of the inner self to the periphery of the world, thus gaining scientifically what for ages past the prophetic voices of the wisest among men were able to express only by images.

To both these men posterity will raise one monument, representing the first, as he sits, self-absorbed and sunk in profound thought, the other, leaning on him, with upraised open glance, as if to embrace the world.

We and many after us tread the path which these mighty heroes have cleared for all after ages, but we must tread it ourselves and independently. Not words, not individual opinions of the immortal masters must guide us, but nature itself, whose inner being they have disclosed to us. Our standpoint is neither empirical nor transcendent, but transcendental, we touch the boundaries and we do not transcend them.

XII. Transcendental Analysis of Empirical Reality

§ 74. The first fruit of the transcendental standpoint is the solution of the problem of perceptual knowledge (raised in § 37), which, being from the empirical standpoint impossible, pointed, for that very reason, beyond it.

The organ of Understanding, on which, as we know, the world depends, appears in physiology as the brain. This, in sending to the sense organs five differently formed offshoots, stretches itself, as it were, towards the five states of aggregation of things (which in the main are the *bhûtâni*, στοιχεῖα, *elementa* of the ancients), the solid, fluid, gaseous, permanently elastic, and the imponderable, and adapts itself, so to say, to them; a thought which permeates all Indian philosophy, while amongst the Greeks we find only uncertain traces of it (compare Aristotle *de sensu* 2). In what way, however, the brain manufactures its sensations into representations, physiology is unable to read in the furrows and convolutions of this curiously constructed organ. Here psychology comes to its aid. To its inner view, the brain appears as the Understanding, which it conceives as a structure, framed of time, space, and causality—that is, as a power of reacting upon the incoming affection in a threefold direction, whereby the perception of the external world arises as follows.

§ 75. It is the Understanding which *first* ranges on its innate thread of **time** all sense affections it receives, into a coherent series. *Secondly*, it takes, by means of its inherent **causality,** each external affection as an effect, which it refers (not intentionally nor reflectingly, but through the immediate impulse of its own nature) to its conditioning cause. This cause, *in the third place*, it projects in **space** (likewise inherent in it by nature), where it appears as the material object.

§ 76. The product, arising from the continually exerted reaction of the intellectual forms upon the thronging affections, is actually ($\kappa\alpha\tau'$ $\dot{\epsilon}\nu\dot{\epsilon}\rho\gamma\epsilon\iota\alpha\nu$) in each moment a limited and narrow circle of ideas; but potentially ($\kappa\alpha\tau\grave{\alpha}$ $\delta\acute{\upsilon}\nu\alpha\mu\iota\nu$) it constitutes the whole aggregate of empirical reality, this itself being nothing more than the consciousness (accompanying all my representations) of that which can be represented, beside that which actually is represented.

Remark.—To exist or to be real, accordingly, means nothing else than to be able to be represented by the senses; while, on the contrary, possible is that the reality of which (that is, its representability by the senses) can be represented.

§ 77. Clearly and incontestably appears, as the result of our inquiries so far, the great doctrine of **Idealism**, this very root of all religion and philosophy: **The whole of nature, immeasurably extended in space and time, exists only under the presupposition of the forms of our intellect and has, apart from them, that is in a metaphysical sense, no reality; for it is nothing more than the un-**

ceasingly generated product of the sensuous affections and the mental forms.—The repugnance to this truth, arising from the physical cast of our intellect, will be lessened, when we consider that the material world in space and time is only the form in which the nature of things-in-themselves appears to us; it will disappear, when (in the second part) we penetrate, by the only possible way, to the knowledge of Being-in-itself, and then pursue in detail how this Being, distorted through the medium of time, space, and causality, appears as that which we call nature.

§ 78. Never would the senses accomplish the wonderful work of perception, if the action exerted by external objects on the thin nerve threads, expanded in our sense organs, were not met from within by the reaction of the nervous matter of the massive and so ingeniously constructed brain; and that, as the Indians have already justly understood: "*cakshur-âdînâm manaḥ-samyogaṃ vinâ vyâpâra-akshamatvâd*, because the eye, etc., without union with the mind, is unable to perform its function" (Wilson, Sâṅkhya-K., p. 100 n.). It is not the senses, therefore, which see, hear, feel, smell, and taste, but the Understanding (represented as brain); as even Epicharmos (B.C. 500) saw and admirably expressed in the verse (Plut. mor. p. 961 A):—

Νοῦς ὁρῇ καὶ νοῦς ἀκούει, τἄλλα κωφὰ καὶ τυφλά—

> What in us hears, what in us sees, is mind,
> And all its organs are but dumb and blind.

§ 79. Nobody should deny himself the pleasure of examining by the light of this truth,—so simple and yet so important (in which Physics and Metaphysics join hands), sensuous perception in detail, and convincing himself how, for instance, the phenomena of vision (physically inexplicable, see § 37) become clear, if only we keep to the fact, that for the Understanding the image on the retina serves as a mere datum from which as effect it passes to its external cause, which, by the aid of touch and of previous experience, it construes in size, position, and distance, accurately in space. A whole series of the most difficult optical phenomena are hereby easily explained; such are: the upright appearance of the inverted image in the eye; the single vision with two eyes; the double vision when the optical angle is not closed; the appearance as body of the flat image in the eye; the perception of the nearness and smallness or the distance and largeness of an object at equal visual angle; the increasing and diminishing of the physiological colour spectrum according as one looks at a distant or a near plane; the illusion of the microscope and the telescope, etc.

XIII. Of the Immediate and Mediate Application of the Understanding

§ 80. The passing from the effect within me to its external cause is the immediate application of the Understanding. But the objects of the external world stand (empirically speaking) not only to me, but also to each other in various relations of space, time, and causality. Now the same organ which builds a bridge between the immediate objects (appearing, § 43, as nerve irritations) and the mediate objects, serves further to trace out the spatial, temporal, and causal relations of the mediate objects to each other, that is, from the metaphysical standpoint, to create them. (The strangeness of this expression will disappear later.) This is the mediate application of the Understanding. Its higher degrees are called in practical life quick-wittedness, in science acumen; the want of it is stupidity, at times associated with great scholarship.

Remark.—Every great discovery depends on the passing from a well-known effect to its hidden cause (discovery of America, of oxygen, of Neptune); each invention is the establishing of a cause which produces as effect some intended result (invention of the alphabet, of printing, of the steam engine, of a manageable balloon, etc.). Accordingly the Understanding is the instrument on the energy of which depends intellectual superiority; far more than Reason, which (apart from the faculty of judgment) is closely allied to memory and scarcely more than a repository.

§ 81. In the immediate application of the Understanding the intellect remains in that state which has been called receptivity, in the mediate it passes into spontaneity. It is of great importance to understand that both depend on that same reaction on the sensuous affections which we recognised as the nature of the Understanding, and that both differ from each other only in degree. In perceiving, the reacting Understanding is, so to say, on the defensive. It contents itself with repelling the attacks of the affections by projecting them in time, space, and causality. As a result of the increase of the brain and its power of reaction in the higher animals and man, the Understanding passes, as it were, from the defensive to the offensive. It not only repels the attacks of the affections, but pursues the aggressor to its farthest retreats, that is, it apprehends things not merely in relation to itself, but in the most distant relations of their spatial, temporal, and causal connection with each other. On a similar reaction of the Understanding, raised to the offensive, depends, as we shall see later, that function of the latter, peculiar to man alone, which is called Reason. For it is, in the main, as will appear, one and the same faculty which, as Understanding, establishes the connection between cause and effect, and as Reason, that between the perceptual world and the predicates abstracted from it.

Remark.—An act of the Understanding can, of course, appear in the form of a logical conclusion (of which later). In itself, however, it is by no means such, but only the intuitive and, so to say, instinctive passing from one relation of the perceptual world to another connected with it. Therefore it belongs, in a certain degree, to the brutes also, which by means of their innate functions of time, space, and causality, practise quite correctly the immediate, and in part even the mediate application of the Understanding.

XIV. Whether there are Innate Ideas?

§ 82. Here is cleared up the old controversy about innate ideas, the existence of which was maintained by Descartes and his school, while Locke disputed it. In the words "*no innate ideas*" lies the real pith of his philosophy. We saw already (§ 65) how this tenet in Hume's hands culminated in a conclusion the untenability of which was obvious. It was this conclusion which roused Kant from "dogmatic slumber" and drove him to his great discoveries.

§ 83. All abstract representations, as we shall show farther on, spring from concrete perception. There are therefore, indeed, no innate ideas, but there are three innate functions of the brain,—space, time, and causality, which constitute the very nature of intellect. They are as innate in the brain as walking in the leg or grasping in the hand. The child brings them ready made with it into the world, though it has not from the beginning the representation of space, etc. For it is only upon the stimulus of external affection that the understanding awakes and its functions become active. Through constant use these are hereafter exerted so spontaneously, that we are not at all conscious of them, so much so, that mankind had to seek some thousands of years before it became aware of that which lay nearest it, and which for that very reason was so difficult to discover. But if children could tell us what goes on in their minds during the first months of their existence, they would lisp Kantian philosophy.

XV. The Theory of Dreaming

§ 84. The nature of sleep might be defined as a periodical separation of will and intellect, which causes a temporary suspension of the conscious will (of which more in the second part). The system of this conscious will in our organism (the eleven *indriyâni*[1] of Indian psychology) embraces three parts :—

[1] The *indriyâni* (originally "the powerful") are therefore frequently not our senses, but the organs of relation; and *vijita-indriya, saṃyata-indriya*, etc., is not so much "whose senses are tamed," as "whose will is tamed," or as Manu (2, 98) paraphrases it : " Whose will is not excited by the perceptions of the senses."

1. The sensory nerves of the organs of sense (*buddhi-indriyâṇi*), which transmit the affections to the brain.
2. The brain, which moulds these affections into percepts and stamps them to resolutions (in this double function corresponding to the Indian *manas*).
3. The motor nerves, which, starting from the brain, terminate in the organs of action (*karma-indriyâṇi*, tongue, hand, foot, etc.) in order to regulate through these the execution of the resolutions.

In a waking state these three parts are held in close unity by the conscious will. In sleep the conscious will becomes latent, and its organs are isolated from each other; therefore Homer gives sleep the unequalled epithet of "the limb-loosening" (λυσιμελής). This isolation of the brain from the motor and sensory nerves is the cause of our having in sleep neither voluntary movement nor perception. With the ceasing of the external affection is extinguished also the reaction of the Understanding, after the representations still occupying it, being no longer fed from without, come to a standstill, in which falling asleep consists. Because this cessation of the conscious will is an indispensable condition of sleep, it is impossible to obtain sleep, like so much else, by force of will.

§ 85. But when external affection and the thoughts and fancies dependent on it are silenced, whence come dreams — these dramas with such plastic scenery, such lifelike characters, of which we are the spectators and creators in sleep?

Nothing happens without cause. There is no perception without affection: so also in dreaming. The affection during sleep cannot come from without, for in that case the isolation would be broken and a half-waking state be the result. It follows consequently, that the affections by which dreams are caused, arise from the interior of our organism. We can with great probability assume the following. As nature uses (or rather causes) the stoppage of the machine, in order to repair it, so it may happen that, through her busy working to and fro, certain gentle shocks penetrate to those parts of the brain which, when affected in a waking state, would produce the perception of the external world. Now when these (like the strings of a piano when dusted) are during sleep affected from within to and fro irregularly and without connection, the Understanding at once performs its accustomed functions (the strings sound) and creates out of these sporadic affections, always of course aided by the memory of previous experience, the perceptions of the dream, so disordered and yet so distinct, so strangely confused and yet so consistently connected.

XVI. Transcendental Analysis of Matter

§ 86. The perception of the material world, and so the material world itself (§§ 38-40), arises, as we have seen, through the Understanding projecting its affections, by means of causality, in space and time (§ 75). Thus bodies are through and through nothing more than affection, that is, force, represented as filling space. Material objects are, according to Kant's excellent expression, force-filled spaces.

If now I take away force, if I deduct from bodies all that by which they affect me, there remains nothing but empty space. Some minds will be perfectly satisfied with this decomposition of matter into force and space. It will be those in whom abstract has a decided preponderance over perceptual knowledge.

§ 87. Others again, with whom the contrary is the case, will, even after thinking away all force, imagine that they still retain something besides space, namely the representation of a dark, confused mass, which, indeed, owing to the total absence of force and consequently of all affection, is neither visible nor tangible nor in any way perceptible, and yet persists as a certain something before their intellect. It is properly this something which, as it remains after the removal of all force from bodies, is opposed to force as matter or substance devoid of all quality. Now, since with the removal of force all reality, that is, all that exists independently of my intellect, falls away, the remaining matter can only be a subjective phenomenon, springing from the forms of our intellect. This phenomenon arises as follows.

§ 88. In perceiving, the Understanding is unceasingly occupied in projecting the most diverse effects, given it as affections, in space and time (§ 75). Now, if I try to efface from my consciousness (what, strictly speaking is, of course, impossible) every single real effect, there remains to me nothing but the general form of effecting, that is causality. Now just as the Understanding continually projects all concrete effects (all effecting ἐνεργείᾳ ὄν) as causes in space, so it continues, even when I set these aside, to perceive the general possibility of effecting (the effect δυνάμει ὄν), that is, causality itself (§ 62), as filling space and persisting in time, where it then appears as that dark phantom of matter or substance. Matter therefore has no proper reality, as even Aristotle recognised, when he defined it as merely δυνάμει ὄν. It is only the possibility of corporeity conceived as corporeal, that is causality, perceived in space and time. Consequently it is the combined totality of causality, space, and time perceived objectively, whereas the same totality perceived subjectively (as we saw, § 74) constitutes the Understanding. Matter is therefore the objective reflex of the Understanding itself, and is to it what space is to the space-function, time to the time-function. It is therefore in the main the same, only viewed on the one side from the empirical, on the other from the transcendental standpoint.

Remark.—Thus matter originates in the abstraction from all concrete effect, just as each concept originates in abstraction from the individual representations underlying it. Curiously enough, however, matter is not an abstract concept but an element of the perceptual world. This, I believe, must have been in Plato's mind when he defined matter as μεταλαμβάνον ἀπορώτατά πῃ τοῦ νοητοῦ and as ἁπτὸν λογισμῷ τινι νόθῳ (Tim. 51 A, 52 B). Abstracting is an act of the reason, which, however, in this case leads exceptionally not to a concept but to a perceptual representation, for which cause Plato pronounced it spurious, νόθος. (Compare on this obscure passage and the various unsatisfactory attempts to explain it my *Commentatio de Platonis Sophista*, Bonn, 1869, pp. 32-34.)

XVII. The Double World of the Half-Philosophers

§ 89. Kant had proved that the three main pillars of nature,—time, space, and causality, are nothing but the subjective forms of our intellect: whence follows inevitably, that the material world, presented in them, is merely the form in which things appear to me, but not what they are in themselves.

§ 90. Admitting the irrefutability of the Kantian arguments, without however adopting their inevitable conclusions, a series of thinkers since Kant have sought refuge in a certain Ideal-Realism, as they call it. According to them, space, time, and causality are on the one hand subjective functions of the intellect, in which we conceive and manufacture into representations the affections coming from things, and on the other hand they are the objective forms of existence of things themselves, so that between the being of things and our representing of them there would be a complete parallelism.

§ 91. The absurdity of this assertion is obvious, since it is nothing but the assumption that everything which is, exists doubly, so that we should have before us not one, but two worlds, resembling each other to a hair's breadth, without however having the least contact with, or relation to, each other. The first of these two worlds is this real, perceptual world which I see with my eyes and touch with my hands. This world is, as we have seen, the product of *a priori* consciousness and *a posteriori* sensations. Behind this world, according to the above assumption, lies another, of which we can never obtain the slightest knowledge, and which therefore probably exists nowhere,—unless perhaps in the imagination of those thinkers, whose names we omit.

XVIII. Kant and the Philosophy after him

§ 92. The distinction between phenomena and things-in-themselves is as old as philosophy itself, nay, all philosophy (so far as empirical science is not concealed under the name) expresses the consciousness of this great contrast. It was Kant, however, who first gave it a scientific basis, by showing that it is the forms of the Understanding, inherent in our intellect, by means of which Being-in-itself becomes visible to us as the material world extended in space and time. The appearance of Kant therefore will remain for all time the turning-point in the history of philosophy, and whoever in the future means to philosophise, must first of all come to an understanding with his teaching. The pith of Kant's doctrine is the transcendental dogma of the a priority of time, space, and causality; each must decide whether to accept or reject it. There are but two grounds on which it can be rejected; there are but two ways open to those who accept it. Accordingly the philosophers after Kant fall into four classes, which include all thinkers, present and future.

§ 93. Those who reject Kant's teaching can have only two reasons for doing so: either, they are unable to convince themselves of the validity of his arguments,—in this case our exposition of these invites to a renewed examination of them; or they go their own way, ignoring Kant's discovery,—they will allow us to do the same with them.

§ 94. Amongst those who admit Kant's doctrine, we distinguish such as accept it, but evade its consequences,—of these we spoke in the foregoing chapter; and such as have the courage to adopt not only the transcendental dogma but also the conclusions which necessarily follow from it.

This was the way taken by Schopenhauer. He stands in many remarkable respects to Kant as Plato to Sokrates. All the rest are at best like the so-called "imperfect Sokratists."

For an Aristotle wait not! Thousands of busy hands are stirring in all corners of the empirical sciences. But a little while, and the whole world—*â pipîlikâbhyas*—will perceive the day that has dawned. Let us hope that under the impending salutary revolution which Schopenhauer's doctrine will cause in the domain of empirical science, the depth of Schopenhauer's thought may not be so overwhelmed as was that of Plato by Aristotle.

APPENDIX TO THE FIRST PART OF METAPHYSICS

REASON AND ITS CONTENT

XIX. Survey

§ 95. Reason is an intellectual faculty, peculiar to man, of forming from perceptual representations (by dropping what is different in them and retaining what is identical) "abstract" representations or concepts, further, of combining concepts into judgments and judgments into syllogisms. In contradistinction to perceptual knowledge the operating with concepts is called thinking.

§ 96. Since concepts, as vibrations of the brain cells or whatever they may be, are not perceptible, we need for their communication an external vehicle. This we have in the words of language, which consist of certain specific vibrations of the air, produced by the sound of the voice and variously modified by the organs of the mouth (throat, palate, tongue, teeth, lips). Thus language, by the manifold combination of a few primary elements, produces an astonishing wealth of material, sufficient to portray in a perceptible form and to communicate to others not only concepts but also the relations of these to each other even to the finest shades of distinction.

§ 97. Speaking is therefore so to say the visibility of thinking. Now thinking among all nations is essentially the same, whereas language shows with different peoples the greatest variety—a fact which is surprising and not easily explained. Logic exhibits everywhere the same problems; the question how these are to be solved in different languages, led necessarily to comparative grammar. This has started by going back from the corrupted forms of the historical languages to the primitive languages preceding them, whereby the problem is not solved but only clearly stated.

§ 98. A thorough discussion of these topics belongs to Logic and Grammar. We shall confine ourselves in the following, (1) to showing how concepts, upon which the whole content of logic depends, spring from perception; (2) to explaining how the functions of Reason have their root in the one and simple reactive faculty of the Understanding; (3) to deriving the difference between man and brute from the faculty of concepts which alone distinguishes them; (4) to hazarding a few conjectures as to the origin of language.

XX. Origin and Nature of Concepts

§ 99. It is very remarkable that nature is neither thoroughly alike nor yet in all parts thoroughly unlike, but shows a variegated blending of identical and non-identical elements. Here I see a red, there a blue flower; I meet the same blue again in the sky, in the bird's wing, or in the stone, which yet have nothing whatever to do with the flower, while again all these objects have much in common with others from which, for the rest, they are quite different. Thus I often notice identical phenomena in different places and at different times. Must these not have some secret affinity to each other, for how else come they to be identical? This thought is the gate by which Plato entered the realm of metaphysics. But of this later. At present we are concerned with nature as an aggregate of identical and non-identical elements only in so far, as it is on this peculiarity that the formation of concepts depends.

§ 100. The brutes also perceive the similarity and dissimilarity of things, often even more perfectly than man. The dog which rambles with the hunter through the woods, distinguishes more sharply than does his master the deer from its like-hued sheltering surroundings. There can be no doubt also, that a dog distinguishes perfectly between an oak and a fir-tree. But its less developed brain does not react powerfully enough, its understanding is not sufficiently independent of things, to see in them anything more than those relations in which, for the moment, its will is interested. Not so man. When in an oak forest he notices how the trees around, in spite of all difference in detail, have yet something identical in them, he proceeds to decompose this perception into its identical and non-identical elements; and in abstracting from what is non-identical and retaining what is identical in the representation, he passes from the various individual perceptions of oak-trees to the concept of oak.

§ 101. Such is the process in the formation of a concept. But this destruction of perception which must take place to obtain a concept (similar to our destruction of the marvellous organisms of animals, for the purpose of eating their flesh), is in reality due to the fact, that it is the natural destiny of the intellect to be an instrument of the will. For what is of interest to the will is not things, but the relations of things to itself. From this standpoint the wonderful continuity of the perceptual world is dissolved into a number of possible relations, which in logic are called predicates, or more characteristically marks (*notae*). They are the provisions which the will lays up in the storehouse of reason for future use. If our intellect were not a servant of the will, in all probability we should form no concepts.

§ 102. The sum of the predicates of a concrete object is infinite. The predicates, however, which are common to it with other objects, are generally, at least for our apprehension, very limited in number. Since the space which every object fills, is always different, and perceptibility depends on space-occupation, all concepts, being abstractions from all that is different, must lose their individual form. They are not to be confounded with images of fancy, which are in fact individual, and for that very reason only single representatives of concepts, containing much which is not common to all objects of the same kind.

§ 103. The concepts of the oak, the beech, the fir, each consist of a number of marks or predicates which are partly different, partly in all three the same. If now, again, of these predicates we drop the non-identical and retain the identical, we obtain the concept of tree, richer in extent but poorer in content of predicates, which comprehends oak, fir, and beech, just as each of these includes the single objects of its kind. By the same process I pass from the concept of tree to that of plant, from this to that of organism, from this to that of body, and so at last to the concept of Substance or Being. This concept has an extremely wide extent, for it comprehends under it all that is; the poorer, however, is its content, for it is restricted to a single predicate. But for that very reason it can have no more general concept above it. In a similar way I can rise from the perceptions of red, round, cold, bitter, fragrant, etc. to the general concepts of colour, form, taste, etc., and from these to the most general concept of quality, which as such is restricted to a single predicate.

§ 104. These concepts of highest generality are, according to *Aristotle*, called Categories, of which he enumerates ten: οὐσία, ποσόν, ποιόν, πρός τι, ποῦ, ποτέ, κεῖσθαι, ἔχειν, ποιεῖν, πάσχειν (Substance, Quantity, Quality, Relation, Space, Time, Position, Possession, Action, Passion), while in India *Kaṇâda* undertook a classification of things under six Categories, which he called *pada-arthâs* (word-things, essences or concepts corresponding to words). They are: *dravya, guṇa, karman, sâmânya, viçesha, samavâya* (Substance, Quality, Action, Community, Difference, Inherency). It might be possible to do with three Categories: (1) Substance (οὐσία—*dravya*); (2) Quality (ποσόν, ποιόν—*guṇa*); (3) Relation (πρός τι—*sâmânya, viçesha, samavâya*);

for ποῦ and ποτέ, as Kant observed, are not conceptual but perceptual, and the verbal Categories (κεῖσθαι, ἔχειν, ποιεῖν, πάσχειν — *karman*) can be reduced to the others by separating the copula, which is not a concept but the linguistic sign of a combination of concepts.

§ 105. The whole system of concepts up to the Categories is accordingly abstracted from the perceptual world, and may be likened to a number of interlocked pyramids with a common and very broad base, namely perception. From this, by the continued comprehension of several specific concepts under a generic concept, we ascend from peak to peak to those few highest summits formed by the Categories. If now, again, we look with a bird's-eye view down on these category peaks and through them to the base, the summits of all special and general concepts will appear projected upon the base. And there they lie in reality; for if on the one hand general concepts comprehend specific **under them,** so on the other hand specific concepts contain the general concepts, up to the Categories, as predicates **in them** (Extent and Content of Concepts).

XXI. On Combinations of Concepts

§ 106. Every judgment is the combination of two (more or less complicated) concepts, in such a way, that one (the predicate) is predicated (κατηγορεῖται, *praedicatur*) of the other (the subject) or (in negative judgments) excluded from it.

§ 107. A judgment is **analytical**, when the subject-concept contains the predicate-concept in it as a characteristic, so that we need only extract the latter from the former (ex. the rose is a flower); a judgment is **synthetic**, when we denote by the combination of concepts a union of two elements of the perceptual world which are not already contained in our concept of the subject (ex. the rose is red). For forming analytical judgments, therefore, we need only the knowledge stored up by previous experience in the system of our concepts and no new experience. In this respect one may say that all analytical judgments are *a priori*, that is, independent of experience (excepting of course the previous experience from which the concept was originally formed). Synthetic judgments, on the other hand, always show a combination of characteristics not involved in the concepts themselves, but contained only in the perceptual world. They would therefore be altogether *a posteriori*, were it not that, as we have seen (§§ 42-68), certain elements of perception are *a priori*. On these elements are based the synthetic judgments *a priori* of the mathematical sciences (§§ 52. 59. 66). This observation is important for metaphysics, because it was Kant's starting-point in the "Critique of Pure Reason."

§ 108. Whatever we think, whatever (by means of words) we speak and hear, write and read, are concepts, for the most part combined as judgments. It is a good exercise to take any book and analyse a passage of it into nothing but concepts, modified by various accessory determinations and connected by the copula (usually contained in the verb).

Remark.—It is the merit of the Greeks to have created a syntax which hides by the cunning of language the monotonous combination of subject and predicate of which the nature of the judgment consists. On Greek syntax depends in the main that of all the civilised languages of Europe. The Indians, on the other hand, led away by the wealth of their case-forms and the extraordinary facility for composition which distinguishes their language, express subject and predicate with their accessory determinations, particularly in scientific prose, by long compounds. As a result, their style generally is in a high degree logical, but at the same time for the reader extremely wearisome.

§ 109. The predicate of a subject-concept is of course valid for all concepts comprehended under the subject-concept (ex. if all Being is created by God, so also is evil, since its concept is comprehended under that of Being). On this depends the possibility of drawing particular judgments from general: a practice we constantly follow in thinking. Its methodical form is the syllogism (*nyâya*, συλλογισμός), of which there are three, or if one likes, four figures and nineteen modes, which we may here omit.

§ 110. Since all concepts whatever are abstracted from perception, every correct judgment is based finally upon a relation in the perceptual world, whether the judgment springs immediately from perception, or whether it is derived by deduction from a more general judgment (§ 109) which itself is in turn obtained from perception by induction. The methodical process of going back from one proposition to another, and by means of this to perception, is called Proof. But perception itself is the base on which all judgments and proofs, whether immediate or mediate, are founded. What we perceive cannot therefore be demonstrated further, that is, reduced to anything else more certain, nor does it require it. This does not, however, preclude our making use of proofs, when the question is to derive from the accessible data of the perceptual world other facts which belong also to perception, but escape our observation, whether through being too far from us in space and time, or because their relations are too subtle and floating to be grasped and retained with exactitude by mere perceiving. On this we may base the justification of Euclid's proofs in mathematics, which Schopenhauer would not admit.

§ 111. From what has been said, it is clear that all concepts and all judgments spring from perception. (The sole exception are the so-called Laws of Thought, together with the nearly related abstract Categories of Kant, in all of which, however, no content is expressed, but only the general form of abstract knowledge.) Accordingly abstract representations both in physics and metaphysics are only to be regarded as an instrument by means of which we grasp the concrete world. This world itself with its content is the sole subject of all sciences (excepting logic), and only the data given by it can guide us to physical and metaphysical truth.

§ 112. The neglect of this principle has caused the gravest errors in metaphysics, whether, like Zeno and others, men, arguing from the mosaic-like and abrupt nature of abstract knowledge, have assumed "contradictions" in the perceptual world, which neither asserts nor contradicts, or whether, obeying the impulse given by Aristotle and Kant, they have regarded concepts (because through them we retain the essence of perception) as the genetic principles of Reality. Both errors have in post-Kantian philosophy given birth to systems which, for a time, succeeded in attracting the attention and the approval of their age.

XXII. Whether Reason is a Particular Physiological Organ?

§ 113. Whatever exists is material (§ 11); so also the intellect[1] (§§ 26. 27) Brain and intellect are two names for the same thing. Their difference arises from the fact that in this case the organ and its functions are accessible by different ways. Psychology knows only the function, physiology, until now, almost only the organ. Both methods supplement, and do not contradict, each other.

§ 114. Now psychology has taught us two functions of the human intellect, that of perceiving and that of thinking. The question is, whether these are to be regarded as manifestations of one and the same faculty or of different faculties,— whether Understanding and Reason are two distinct physiological organs or only two specific functions of the same organ.

§ 115. The following reasons determine us in favour of the latter view, by means of which the unity of the human mind is maintained,—a fact of importance for our later inquiries.

---

[1] Primum animum dico, mentem quam saepe vocamus,
In quo consilium vitae regimenque locatum est,
Esse hominis partem nilo minus ac manus et pes
Atque oculei partes animantis totius extant.
       Lucretius III. 94-97.

1. The structure of the human brain corresponds in all essentials to that of the higher animals, although its single parts appear in different proportions and in much higher development. From this certain ignorant physiologists would fain draw the conclusion that brutes also to a certain degree "think" (!). We, however, infer from this, that thinking is nothing but a distinct operation, peculiar to man, of the perceiving faculty, that is, of the brain.

2. Knowledge is very likely the product of a single organ in our head, the brain so far as it consists of the cerebral hemispheres. In its place we should find two organs, if Understanding and Reason were two separate faculties.

3. Our intellect is continually occupied in subsuming perceptions under concepts. We pass from perceiving to thinking, from thinking to perceiving, with the greatest ease and without any feeling of interruption. This would scarcely be possible if these functions were assigned to two different organs.

4. In the scale of beings we see the development of the intellect keeping pace with that of the nervous system centralised in the brain. The more perfectly formed the brain, the more energetically does the Understanding fulfil its office, the more powerful is its reaction upon the affections coming from without (§ 74). In consequence, the products of this reaction, that is, represented things, are more distinctly

detached, as it were, from the knowing subject, and gain through this greater independence and objectivity.—Plants, to begin with, are without any knowledge. They do not react at all (in the sense in which we have used the word) upon external affection. In them the receiving of impressions and the being determined by them completely coincide, in which essentially the nature of irritation consists (§ 20_2). In the brutes these two elements are sundered. Thus the brute reacts upon external impressions, but only so far as is necessary to distinguish itself from external objects, that is, to establish between itself and the objects of the outside world (and partly even between the different objects themselves) the spatial, temporal, and causal connection springing from the forms of the intellect (§ 80). However, the brute intellect is still wholly absorbed in things, and animals are therefore at every moment totally dependent on surrounding impressions. From the brute to man nature takes in this direction the last possible step by augmenting the reactive faculty of the intellect to such a degree, that things appear completely isolated from the knowing ego and therefore in full objectivity. The result on the subjective side is the passing of consciousness into self-consciousness, while on the objective side it becomes possible to the intellect, by means of its isolation, to dissolve perceptions into their elements, that is, their characteristics, and to grasp and retain these in new combinations as concepts, wherein the whole mechanism of Reason consists.

§ 116. It is therefore essentially one and the same reactive faculty which, developing by degrees, establishes as the immediate application of the Understanding the connection between the affections of the subject and the external world, as the mediate application of the Understanding the connection between external objects themselves, and as the faculty of Judgment the connection between the perceptual world and its predicates, classified as concepts. The faculty of judgment is the tie which unites concepts with each other and finally with perception. It is reflecting, when extracting the general from the particular; subsuming, when ranging the particular under the general. If we take away from Reason the faculty of judgment, there remains to us only Memory, the function of which is, to reproduce in part perceptual, but chiefly abstract representations. On this account the brutes possess it only to a very limited degree, because they lack abstract representations and with these the possibility of a connected remembrance.

Remark.—Memory is, strictly speaking, not so much a faculty of retaining representations once had, as rather a facility for reproducing these by means of "association of ideas," which (like a gymnastic exercise) becomes the easier, the oftener it is practised. For the rest Memory is not, like Understanding and Judgment, that which makes intellectual superiority, being rather antagonistic to it. Only the fact that education, instead of cultivating before all things the Understanding and the Judgment, burdens the memory, can explain the circumstance, that the minds which on an average are most gifted by nature, and on the cultivation of which most pains have been bestowed, that is, those of scholars, have by no means always the intellectual ascendency to which they otherwise might have claim.

XXIII. Retrospective View of the Human Mind in General

§ 117. The intellect is, as we have shown, nothing but a component part of the animal organism and accordingly, like all members of the body, an organ of the Will (of which later). It is not, therefore, metaphysical and immortal like the soul, that is, the Will, but physical and perishable, like the body. This is the less to be regretted, since it is the constitution of our intellect which bars our view into the inner being of things. Nay, the sinfulness of our earthly life is intimately connected with the existence of our intellect, since it is intellect which by its forms creates plurality on which all egoism and discord depend.

Remark.—Yet the world created by the intellect is only the visibility of sin, while the real root of sin lies still deeper (in the freedom of the Will), and remains, therefore, inaccessible to our intellectual apprehension. But this can only be fully understood later on.

§ 118. The human intellect is, as we saw, an organ of perfect unity with two functions: (1) that of producing representations, on which depend the immediate application of the Understanding, the mediate application of the Understanding, and the faculty of judgment; (2) that of reproducing representations, wherein consists the nature of memory and imagination. The latter differs from memory chiefly by the fact, that its images arise without the consciousness of reproduction, and show therefore no connection in time, space, and causality with the present. On this depends the value of imagination in works of art and its unfitness for use in practical life.

Remark I.—It may be that of these two chief intellectual functions the productive is dependent on the quality of the brain (fineness of texture, proper nourishment, etc.) and the reproductive on its quantity (in comparison with the nervous matter of the whole body).

Remark II.—It is interesting to compare our division of the intellect with a very similar one of the *buddhi* in the Nyâya- and Vaiçeshika-Philosophy (see for instance *Bhâshâpariccheda*, v. 50. 51).

XXIV. Man and Brute

§ 119. Inner and outer perception are common to us with the brutes. Now these two are the only sources from which we obtain all our knowledge.

We have accordingly, as regards the content of our knowledge, no advantage over the brutes, and our whole superiority to these is due to the fact that we can give our perceptual knowledge another form, namely the abstract form of concepts.

§ 120. At first sight this difference may seem to be a slight one. It is, however, the result of a qualitative and quantitative development of the brain which is probably the most difficult work accomplished by nature. None of the innumerable species of animals even distantly approach it, no being known to us has surpassed it. If now it is the faculty of concepts, that is Reason alone, which raises man above the brute, all that distinguishes human life from that of the lower animals and stamps it with so distinctive a character, must be derived from Reason.

§ 121. Animals are restricted to perceptual knowledge. This embraces (apart from single recollections) nothing more than the immediate present. For its connection with what is absent, past, or future is only representable by means of concepts, which the brute lacks. It lives, therefore, only in the present, which, like a mighty stream, sweeps unceasingly past it, leaving but a few perceptual images impressed on its memory. Hence the limitation of its horizon.

§ 122. **Not so Man.** Continually is he occupied in grasping what is essential in the fleeting present, by storing it in concepts which comprehend under a few categories the immeasurable variety of the perceptual world. Thus we have in concepts, instead of the fragmentary perceptual recollection of the brute, a connected consciousness of the past, even though the amount of perceptions we retain in them is but limited. By means of concepts we control, besides the narrow circle of the perceptual present, the immeasurable totality of the absent and reckon with it in all our thinking and acting. Through concepts we anticipate nine-tenths of the future. It but seldom happens that the capricious course of things does not confirm the calculations we have made beforehand in abstract concepts.

§ 123. Thus is opened to our view the whole of the world, the reproduction of which in a system of methodically arranged concepts is the aim of all Empirical Science. At the same time we become aware of the sorrowful and fleeting nature of our existence. Death, which is unknown to the brute until the moment of dying, stands before our eyes as an ever-threatening necessity, and the fear of possible suffering torments us more than actual distress. Both drive us to Philosophy; it is, according to the Indian view, the remedy for all the ills of existence; it is, as Plato says, a preparing for death (Phaedon, p. 64 A).

§ 124. Again, the planned action of one or of several individuals in co-operation is only possible through the faculty of concepts. On it depends all that serves to protect and adorn our existence: art and science, education, government, justice, law, agriculture, industry, commerce—in short, whatever we oppose to nature as civilisation, and by which human life presents such a striking contrast to that of the brutes. All these great institutions are unknown to the brute, and its intellect, confined, as it is, to the present and unaware of the greatest wants and dangers of the future, would not suffice to guarantee the safety of its existence, if all-wise Nature had not provided a means, where knowledge is insufficient, for guiding the steps of the brute without knowledge as though it were with knowledge. This provision of Nature is instinct, one of the most important facts for philosophy, with which we shall have to deal later.

§ 125. The action of brutes is throughout determined by perceptual motives confined to the present: hence the transparency of all that they do. Man, on the contrary, has not only perceptual but also abstract motives, which allow him a deliberate choice, since, before he acts, he can reflect, that is, allow the different motives to try their power on his will, in order to experience which of them is the strongest. For by the strongest motive his action is in every case determined, and his decisions are never free, though the determining motives may often not be apparent to us. The acting according to abstract motives is called **reasonable**, and in it lies a great prerogative of Man: for his power increases in proportion as he is able to free himself from present impressions and be guided by the consideration of the totality of things (present to him in abstract representations). The moral worth of a character, however, depends on what sort of motives influence the will, and not on the form, whether concrete or abstract, which they adopt to determine our actions.

XXV. On the Nature and Origin of Language

§ 126. Concepts, as modifications of the substance of the brain, are not perceptible. In order to be communicated, they need certain external symbols. These are the words of language, peculiar to man alone. The relation between concept and word cannot be an accidental one; and yet it is not a thoroughly necessary one, as appears from the diversity of primitive languages.

§ 127. The sounds of language had to express two things: firstly, concepts and, secondly, the relation of concepts to each other. Hence the necessity for two elements of speech: signs of signification and signs of relation. In all languages these two must appear either separated or united as words. In the latter case the union is either a merely external one and causes no change in the signs, or it is internal, so that the two elements mutually influence each other (whether by strengthening of the root or weakening of the termination). Hence we have three possible stages of speech, which include all known languages.

1. The isolating languages (ex. Chinese) range signs of signification and signs of relation (as far as the latter are not entirely suppressed) together, without any union.

2. The agglutinative languages (ex. Finno-Tartaric, Polynesian, and the majority of languages) combine both elements without altering either.

3. The inflectional languages (Semitic and Indo-Germanic) make of the two elements an organic whole in which one modifies the other. This proves, perhaps, that man at this stage of language first attained the intellectual energy to grasp the concept and its relation as a unity.

§ 128. Just as comparative anatomy regards the higher organisms of the animal kingdom as a more perfect development of the lower, so the anatomy of the primitive languages leads to the assumption that the inflectional languages were originally agglutinative, and these again isolating. The supposition is obvious that these three stages of language correspond to three stages in the growth of the thinking faculty. We may leave undecided, how far the isolation of the concept-sign and the relational sign to which modern languages have in part returned, bears witness to a deterioration of thought.

§ 129. But suppose we had reduced all languages to that stage in which all concepts were expressed by isolated monosyllabic roots, the chief problem would still remain unsolved ; for how came men to choose for a particular concept just these sounds and no others? The theory, that the denotation of concepts by sounds was due to convention ($\theta \acute{\epsilon} \sigma \epsilon \iota$), falls to the ground, for all convention is only possible by means of language. Moreover concept and word have certainly grown one with the other, as the skin grows together with the body and is not drawn over it afterwards.

§ 130. The following theory (together with onomatopœia and other subordinate influences) might lead to a satisfactory explanation of the origin of speech ; whilst the diversity of the primitive languages might be attributed partly to original physiological race-differences, partly to the deeply-moulding influences of climate, soil, occupation, food, etc. Imagine man in the condition of the brute, restricted to perception and like the brutes absorbed, as it were, in it. By degrees the reactive faculty of the intellect increased (§ 115,$_4$), the apprehension of the surrounding present became more and more objective, and the subject opposed itself more and more determinedly to external objects. This awakening of man was expressed through his denoting his relation to the outside world by gestures (of the hand, foot, eye, etc.). Herewith the animal state was passed, for no animal attains to a real gesture language. Now in the same way as to-day the (untrained) deaf and dumb accompany the gestures with which they make themselves understood, by more or less articulate sounds, so it might happen that the desiring, refusing, pointing at, grasping, seeking, etc. which were manifested through that primitive speech of the limbs, were at the same time accompanied by a corresponding movement of the organs of the mouth. Thus, for instance, the pointing with the hand might be accompanied by a pointing of the tongue, which however was not visible, but as *ta* (the demonstrative pronoun) became audible and so perceptible even in the dark. Little by little perhaps these gestures of the throat, tongue, and lips would take the place of the analogous gestures of the limbs which formerly they had accompanied. In this way exchanging visibility for audibility, they were able, even in the absence of the object to be denoted by them, to refer to it. Thus on the one hand the mind became independent of the corresponding present, while by the same process on the other hand the perceived object passed into its fancy image and—by restricting the reproduction to the essential outlines of the object—into its concept.

§ 131. The process and the further development of language to its highest perfection belongs entirely to the sphere of conscious Will, and yet it cannot be admitted that languages are the product of conscious design. For it is impossible that the childlike consciousness which meets us in the hymns of the Ṛigveda, should have created a language the analysis of which demanded all the penetration of a Pâṇini. Language therefore belongs to the unconscious creations of the Will within the sphere of consciousness, that is, to the productions of instinct, and we must explain the high perfection of primitive speech in the same way as we do the geometrically-woven web of the spider and the wonderfully-ordered communities of the bees and ants.

THE SYSTEM OF METAPHYSICS

PART II

THE METAPHYSICS OF NATURE

I. The Problem

§ 132. "What is the World?" This is the simple fundamental question of all philosophy. The immediate answer would be: "Well, the world is nothing but the world. It lies extended before your eyes, and moreover all empirical sciences are engaged in investigating more and more minutely every part of the universe."—Those who do not acquiesce in this answer are called philosophers. Even after all the instruction of empirical science, they cannot get rid of the tormenting question: "But this so much investigated and well-known world—what is it in its real essence?"—Their continued asking shows that they distinguish the What of the world from the world itself, that they regard the world as the appearance of an essence which in itself does not appear, and which no progress in empirical science can ever reach.

§ 133. It is this real essence of the world which philosophy has sought since the most ancient times as the **principle** from which the existence of the world with all that it contains, may be derived and explained. The character therefore of every philosophical system is determined by the two questions: (1) what principle of the world it establishes, and (2) how from this principle it explains the world. Almost all pre-Kantian philosophers erred mainly in this, that (as is already indicated by the name ἀρχή, *principium*) they transferred the forms of our understanding, space, time, and causality to the principle of the world, and further used these forms as a bridge to go back from the world to its principle. Kant, however, proved that it is just by means of these innate functions of our Understanding, that the principle of the world, which he called the **thing-in-itself** (Ding-an-sich), is presented to our eyes as the universe extended in space, time, and causality. Hence we must neither transfer these forms of knowledge to the thing-in-itself, nor abuse them, to derive from it the world which is its appearance.

§ 134. The impossibility of establishing a spatial, temporal, or causal connection between phenomena and the thing-in-itself becomes evident to us even in an empirical way, if we try, by means of facts and with the help of bold hypotheses, to picture to ourselves the life of the Universe as it exists in infinite space through infinite time. However far we may go by the clue of causality backwards, forwards, and on all sides in space and time, we reach only what is in nature, but never that which (to speak figuratively) lies behind it, that is, we are always restricted to Physics without ever being able to penetrate to Metaphysics.

Remark.—In contradistinction to Physics or the science of Nature, the science of Being-in-itself (des An-sich-seienden) is happily expressed by the name Metaphysics, though (like the beautiful name *Vedânta*) we probably owe it to a mere literary accident.

§ 135. The natural sciences show us the world as a totality of matter which perpetually changes its qualities, forms, and conditions (§ 14). Now all these changes in matter and also (as we showed, §§ 74-76. 86-88) material objects themselves are finally only a sum of effects; and these effects are one and all nothing but the varied manifestations in space, time, and causality of that which in itself does not exist in space, time, and causality, and is therefore absolutely unknowable. It is this unknowable essence which scientists call **force**, and which in a series of original phenomenal forms (the physical, chemical, and organic forces of nature) is manifested in all those effects, constituting nature. In so far as these effects concern our body and thereby make us conscious of the existence of things, they have been mentioned already under the name of **sensations** or **affections** (§§ 43. 69,₃. 75).

§ 136. The scientist or student of nature can accordingly only indicate **how,** that is, in what form of space, in what sequence of time and under what causal conditions force is manifested; but he does not know **what** force in itself may be, because it exists neither in space nor time, nor is it to be found by means of causality (§ 24). From this it becomes clear that the same entity which philosophers seek as the principle of the world, is that which is pre-supposed by Kant as the thing-in-itself, and by natural science as force, and by both given up as unknowable.

§ 137. Philosophy meanwhile is engaged in explaining the world from this principle, this force, this thing-in-itself (§ 133). Now all explanation is the deriving of the unknown from the known and not the reverse. If therefore the problem of philosophy is not absolutely insoluble, there must be some point from which the thing-in-itself is not only accessible, but even more immediately and more intimately known than the whole phenomenal world which is to be explained from it.

There is such a point, and there is but one.

§ 138. All knowledge is a process in our intellect. The latter is for ever bound to the forms which constitute its nature (§ 69$_4$). Now it is in these forms that the thing-in-itself appears expanded as the world. Consequently, so long as we perceive things through our intellect, that is, so long as we are human beings, a knowledge of the thing-in-itself is impossible to us.—So argued Kant. He believed to have thereby overthrown Metaphysics for ever.

§ 139. Kant's conclusions would hold good for all time, if our intellect and its three forms were the only way to reach things.—But this is not so. More intimately known to me indeed, than this whole world, is the intellect in and through which all its manifestations are presented to me; but there is one thing still more intimately known to me than my intellect, and that is I myself. In our own inmost self therefore, if anywhere, must lie the key which opens to us the inner understanding of nature. Here it was found by Schopenhauer.—No sculptor's chisel, no poet's hymn can worthily celebrate him for it.

§ 140. Plato deplored that our intellect, in which he placed the centre of the soul, should be bound to a body which dims the purity of our perception of things (Phaedon, pp. 66 B. 79 C). But we must rather praise this dispensation, since our body is the only thing which we apprehend, not merely, like everything else, from without, but also from within. Before, however, guided by Schopenhauer, we make use of inner experience to open to us the understanding of the external world, let us cast a glance at nature, as it would appear to us, if we were, as Plato wished, pure bodiless intelligences, that is, if external experience alone and not internal as well were at our command.

II. Nature, viewed from the Standpoint of Pure Intellect, that is, from without

§ 141. The *a priori* forms of our intellect: time, space, and causality, are perfectly familiar and comprehensible to us. The *a posteriori* force, given as sense-affection, which we weave with these forms into the totality of nature (§§ 45. 75), remains entirely unknown and inconceivable. Hence follows, that the intelligibility of nature reaches just so far as the *a-priority* in it, and that the phenomena of the inorganic and organic world become gradually more mysterious and incomprehensible in proportion as *a-posteriority* prevails in them.

§ 142. All that the investigator of nature can determine, is the manifestation of force in a certain place, at a certain time, and as the result of a certain cause. In this alone lies the comprehensible part of phenomena. Accordingly what we understand is the spatial form and the temporal sequence of phenomena, but not what appears in this form and this sequence. Likewise the causality of phenomena, that is, their being conditioned, is comprehensible, but not that which, occasioned by cause, appears as effect; and one can follow, step by step, how the comprehensibility of natural phenomena decreases in proportion as, in the scale of mechanical, physical, chemical, and organic phenomena, the effect gradually overwhelms the cause, in becoming, in comparison to it, more and more dissimilar, mighty and independent; which is due to a gradually increasing susceptibility or, so to say, sensibility of organic and inorganic beings. While namely the force, embodied in all nature from the stone to man, becomes more and more susceptible to the causal influence, which thereby turns from cause in its narrower sense into irritation, from irritation to perceptual and finally to abstract motives (§§ 20. 115$_4$), the causes become ever more heterogeneous, insignificant, and remote in comparison to the effects which they produce, and for this reason the comprehensibility of the effect, consisting in its causality, becomes slighter and slighter.

§ 143. Among all sciences geometry, arithmetic, phoronomy, and logic are alone absolutely clear, because they lie entirely in the *a priori* domain. But already even in mechanics an obscuring element makes itself felt in the *a posteriori* given force, although the mechanical action of forces, due to the preponderance of a-priority in it, has for us the greatest possible comprehensibility. Hence our natural inclination to interpret every effect as a mechanical one. Less comprehensible to us than pressure and impact are the phenomena forming the subject of physics and chemistry, because in these we see the effect becoming more and more unlike its cause, and are therefore unable to understand how, for instance, expansion should be caused by heat, electricity by friction, or chemical decomposition by light. Yet the susceptibility of force to causal influence remains slight in all inorganic nature. Here therefore with the degree of the cause that of the effect increases and decreases, and the change in the cause is as great as that which it imparts to the effect ($\S$ $20_{,1}$).

§ 144. Neither of these two laws holds good, once we pass from the inorganic to the organic world. The susceptibility of things to causal influences, manifested even in inanimate nature, appears in an intensified form in the life of plants and animals, and for this reason effect and cause become more and more foreign to each other. Effect here shows itself in the phenomena of life;—cause, for the involuntary changes in plant and animal life, in irritation; for the voluntary movements of animals, in motives. Already in the case of irritation increase of cause may lead to a contrary effect, and changes in the effect take place without corresponding changes in the cause, whereby even the phenomenon of life gains such a mysterious independence. Yet, in the case of irritation, the action is always conditioned by contact in space and a certain duration in time; also the receiving of the impression and the being determined by it still completely coincide.

§ 145. In the voluntary movements of animals these two are sundered; the cause appears here as motive, the effect as bodily movement. The medium between the two is the intellect. The latter is at bottom nothing else but that same susceptibility to the causal influence, inherent in everything that exists, which appears here, in conscious beings, in an intensified form as a specific organ, namely, the brain. In proportion as the intellect becomes perfected in the animal scale, the gap between cause (motive) and effect (movement of the limbs) becomes ever wider, and with that the incomprehensibility of the causal influence ever greater. This incomprehensibility reaches its highest degree in the action of Man, since this is determined not only by perceptual but also by abstract motives

(§ 125). Here the effect is even no longer confined, as in the case of the animal, to the presence of the cause; the thread between cause and effect has become so thin, that many have even ventured to deny its existence and to declare the action of man as (empirically) free, that is, as conditioned by no cause whatever.

The external comprehensibility of natural phenomena, which consists in the transparency of the nexus between cause and effect, has here at the highest stage completely vanished, and consequently the manifold and ever-changing movements of our own limbs would be for us the darkest point in all nature—were they not of all the most clear, because, by a particular chance, the philosophising intellect itself forms here a link in the secret chain, and is thus initiated into the mystery of Nature at the very point where it appears in its highest development.

Remark.—To the increasing incomprehensibility of natural phenomena corresponds, in a practical respect, an increasing difficulty in the management of them; for every influence is possible only by way of causality, and that, as has been shown, becomes obscurer, the higher we ascend in nature. Hence inorganic bodies are more easily managed than plants, these than animals, and animals than men. Compare from this point of view the increasing difficulty in the task of the mechanic, the chemist, the gardener, the physician, and the teacher.

III. The Way into the Interior of Nature

§ 146. We have shown how the viewing of things from without, whether by the subjective method of Kant or the objective method of empirical science, leads finally to an inscrutable entity (the thing-in-itself, affection, force), which is for ever unattainable by way of external experience. For wherever we may turn to grasp the thing-in-itself,—there stand ever between it and ourselves, as a darkening medium, the innate forms of our intellect, showing us how it appears in time, space, and causality, but not what it is in itself.

§ 147. All things in the world are accessible to me only from without,—with one exception. This exception is my own self (*âtman*), which I am able to comprehend *firstly*, like everything else, from without, and *secondly*, unlike anything else, from within. In both cases that which comprehends, is the intellect, woven of time, space, and causality, that which is comprehended, the sensation, given to the intellect as nerve-irritation. Thus far internal and external experience are similar. But the great difference between the two is this. On the one hand I know my ego as an object of external experience, like every other thing, by construing in space, with the help of causality, the affections given to the external senses, through which process my Self, just like everything else, appears in my perception as a through and through material body. Now, on the other hand, I do not conceive the affections coming from within, like those from without, as effects which I project as causes in space and time. On the contrary, my ego, as object of inner experience, is free from space and causality, and there remains only the form of time in which expanded inner experience is reflected in the intellect. Thus time is the only barrier which hinders me from knowing by the inner view, what I am as thing-in-itself. The question is, whether it may not be surmounted.

Remark.—The outer world and the inner world both lie as feelings in our consciousness and are both for the intellectual ego something foreign, something else, a non-ego. And yet we treat them both differently. For we consider the external impressions, given by the senses, as aliens and expel them from us by means of causality. The internal or subjective feelings of volition, pleasure, and pain on the contrary receive from us the rights of citizenship and remain, as belonging to our ego, untransformed. This is explicable only by the fact, that the intellectual ego is not the final point of unity in ourselves, but recognises above itself another and a still higher ego, from which these internal sensations spring. We are about to disclose this higher ego in us as the willing ego.

§ 148. When I move any limb of my body (ex. hand or foot), this process, regarded from without, appears as a bodily change in space, time, and causality; regarded from within, as a volition, that is, as **Will,** expanded in time. We distinguish here three things: the bodily movement, the volition accompanying it, and the Will manifested in it. But these three are not different in themselves but only so for our intellect, because their difference springs only from a different relation to our intellect. (1) Bodily movement lies always in time, space, and causality. (2) The volition, corresponding to it, does not lie in space; it lies in causality, so far as every volition is determined by a motive, and again it does not lie in causality, in so far as I do not conceive inner like outer affection (§ 75) as an effect, which I refer to its external cause. Finally, every volition fills a certain time and consequently appears certainly and necessarily in the form of time. (3) Will itself, however, which appears to the external senses as bodily movement and to the internal sense as the single acts of volition, lies neither in space, nor in causality, nor in time. It lies therefore beyond the reach of our intellect and remains thus in itself absolutely unknowable. We know it only in so far as it is mirrored in the intellectual form of time, in which it appears extended as volition.

§ 149. That which appears to our intellect as bodily movement, is in itself Will. But just as not only the changes in matter, but also material objects themselves are nothing but sensation which we construe as bodies in space, time, and causality, so also, as will appear in the following, not only the movements of my limbs, but also the limbs themselves of which my body is composed, are intrinsically and in themselves Will. The understanding of this truth is somewhat difficult, because in a normal state I am little or not at all conscious of my body. I become conscious of it however, the moment some outward influence affects it, which inwardly makes itself directly felt as sensation. This sensation is (with the exception of normal sense-affections) either pleasure or pain, that is, a willing or a non-willing imposed on us by the corresponding impression. From this it appears, that not only the movement of the body, but also the body itself, as far as I am at all conscious of it, enters into my consciousness as Will.

Remark.—Let it be said here once for all, that by Will we do not mean, as one might expect, the acquired sovereignty of the reason over the claims of desire, nor mere intentions, resolutions, or decisions, which are nothing but calculations of motives concluded in the intellect and provisionally and revocably approved by the Will. But Will here and throughout is for us that which is better known to us than anything else and therefore inexplicable by anything else, that which indeed underlies all inner emotions, all desiring, striving, wishing, longing, craving, hoping, loving, rejoicing, grieving, etc., but of which we first become fully conscious in performing externally any movement of our limbs, or in experiencing any influence on our body (hunger, thirst, pleasure, pain, etc.).

IV. Conscious and Unconscious Will

§ 150. All changes by which the life of my organism is sustained, are either voluntary (animal, conscious) and result from motives, or involuntary (vegetative, unconscious) and produced by irritation. The first are all, as we saw, manifestations of Will. The question is, whether we must assume for those involuntary functions which serve for the nutrition of the body, a different principle from Will, or if in both cases it is the phenomenal form alone that varies, while that which appears in it remains the same.

§ 151. The following reasons lead us to the highly important conclusion, that it is one and the same force which appears, on the one hand in the voluntary movements of the limbs, on the other, in the involuntary vital processes of digestion, circulation of the blood, breathing, etc.

1. The fundamental character of every natural force is the striving to take possession of matter, by driving back or subduing those other forces, which till then had the mastery of it. Hence arises that hostile behaviour towards each other of natural forces striving for manifestation by reason of which nature everywhere and always presents the spectacle of a struggle of opposing forces. Also in the service of our organism a whole series of physical and

chemical forces are continually active. But all these are, in a state of health, kept down and governed by a higher central force which manifests itself in the unity of the whole notwithstanding the diversity of the parts, in the unity of the aims notwithstanding the variety of the efforts. For the unity of these aims we see voluntary and involuntary vital functions co-operating in perfect harmony. They are not, therefore, like the physical and chemical agencies in their service, the manifestations of opposed forces, held temporarily in reluctant subjection, but it can be only one force which manifests itself in both in different ways.

2. As in the whole, so in all its parts this unity of conscious and unconscious life is apparent. Thus, for instance, the use of the hand belongs to the voluntary manifestations of life, but its form is the work of those involuntary functions to which the nutrition of the body is due, together with its formation, renewal, and healing. Now the function of the hand is predetermined in its whole structure. Therefore that which uses the hand, cannot be only accidentally related to that which forms and nourishes it. This would, however, be the case, if the forming power and the employing power were fundamentally different.

3. Every organic movement, whether voluntary or involuntary, is, physiologically speaking, the contraction of a particular muscle. No muscle can

contract without being irritated by the nerves ending in it. This nerve-irritation springs, in the case of the muscles of voluntary movement, from the cerebral system, in that of the muscles of involuntary movement, from the sympathetic system. Now that which is essential in every movement, is the effect, appearing as contraction of the muscle; that which is accidental (and therefore capable of being replaced by other influences, for instance, by electricity), consists in the conditioning cause, appearing as nerve-irritation. Accordingly voluntary and involuntary movements differ not in what is essential but in what is accidental, not in the effect but in the kind of causation which provokes it. We must therefore conceive them as manifestations of one and the same force which appears in two different forms.

Remark.—It is of great importance to understand, that the difference between the voluntary and involuntary functions appears so considerable only to us, that is, to our knowing intellect, because in the case of voluntary movements the intellect by chance forms itself a link in the chain irritating the muscles (§ 84), while it is absolutely excluded from any participation in the involuntary movements. But in itself it is only a secondary and unimportant difference, that the nerves, stimulating the muscles to contraction, should take their way in the one case through the brain, in the other through the ganglia.

§ 152. It is therefore one and the same force

which is manifested through two diverse but harmoniously co-operating phenomenal forms in the voluntary and involuntary processes of life. It is this force which has been called by physiology and psychology (in their best moments) **vital force** and **soul** respectively. Yet these two names signify as much as x and y, that is, a something perfectly unknown, and therefore do not further our understanding. Now this force, as far as it appears in voluntary, that is, conscious movements, is not only known to us, but even better known than anything else in the world, under the name of **Will**. Again we have shown that the being accompanied by consciousness concerns only the causality of will-phenomena, that is, what is accidental and belonging only to the forms in which Will appears, and that, apart from the kind of causation, it is one and the same force which produces on the one hand, by means of motives, the conscious and voluntary phenomena of life, and on the other by irritation the unconscious and involuntary. Accordingly philosophy here makes use of its right to give to the popular significations of words the sense, resulting from a more accurate conception of nature, and so requires that we accustom ourselves to recognise Will even there where it is not, as in voluntary movements, accompanied by consciousness. We call that, therefore, which operates in the vegetative functions of the organism, the unconscious Will.

§ 153. Thus that of which I become aware (in that part of the phenomena of life alone accessible to inner experience) in each movement of my body (§ 148), in each sensation of pleasure and pain (§ 149) as Will, even this entity, more familiar to me than anything else, it is which, without the aid of intellect, accomplishes as unconscious Will, namely as unknowing impulse, blind instinct, determined by irritation, all the involuntary processes in my organism; on which processes depend through digestion, circulation of the blood, breathing, secretion, etc. not only the nutrition, but also the whole growth and development of the body. From that, therefore, which immediately enters into our consciousness as Will, we need only deduct the share of the intellect, to retain that which, as the inner impelling principle of our whole life, not only perpetually sustains, by the assimilation of new and the elimination of waste materials, the integrity of our body, heals its wounds, combats foreign forces intruding as diseases, and (if not overcome by these in death) subdues them, but which also produces all growth of the body from birth and its original formation before birth, after it has burst into existence (in generation) with that impetuosity, characterising the manifestation of all forces of nature. Thus every man is, in the deepest sense, his own work: for each is through and through the objectity of his own Will, which, originally and essentially unconscious, accomplishes as sexual impulse, generation; as plasticity, formation in the womb and growth after birth; which in unconscious wisdom—unattainable by any consciousness—shapes from the beginning all organs of the body in conformity to its original aims; and amongst these, as a regulator of its relations to the external world, the brain, that is, the intellect, through which at last it emerges, in the full light of knowledge, as that which it essentially and originally is, namely as Will.

V. On the Soul and its Relation to the Body

§ 154. The human organism with all its different parts and functions forms throughout a perfect unity. Yet men have always distinguished two elements in it: firstly, the material body, given as an object of external experience; secondly, the immaterial soul, accessible only to the inly-directed consciousness. In remarkable coincidence, explicable only by the fundamental tendencies of human nature, we see in Indian, Greek, and modern philosophy the error arise, that the soul is essentially and in the first place a knowing being, whereas on the contrary all facts of psychic life unmistakably prove, that the centre of man is to be sought not in the head, but in the heart, not in knowing, but in willing. To this in particular the following facts bear witness:

1. The intellect develops, like all organs of the

body, in childhood, and decays with these in old age, as is well and truly described by Lucretius (III, 445-458). Will alone in man does not age; for as already the *Mahâbhâratam* (xiii, 367) has it:

*jîryanti jîryataḥ keçâ, dantâ jîryanti jîryataḥ,
cakshuḥ-çrotre ca jîryete, trishṇâ ekâ na tu jîryate;*

> "Of him who grows old, the hair grows old,
> The teeth grow old of him who grows old,
> The eyes grow old, the ears grow old,
> Desire alone does not grow old."

2. The intellect suspends its activity periodically in sleep, the Will, as unconscious Will, is, like the heart, unwearying.

3. The intellect is, like all organs of the body, an instrument of the Will, as the submissive servant of which it throughout appears, while the dominant factor is the Will; a truth which, if not perhaps apparent in the study, is seen everywhere in practical life.

4. Descending in the animal scale, we see the intellect more and more diminishing, while Will, as we shall show, animates everywhere with the same vehemence even the lowest animal.

5. Excellences and defects of intellect are not taken into account at all, when it is a question of determining the real, that is the moral worth of Man.

But to the deeds of a man, and to them alone, as manifestations of the quality of his Will, we attribute a significance reaching beyond the tomb.

Thus is shown everywhere, that what is primary and radical in man, is the Will, while all that is connected with the intellect, belongs only to the physical and perishable form in which our Self (*âtman*) appears, but not to the metaphysical and eternal substratum of it, that is, the soul.

§ 155. So long as we place the essence of the soul in intelligence, we shall, notwithstanding all the proofs for immortality adduced by a Platonic Phaedon, be ever driven back by consideration of the facts to the conclusion of the candid Lucretius (III, 462):

quare participem leti quoque convenit esse;

for nothing is more certain than the annihilation of the intellect by death. Only when we resolve to break with tradition, and, in accordance with the facts of inner consciousness, to place the essence of the soul not in the intellect, but in the originally and essentially unconscious Will, shall we succeed in establishing, in spite of all attacks of materialism, **the immortality of the soul;** and that not by artificial and easily misleading arguments, but as a simple and inevitable conclusion, drawn from the tenets of Kantian philosophy here set forth by us.

§ 156. Like everything else in nature, I myself am on the one hand **phenomenon** and on the other **thing-in-itself**. As phenomenon, viewed through the forms of my intellect, my being appears as **body**, which, like all that exists, is through and through material. Now the same entity which, viewed externally, appears as the body, moving in time, space, and causality, when viewed from within, apart from space and causality, enters my consciousness as volition, or, when I strip off the form of time, as **Will**. We have shown that Will is the principle not only of the voluntary movements, but also of the involuntary nutritive functions, on which the nourishment, growth, and origin, and consequently the whole existence of the body, depend. Accordingly my body is nothing but Will itself, objectified in space and time through causality, and all its members, hand, foot, brain, stomach, genitals, etc. are the objectity of the various tendencies of Will.

§ 157. Hence follows, that that which as thing-in-itself, and so independent of time, space, and causality, is **my soul**, that is, **my Will**, appears in phenomenal form as **my body**, extended in space, existing in time, and subject in all its manifestations to causality. Now all becoming and perishing, all being born and dying is possible only in time by causality. Consequently as body I had a beginning and shall have an end, as **Soul**, that is as

Will, I am on the contrary uncreated and immortal.

Τὼς γένεσις μὲν ἀπέσβεσται καὶ ἄπιστος ὄλεθρος.

§ 158. My organism appears as a variety of material parts which co-operate for the maintenance of the whole harmoniously and in conformity to its original aims. This unity in plurality remains for empirical science an absolutely inconceivable miracle. Even the conception of the body after the analogy of human works of art, as the planned work of an all-wise Creator, does not explain the facts. For apart from its being objectionable on moral grounds, this extremely bold hypothesis would only suffice to explain a mechanism but not an organism. The solution of the riddle from our standpoint is extremely simple. The Will as thing-in-itself is a perfect unity. Our body is just this undivided Will, as it appears viewed through the forms of our intellect. These cannot make any change in its essence, and therefore the phenomenon, though appearing extended in space as body, and in time as life, shows the same unity which it possesses as thing-in-itself or Will.

VI. The Will in Nature

§ 159. My own ego alone is accessible to me in two ways: firstly, from without as representation, that is as body; secondly, from within as Will, that is as soul. All the rest of nature is given me from one side only, namely as representation. The question is, whether it is merely this, and consequently a phantom without reality, an empty semblance, an illusive apparition, or whether, being externally like myself appearance, it may be also internally the same as I am, namely Will.

§ 160. No one will seriously doubt that all human beings, like himself, are inwardly conscious of themselves as willing, and that consequently their bodies, like his own, are objectifications of Will, even though no actual proof of this can be adduced, since all proof leads from one point of the represented world to another, but never beyond representation in which alone the external world is given to me. But we meet here a case where analogy is more convincing than any proof could be.

§ 161. After admitting that all men, just like ourselves, are objectifications of the Will, we shall find it impossible to deny the same in the case of the brutes. For what distinguishes man from the brute, is the organisation of the intellect (§§ 119-125). Now intellect belongs to the form of appearing, but not to that which appears through this form (§§ 154. 155). Consequently Being-in-itself (das An-sich-Seiende) in man and brute is the same, thus here as there, Will.

§ 162. Diverse as are the different animal species as regards their external appearance, they are yet identical as regards that which they will. All animals, from the highest to the lowest, are embodiments of the Will to life, which in all stages strives equally to conserve itself. Hence all exertions of the brute are concentrated in the two tendencies, to preserve the individual by nourishment and protection, and the species by propagation and care of the young. This is the everywhere identical problem. The consideration of how it has been solved by nature in the endless variety of animal species, ever differently and yet ever in like perfection, forms an inexhaustible source of entertainment. From this point of view zoology gains an interest which no other could give it.

§ 163. The Will as the objectification of which every man and every animal appears, is originally and essentially unconscious. It is only in a limited sphere of animal life, becoming narrower as we descend the scale, that it furnishes itself with consciousness. Nothing proves more clearly the secondary and so to say borrowed nature of all conscious life, than the necessity of sleep. In sleep, owing to the isolation of the brain from the motor and sensory nerves, consciousness is periodically extinguished, that is, the union between will and intellect is suspended, and the latter, for the sake of its (that is the brain's) nourishment, is merged completely in unconscious life, which, as the central and essential entity, unweariedly exercises its functions, whether we sleep or wake. This is already taught by a passage of the Veda in the *Çatapatha-brâhmaṇam* x. 3, 3, 6: *Yadâ vai purushah svapiti, prânam tarhi vâg api-eti, prânam cakshuh, prânam manah, prânam çrotram. Sa yadâ prabudhyate, prânâd eva adhi- punar jâyante.* (When a man sleeps, speech is merged in life, eye in life, mind in life, ear in life. And when he awakes they are reborn from life.)

§ 164. The intellect is nothing but a material organ with which the Will provides itself for the sake of regulating its relations with the outer world. Hence it is, that all productions of the conscious Will bear the stamp of outwardness, artificiality, mechanism as opposed to the inwardness, naturalness, organisation which distinguishes the creations of unconscious Will. Therefore with these no work of human skill can be even remotely compared. The unconscious Will operates in the vegetative functions of the organism throughout with adaptation, yet without consciousness, and thus without knowledge of the end to be attained. But marvellous indeed is the encroachment of this unconscious Will with its blind and yet adaptive activity on the sphere of conscious Will which is manifested in Instinct and the artistic impulses of animals. That which operates in the bird building its nest, is obviously Will. And yet the year-old bird can have no consciousness of the purpose for which the nest is built. Consequently it must be unconscious, not conscious Will, Will working by irritation, not by motives, which appears in these instinctive operations, though the details of execution may be regulated by motives. Thus the same unconsciously-purposive action which prevails in the nutritive functions as the rule, trenches exceptionally as instinct on the domain of conscious life, and that always in such cases where the intellect is insufficient for the purposes of nature. Hence in man, owing to the perfection of his intellect, it shows itself but rarely (for instance, in sexual love). In animals it appears more frequently, and most strongly where the intellect is least perfect, while at the same time the vital operations remain complicated. Accordingly it reaches its climax in the social instincts of the insects. In proportion as the cerebral and sympathetic nervous systems in these coincide in the ganglia, their voluntary actions are regulated throughout by instinct and consequently stand under the same guidance as the involuntary functions of nutrition. Accordingly we might go so far as to consider a swarm of bees as an organism resolved into its component parts. Like the unconscious life of a single organism, the whole social life of bees and ants is dependent on irritation, with this exception, that in details it is replaced by slight motives, because the contact is removed by which the operating of irritation is conditioned.

Remark.—The distribution of the different organic functions (nourishment, propagation) amongst different individuals, whether co-existing (queen bee, drones, and workers) or succeeding each other (caterpillar, butterfly), differs only in degree from the separation of the sexes among the higher animals and men, and operates, like the latter, under the guidance of instinct.

§ 165. Descending in the scale of organic beings we see conscious voluntary life ever retreating before the unconscious operation of the Will, until the former utterly disappears. The point where the last remnant of consciousness and voluntary movement is extinguished, marks the transition (difficult to determine empirically) from the animal to the vegetable kingdom. In the plant unconscious life, serving the purposes of nourishment and propagation, fills therefore the whole sphere of its existence. Now, as we have seen, unconscious no less than conscious life is the manifestation of Will. Consequently the life of the plant must be conceived as an unconscious, involuntary willing, and every plant, like animal and man, is an objectification of the Will to life. This is difficult to grasp only for the reason, that the sphere in which we immediately know Will, has here utterly disappeared, and that sphere alone remains in which we can approach it only mediately and by inference.

Meanwhile not only are the exertions which fill up the life of every plant, obviously the same as those of animals, namely, nourishment and propagation, but also their bodily organs show a striking analogy, since, for instance, the digestive organs reappear as roots, the respiratory organs as leaves, the genitals as blossoms. Further, a number of the manifestations of vegetable life, as, for instance, the striving of the root after good soil and moisture, that of the branches after light and air, as well as many single facts are inexplicable, unless we assume, as the inner principle of vegetable life, a desiring, a craving, a striving, in short a willing, albeit an unconscious one.

§ 166. No sharper boundary line is drawn in the whole of Nature than that between organic forces, appearing as living organisms, and inorganic forces, variously manifested in the physical and chemical processes of inanimate nature. Nevertheless considerations like the following show that the great difference between organic and inorganic forces after all concerns the form of appearance alone, but not that which appears in these entirely different forms. (1) In all effects, whether belonging to the sphere of animate or inanimate nature, that which manifests itself is force. Now force is related to its manifestations not merely as a general concept to its different underlying perceptions (§ 100), but as the thing-in-itself to the phenomenal world (§ 136). Consequently the identity, denoted by the word force, is not an abstract but a concrete identity, and the diversity of operating forces springs not from the nature of force in itself, but from the forms of its appearance. (2) Accordingly the great diversity in the action of organic and inorganic forces is to be explained for the most part by their relation to the forms of appearance, that is, by circumstances of time, space, and causality. It is first of all causality which, as cause in its narrower sense, occasions inorganic, as irritation and motives, organic change (§§ 142-145), and thereby draws between both a boundary, admitting of no intermediate links. After causality it is time and space out of which arise the profound differences between organic and inorganic phenomena. While namely every organic force (plant or animal) succeeds in giving full expression to its being only in a variety of spatial parts (as organism) and in a succession of temporal conditions (as life), every inorganic force on the contrary reveals its whole inner being in an undivided and everywhere identical manifestation, admitting only of differences in degree. (The only exception is crystallisation, which may be regarded as a first attempt at organic life seized by rigidity in the very process of formation.) Hence is clear that the essential differences between organic and inorganic forces find their explanation in relations of time, space, and causality, from which follows, that they do not originate in Being-in-itself, but only in the forms through which it appears to us.

We have only therefore to take that force-manifestation in which alone the being of force becomes accessible to our inner apprehension as Will, namely, our own self, and to strip from it all its appearance-forms, to which not only consciousness, but also life, and organisation belong, and we shall retain in the unconscious, inanimate, inorganic Will that which is manifested as inner impelling principle in all forces of inorganic nature.

Even clearer than by proof will this truth become, when we observe in detail the action of inorganic forces: when we see the eagerness with which substances enter into chemical combination, the vehemence with which the electric poles strive after union, the impetuosity with which the dammed-up water everywhere seeks an outlet, or when, in lifting a heavy weight or pressing against a solid body, we immediately feel how our striving is resisted by a contrary striving which fundamentally must be identical with the striving in ourselves and thus, like that,—Will, even though as gravity and impenetrability it shows the greatest possible distance in its form of appearance from our own Will.

VII. Transcendent Reflections on the Will as Thing-in-itself

§ 167. All is matter. Such is the final conclusion from the standpoint of physical science (§ 26). Kant's doctrine alone leads beyond this, when proving that the essential conditions of corporeal existence, space, time, and causality, are only subjective faculties of our intellect, and that consequently the materiality of things is only the form in which the being of the thing-in-itself appears to our eyes. What that Being-in-itself is, was found in the only possible way by Schopenhauer. It is nothing but Will which, as physical, chemical, and organic force, intrudes into time, space, and causality, thereby appearing in all changes of bodies and in bodies themselves. To him who has understood Schopenhauer's teaching aright, every phenomenon of the universe, wherever we may look, is resolved into Will. Hence the final conclusion of metaphysical science is: All is Will.

§ 168. That which makes Will appear to us as world, is the innate forms of our intellect. As we cannot get rid of them, and Will as thing-in-itself lies beyond them, only negative assertions about Will are possible to us.

1. The Will as thing-in-itself is not in space

and time. Now all plurality is conditioned by a spatial co-existence or a temporal succession of parts. Although therefore the Will is manifested as a plurality of phenomena in space and time, in itself plurality is unknown to it. This truth has at all times been felt (ἐν καὶ πᾶν, One and All), but the proof of it is only possible by Kant's philosophy.

2. Like plurality, divisibility is also conditioned by space and time. The Will as thing-in-itself is therefore indivisible. We must not think of it as divided amongst its phenomena; for each of these contains it entire, every being in nature is a manifestation of the whole and undivided Will to life, just as each of the thousand images of the sun in the water reflects the entire sun. When therefore Plato (Parm. p. 131 E) asks: τίν' οὖν τρόπον τῶν εἰδῶν τὰ ἄλλα μεταλήψεται, μήτε κατὰ μέρη μήτε κατὰ ὅλα μεταλαμβάνειν δυνάμενα;—the *Bhagavad-gîtâḥ* (xiii, 16) may answer:

avibhaktaṃ ca bhûteshu, vibhaktam iva ca sthitam

(undivided he dwells in beings, and yet, as it were, divided); and Kant may furnish the key to this enigma by his doctrine that space and time do indeed separate the manifestations but not the manifested, so that every one finds and feels himself to be the entire, limitless Will to life, the totality of all that is real. Hence it is, that the natural man (ἄνθρωπος ψυχικός), as his deeds show, restricts all reality to his ego; he knows everything in himself. And hence it is, that the regenerate (in the Christian sense) extends his ego to all reality; he knows himself in everything. He celebrates solemnly (in the Communion) his unification with all creatures as a member of the body of Christ, τοῦ τὰ πάντα ἐν πᾶσι πληρουμένου (Ephes. i. 23), and Nature thousand-tongued greets him with the "great word," which we shall have later on to consider: "*Tat tvam asi*" (That art thou), while from his inmost being re-echoes the consciousness: "*Aham brahma asmi*" (I am Brahman).

3. All phenomena of the Will to life are subject to causality, and therefore, in all their manifestations, to necessity. On the contrary the Will, as thing-in-itself, does not lie in causality and is consequently uncaused and free. Here is the meeting-point of two great truths, that of the freedom of the Will, and that of the necessity of all its manifestations. It is true that our deeds are the necessary and inevitable results of our innate character (expressed in corporisation): and yet we cannot get rid of the consciousness of responsibility for our actions which is called conscience: and rightly so: for this innate character is after all our own work (§ 153), and our whole life is only the empirical and therefore necessary development of our in itself free willing. This

truth finds its mythical expression in the Indian doctrine, that all deeds and destinies of our existence are the inevitable, though not immediate (*apûrva*), consequence of our own actions in a previous life, and so dependent on ourselves. And the same truth seems to be in Plato's mind, when he describes (Rep. x, p. 617 D sq.) how the soul before its birth chooses with freedom from the lap of Lachesis the lot which predestines with necessity its fate and, with its fate (618 D, E), its actions in the future life.

§ 169. Will as such has two possible modes and two alone: **willing** and **not-willing**. In reference to earthly existence willing appears (as we shall show in the metaphysics of morality) as the affirmation of the Will to life, of which this whole world is the manifestation; not-willing as the denial of the Will to life, the manifestation of which has been called by religions in their figurative language bliss, *unio mystica*, Kingdom of God, Kingdom of Heaven, etc., but which, apart from its breaking through in every moral action, remains completely unknown to the intellect, nay is absolutely inconceivable by it. To the intellect therefore it appears as the negation, the extinction (*nirvânam*) of all existence. Yet it is well to notice that it is only to our understanding, bound to the finite and its limits, that this world of affirmation appears as the existing, and negation as the non-existing. On the contrary, viewed from the highest standpoint, the world of denial, unknown to us, yet transparent in every moral deed, is that which really and truly is (τὸ ὄν), while on the other hand this whole world of affirmation metaphysically speaking is that which is not (τὸ μὴ ὄν), and in a moral sense that which should not be.

VIII. Mythical Representation of the World-Process

§ 170. There where there is no longer a Where,—therefore here, everywhere and again nowhere,—then when there is no longer a When,—therefore now, in all eternity and again at no time,—was, is, and will be **the Will** (the Deity, the Brahman, the Thing-in-itself), and besides it nothing. Each of us is this Will, and again each of us is not this Will: for we are all estranged from its original nature, which is Denial—without sin, without sorrow, without existence.

§ 171. Now there was formed,—not at any time, but before all eternity, to-day and for ever,—like an inexplicable clouding of the clearness of the heavens, in the pure, painless, and will-less bliss of denial a morbid propensity, a sinful bent: the affirmation of the Will to life. In it and with it is given the myriad host of all the sins and woes of which this immeasurable world is the revealer.

§ 172. When in the life of our body some serious disorder has taken place, nature by a violent augmentation of the vital processes summons all her powers for the purpose of curing it. Thus arises fever, which is at the same time the symptom of disease and an attempt at cure. What fever is to disease, that is this whole world to the self-affirming Will. It is the visibility of affirmation; and in giving to all sin and its train of evils the most full and terrible expression, it holds up to the erring Will a mirror of its own striving, guilty of all the woe of existence, if haply it might attain to a full understanding of itself, and thereby come to a turn, to a return, to salvation.

§ 173. Salvation springs from knowledge (*jñânâd muktiḥ*, Kapila 3, 23). Now the full knowledge of the world is only possible by means of the human intellect. Therefore all nature up to man is but the way which the affirming Will travels in gradual development, in order to attain to the human intellect and by it to saving self-knowledge. But also as man it passes through long series of generations, furnishing itself in every womb with a new intellect, in order to approach by progressive purification the realm of denial (§ 250).

§ 174. Long periods in the life of nature had to elapse before an intellect could arise. On the other hand all these past world-epochs are only possible through time, and this again through intellect. Herein lies a contradiction only for our imperfect understanding, because of its being bound to temporality. This, however, in the process of the world has no significance. Therefore the fall of the spirits took place from time immemorial, and again it takes place now and at each moment. But saving denial also is ever present, and in denying, the individual saves himself and in himself all creatures, even because he is in himself the entire Will to life. When therefore it stands in the Veda (*Chândogya-upanishad* 5, 24, 5):

Yathâ iha kshudhitâ bâlâ mâtaram pari-upâsate evam sarvâni bhûtâni agnihotram upâsate,

"as here below hungry children sit round their mother, so sit all beings round the fire-sacrifice (brought by him, who has the knowledge of Brahman),"—we might perhaps add as explanation in the language of the Bible (Rom. viii. 19): ἡ γὰρ ἀποκαραδοκία τῆς κτίσεως τὴν ἀποκάλυψιν τῶν υἱῶν τοῦ θεοῦ ἀπεκδέχεται. Thus the regenerate saves himself and the groaning creation: and yet affirmation still continues, even after he has found the way out of its circle. Also this world for ever and aye will exist, will affirm, will suffer,—but again all time in the light of denial is nothing, and all that it contains fades away as the shadow-play on the wall for the Will, when it has turned.

Thus contradictory appears metaphysical truth, when we attempt to clothe it in the words and conceptions of empirical thought.

IX. God and World

§ 175. There is nothing but Will; its true state is denial (as is proved by the approbation we give to every moral, that is denying action). An aberration of the Will is affirmation, of which this whole world is the manifestation and the purifying process.

In these words, which can only be thoroughly understood later, lies the metaphysical truth, which for all times and countries is one and the same. Accordingly we see it springing up wherever the human mind penetrates to the depths, even though the form in which it appears, shows the greatest varieties.

To exhibit this identical content and to derive its various forms from the influence of the respective civilisations, is the subject of the history of metaphysics. Here we must content ourselves with pointing out some of the most important of these forms.

§ 176. In India we can trace metaphysics back almost to its first beginnings. The forces, appearing in the manifestations of nature and more especially in the striking phenomena of fire, thunderstorm, the firmament, etc., are presented in the hymns of the Rigveda in transparent personification as the gods *Agni, Indra, Varuṇa,* etc. Nay, to a certain extent we see the forces of nature even in the hands of the poets crystallising into personal gods. This primitive view of the world is true, so far as man recognises in all action of nature his own being (Will); it is untrue, so far as he transfers not only his own being, but also its form of appearance (personality) to the forces of nature.

We know that these forces from the lowest to the highest are only the original forms in which the Will to life variously appears. This truth came to light in the second period of Indian life in the conception, that there is but one Being, the (impersonal) *Brahman*, and that all gods, men, animals, plants, and inanimate beings are the diverse manifestations of it. The relation between phenomena and the thing-in-itself is conceived figuratively as an emanation of the world from *Brahman*, compared to the coming forth of the web from the spider, the plants from the earth, the hair from the body. But at the same time the eternity of the souls, for ever circulating in the *Saṃsāra* (that is in the phenomenal world) is maintained; from which follows clearly, that their relation to *Brahman* is to be conceived not as the temporal relation of the effect to its cause, but as the relation of the time-conditioned to the timeless, that is, of phenomena to the thing-in-itself. With this metaphysical antithesis between the undivided Brahman and the manifold world, as which it appears, is immediately connected the ethical between denial and affirmation in the sense of the celebrated "*Tat tvam asi*" (That art Thou), a sentence which expresses in three words at once the deepest mystery of metaphysics (the ἓν καὶ πᾶν) and the highest aim of morality (the ἀγαπήσεις τὸν πλησίον σου ὡς σεαυτόν). As an interpretation of this great truth we may consider, as in a wider sense our whole work, so already the motto prefixed to it, which we here translate:

> "The Lord of all things dwells
>   In ev'ry living being,
> Not dying when it dies.—
>   He who sees him, is seeing.

> "Such will not, when in all
>   This highest Lord he knows,
> Wrong through himself himself,
>   And to perfection goes."

§ 177. In the Bible we have before our eyes the grand spectacle of the real and eternal truth breaking its way forcibly as Christianity through the diametrically opposed teaching of the Old Testament.

The fundamental dogma of primitive Judaism is Theism, according to which the world is created by a personal Being, similar to ourselves (Gen. i. 26, 27), —a hypothesis at the boldness of which we are not surprised only because we are accustomed to hear it from our youth up. The first consequence of Theism is Optimism. If the world is created by God, it must be good, and this is expressly asserted (Gen. i. 31). A further consequence is complete Annihilation by death: only what is uncreated can be immortal; if the soul has arisen from nothing, it must return to nothing: τὸ μηδὲν εἰς οὐδὲν ῥέπει (what is nothing turns to nothing). Accordingly the Old Testament (with the exception of the latest books) does not admit the immortality of the soul. Now, if our existence is limited to this life of affirmation, our aims can be only immanent and consequently egoistic. Therefore the Law appeals solely to egoism, in making its incentives fear of punishment and hope of reward (one may read Lev. xxvi. Deut. xxviii.), on which account it was rejected by the deeper conception of Christianity (Rom. iii. 28).

This view of the world, in which Theism, Optimism, Nihilism, and Eudæmonism cohere with admirable consistency, seems to have been not so much a result of natural development, as rather the inspiration of a single man,—perhaps of Moses,—whose greatness it is not easy to overrate,—who found in it the means of disciplining a race corrupted by slavery. With the people it never became very popular, as the frequent, and otherwise rather inexplicable attempts at apostasy seem to prove. But also the thinkers of Hebraism struggle against it in many passages of the Old Testament. So already in the narrative of the Fall, which cannot be reconciled with the creation of the world by an all-wise and good Being. Still less could the human mind acquiesce in the doctrine of the punishment of the evil and the reward of the good in this life, a theory contradicted by experience at every step (compare Job and Psalms xxxvii. lxxiii).

A fundamental change took place in Hebrew metaphysics during and after the Babylonian Captivity through Persian and Greek influence, which prepared the ground for Christianity. To Theism was added the doctrine of Satan (that is *Añhromainyu*), which made it possible to exonerate God from the authorship of evil (still ascribed to him for instance in Isa. xlv. 7, 2 Sam. xxiv. 1, but no longer in the post-exilic parallel passage in 1 Chron. xxi. [xxii.] 1), and to maintain him as the principle of denial, that is morality. At the same time the belief in the immortality of the soul and with it a transcendent morality, not founded on egoism, broke way, while Optimism, in consequence of bitter experience, gradually gave place to Pessimism, which is the basis of every real religion.

In this intellectual atmosphere we see the eternal and everywhere identical truth as Christianity struggling painfully upwards, like a plant through rock and rubble, towards the light. Adapting its theory to the Old Testament and to the historical traditions of the life of its founder, Christianity personifies (Rom. v. 12-21) the affirmation of the Will to life in Adam, the denial of it in Christ. We are all (according to the theory of original sin) Adam, and we all shall become Christ through his being formed in us (Gal. iv. 19). This cannot be effected by the Law (not so much, because, according to the Pauline theory, it cannot be fulfilled, but rather because it is founded on egoism, and therefore, even if fulfilled, does not lead beyond this). To Christianity therefore the springing up of metaphysical knowledge, independently of our Will while in the state of affirmation, appears as Grace, which accomplishes in us regeneration, that is the returning of the Will to denial. Thus the truth as Christianity burst the hardened bark of the contradictory and in itself untrue Mosaic teaching, the consciousness of which inspired the fourth Evangelist (chap. i. 17, 18), with the words: ὁ νόμος διὰ Μωϋσέως ἐδόθη, ἡ χάρις καὶ ἡ ἀλήθεια διὰ Ἰησοῦ Χριστοῦ ἐγένετο (thus not by Moses). Θεὸν οὐδεὶς ἑώρακε πώποτε (thus not even Moses, as is maintained, Num. xii. 8, Deut. xxxiv. 10), ὁ μονογενὴς υἱός, ὁ ὢν εἰς τὸν κόλπον τοῦ πατρός, ἐκεῖνος ἐξηγήσατο. Compare the sideglances he occasionally throws (for instance chaps. iii. 10, iv. 21, v. 39, vi. 49 [viii. 6], viii. 58, x. 8) on the religion of the fathers.

§ 178. Also the gods of the Greeks, as is apparent from the etymology of their names and the character of many of their myths, were originally personified forces of nature (comp. Plato, Kratyl. 397 C), moulded by the poetic genius of the Homeric age into ideal human figures (Herodot. 2, 53). In opposition to the necessarily discordant plurality of gods Xenophanes proclaimed the unity of the Divine. His disciple Parmenides (as already Xenophanes in part himself) denied to this unity personality and change and opposed it as Being to this world as Non-being: whereby the distinction between phenomena and the thing-in-itself was very sharply expressed. Proceeding from Parmenides Plato examined the nature of Being. In the phenomenal world with its ceaseless becoming and perishing he discovered a series of constant forms which, as eternal types of things, find expression in all that exists, but are themselves untouched by the flux of becoming. These prototypes of things, lying beyond time, space and causality (§ 47), each of which is manifested as a formative principle of being in a plurality of similar individual things, were called by Plato Ideas (ἰδέαι, εἴδη, that is, perceptual forms). What he sought under this name can be nothing but the series of formative forces through which the Will finds expression in all manifestations of nature. Ideas therefore must be well distinguished from Concepts, which indeed share with them their universality (the ἓν ἐπὶ πολλῶν), but lack their concrete form and thorough-going determinedness, for which reason Platonic Ideas were rightly denoted by Aristotle as αἰσθητὰ ἀΐδια, though not rightly as such rejected by him. Meanwhile it is not to be denied that in the philosophy of Plato, to whom was lacking on the one side knowledge of nature and on the other a complete system of logic, Ideas and concepts are not duly discriminated. Thus we can consider ourselves as Platonists only so far as we are permitted to retain in the case of Plato (as in other respects in that of Kant) what is true and excellent in his teaching, purified from wrong ingredients. Here therefore we distinguish strictly once and for all between the Idea as unity, not yet broken up into plurality of individuals by its entrance into the forms of time, space and causality, and the Concept, which is unity re-established by abstract thought out of the plurality of individual things. Accordingly, to Concepts, as abstract outlines of perceptual representations, we can grant no other existence than that in the human mind, while by Ideas we understand, neither (with Plato) mere abstractions as the Good, the Beautiful, nor (with Kant) certain concepts of reason transcending the possibility of experience (soul, universe, God), but solely the physical, chemical, and organic forces underlying all action in nature, since these are the forms through which the Will to life gives, in gradually increasing distinctness, expression to its essence. In this sense therefore we appropriate the Platonic Ideas, and make them the starting-point of our further considerations.

X. The Will and the Ideas of Plato

§ 179. Retrospect and further problems. We have recognised Will as the inner principle of all manifestations of nature and have given some characteristics of its essence (necessary to the understanding of what follows, though themselves only to be clearly comprehended in the course of our whole inquiry). We have further pointed out the harmony of our fundamental theory with the culminating points of metaphysics in all ages and countries. There now remains for us to show in this second part devoted to nature, how the thing-in-itself appears as the world, that is, how the one, free and existence-denying Will (by means of a change not further explicable to us, but originating in its freedom) affirming itself in the forms of our intellect, time, space and causality, which are the principles of the visibility of affirmation, appears as a plurality of beings, subject to the constraint of causality, separated by space and time, and (in so far as they do not penetrate the illusive nature of the order imposed by the intellect and its form) persisting in mutual hostility.

§ 180. The affirmation of the Will to life is its state of being split into plurality in the forms of our intellect: space, time, and causality. Now the Will in itself is absolutely unformed and therefore completely heterogene to these forms of the subject. In order therefore to appear in them, it must to a certain extent adapt itself to them. This the Will does in shaping itself to a series of operative forms of existence, through which, in self-combat, it forces its way into time, space and causality, and comes to appearance in all individual existence. These original Will-forms, opposed to perishable things as their imperishable prototypes, are precisely what Plato sought and partly found under the name of Ideas, and what we shall have shortly to enumerate as the Forces manifested in the life of nature. They are called the grades of objectification, because through them the Will to life with ever-increasing distinctness brings its being to appearance. Thus these Ideas are the footprints on the road, by which the affirming Will, sunk to existence and striving after deliverance, painfully works its way upward to its complete revelation in Man. This, being its real and final goal, was only possible by the long preceding series of grades; for mankind presupposes both the animal and the vegetable worlds, as these again presuppose inorganic nature for their existence as well as subsistence.

§ 181. Since Ideas lie beyond empirical reality, that is where nothing is to be found but the thing-in-itself, they are at bottom identical with this, but they are the thing-in-itself as it appears to our eyes, when we conceive it objectively and, so to say, regard it through the atmosphere of the phenomenal world. They are the coloured pictures in the glass of the magic lantern through which the light of the Will throws on the wall of time, space, and causality the shadow-play of the phenomenal world. Or we may compare the Will to a harper, and its appearance in the life and action of nature to the music. The Ideas would then be the not very numerous strings of the instrument from the ever-varying combination of which proceeds the inexhaustible wealth of the progressing harmony.

§ 182. Ideas are concrete forms adapted to space, moreover a plurality. Yet, as even Plato saw (§ 47), they do not lie in space. From this contradiction it becomes clear, that they can only be regarded as an imperfect attempt to make conceivable to us what is in its nature inconceivable. From the plurality of Ideas spring all differences in nature, for, since these do not originate in the intellect, which remains one and the same towards all diversity, all differences must be rooted in the thing-in-itself. But how the unity or rather non-plurality of being-in-itself can be reconciled with the differences of the phenomenal world rooted in it, is, like the possibility of a plurality of Ideas, a transcendent question, which passes our comprehension. For us indeed unity and plurality are opposites, for the thing-in-itself both and with them their opposition are nothing.

For the rest Ideas do not thoroughly suffice for the explanation of the phenomenal world, for the variety in the individuals representing one Idea can be satisfactorily explained neither by the more or less imperfect subdual of the matter, seized upon and moulded by the Idea, nor by the adaptation to external circumstances (by which are conditioned the varieties of species). On the contrary in man as in part already in the higher animals (also in this respect his precursors) the specific character, in which is expressed the idea of the species, is supplemented by the individual character, which for us is an impenetrable mystery (*omne individuum est ineffabile*) and seems to indicate the stage which every individual has reached on its way to denial. This dark point will receive some more light in our further considerations.

Remark.—If one compares antique sculpture with mediæval and modern painting, the characters of Sophokles with those of Shakespeare, and lastly, the Platonic doctrine of Ideas with Schopenhauer's doctrine of Will, one might, inferring the nature of the age from these its highest manifestations, conjecture that the individuals of classical antiquity had more of the typical, less of the individual in them than those of modern times, that consequently the modern man has become more conscious of himself, perhaps even has approached nearer to denial than the ancient. This assumption, which might be interpreted very much in favour of Christianity, must at any rate be understood, not as a progress of mankind in general, which in the main was and ever will be impossible, but rather as an approaching ascent of the individual towards denial.

XI. The Objectification of the Will in Nature by means of the Ideas

§ 183. Every physical, chemical and organic force is a Platonic Idea, that is, one of these primary forms through which the Will comes to expression in all manifestations of the universe. To facilitate the understanding of this doctrine we here draw up tentatively a list of all primary forces, which however contains much that is questionable, and without doubt will admit of many improvements. The goal which by this means we aim at rather than reach, is the enumeration of the total content of what is *a posteriori* in nature, that is, of that part which remains when we take away the *a priori* elements of time, space and causality with all that belongs to them (such as extension, divisibility, inertia).

A. Physical Forces:

(1) Impenetrability; its mere negation is Porosity, on which depends the Compressibility of bodies.

(2) Gravity, perhaps connected with cohesion.

(3) Cohesion, appearing in three degrees as solid ($\phi\iota\lambda\iota\alpha$), liquid, and gaseous ($\nu\epsilon\hat{\iota}\kappa o\varsigma$). Different varieties of the same are hardness and softness, brittleness and toughness, ductility and perhaps elasticity.

(4) Adhesion, closely related to cohesion; to it may be referred the capillarity, endosmose, and absorption of gases.

(5) Heat (Temperature); connected on the one hand with cohesion, the three forms of which are conditioned by it, on the other in a peculiar way with light.

(6) Light, perhaps to be regarded neither as a body (according to the emission hypothesis), nor as a change of body (according to the undulatory hypothesis), but rather as a force which, appearing like every force in consequence of certain causal influences, is manifested in all bodies, on the one side in luminosity, on the other in visibility as its correlative.

(7) Magnetism and Diamagnetism, probably more or less common to all matter.

(8) Electricity, closely related to magnetism,

appears as a polaric contrast (usually latent in bodies, but manifesting itself in consequence of certain causal influences), the poles of which striving after union attract their complement in other bodies.

(9) Crystallisation, a striving, perhaps common to all matter, to assume in its transition from the liquid to the solid state a regular form, according to the nature of each substance: a prelude to organic force.

B. Chemical Forces :
(1) Each of the 66 Elements.
(2) Every Chemical Combination.

C. Organic Forces :
(1) Each species of plant.
(2) Each species of animal.
(3) Man.

§ 184. In this list (presupposing its correctness) we have before our eyes the whole apparatus of Ideas, that is of forces, through which the Will to life affirms itself, in penetrating through these into time, space, and causality, and appearing in all changes of bodies as well as in the bodies themselves. One should accustom oneself to see in every process of nature a mutual interpenetration of forces, and to regard that which alone is operative in these forces as identical with what works and strives in us as Will. For, as already a very ancient passage of the Veda (*Brihad-âraṇyaka-upanishad* 3, 7, 15) says: "*Yaḥ sarveshu bhûteshu tishṭhan sarvebhyo bhûtebhyo 'ntaro, yaṃ sarvâṇi bhûtâni na vidur, yasya sarvâṇi bhûtâni çarîraṃ, yaḥ sarvâṇi bhûtâni antaro yamayati,—esha te âtmâ, antaryâmî, amṛitaḥ*"—"he who dwelling in all beings differs from all beings, who is not known to all beings, of whom all beings are the embodiment, who from within governs all beings,—he is thy soul, thy inner ruler, thy immortal part."

Remark.—Such passages as the above show clearly, that the *Brahman* of the Indians, which, as we saw, lies outside of time, space, and causality (47), which "in the sleeper remains awake, forming and working at pleasure" (comp. § 163), in which, according to other texts of the Veda, "the sun rises and sets," "on which all gods depend" (§ 176), "all worlds are founded," and which yet again "dwells in size as a thumb-breadth in the cavity of the heart,"—that this *Brahman*, the unity of which with the soul (*brahma-âtma-aikya*) is the fundamental dogma of the Vedânta, notwithstanding the intelligence ascribed to it (§ 154), is after all nothing else but what we call Will. This might explain what is already said in a hymn of the Rigveda (10. 129), that out of the *Tad* (that is Brahman) there arose through *tapas* (self-renunciation, turning of the Will, here to affirmation) first *Kâma* (Ἔρως, also according to Hesiod and Parmenides the eldest of the gods), that is affirmation, and that this became the first germ of *manas*, that is of intellect (§ 84), which also according to our system is only the principle of the visibility of affirmation (§§ 117. 172. 173. 179. 180).

Thus, apart from errors in details, the Brahman of the Indians, the Ideas of Plato, the Creator and Saviour of Christianity, the Thing-in-itself of Kant, the Forces of natural science, and the Will of Schopenhauer, constitute an indissoluble totality of metaphysical truth.

§ 185. All the above-named forces, through which the Will objectifies itself in order to appear in time, space, and causality, are restricted to matter (§§ 86-88) as their place of appearance. Yet the relation of physical, chemical, and organic forces to matter is a characteristically different one. While namely the relation of **organic** forces to matter is, as we shall see, an accidental one, the **physical and chemical** forces on the contrary are attached to it with necessity, and that so that in every substance are inherent (as it seems) all **physical forces**, but only certain, alternating, and mutually exclusive **chemical forces**. These chemical forces appear to our space-bound comprehension as the various substances in nature, and their general character seems to be, that each of them constitutes an aggregate of all the physical forces, but shows these in gradually and characteristically determined combinations. Thus one might regard the physical Ideas as the real combatants, the chemical as the commanders of the troops in this *bellum omnium contra omnes*.

§ 186. The physical forces inhere one and all, as it seems, in every substance, though in variously graduated differences of intensity, in which indeed consists the diversity of inorganic bodies, that is, of all chemical elements and combinations occurring in nature. Accordingly all bodies, the moment causality permits, should show themselves as (1) impenetrable; (2) more or less heavy; (3) striving to hold together or to scatter their particles; (4) more or less adhesive; (5) more or less warm; (6) more or less visible (colours); (7) magnetic or diamagnetic; (8) electric; (9) capable of crystallisation.

§ 187. Chemical forces, like physical, are also necessarily inherent in matter, yet they do not appear like these in every substance, but each of them in one particular substance, to which it is restricted once and for all. Thus, for instance, gold is a chemical force, which shows certain distinct physical properties, that is, it holds the physical forces captive in its service in certain relations, modifiable in a particular way by causality. This force, as a chemical one, is restricted once and for all to a particular place of appearance, movable in space, into which we project it and so construe it as body. In this sense every part of matter is the place of appearance of particular elements and particular chemical combinations, which, being equally primary forces of nature and captors of physical Ideas, wrestle with each other for the possession of matter, while causal influences decide which force remains victor over matter, and which is temporarily subdued. Thus, for instance, a certain substance appears now as oxygen and hydrogen, now as water, according as causality favours the one or the other. For water is by no means a regular aggregate of oxygen and hydrogen, but like these a throughout homogeneous substance, and therefore just as much as the elements to which it temporarily yields the field, the objectification of a primary force of nature, which, however, in order to become manifest, is restricted to the same substance as the elementary forces in competition with it. In order to maintain the purity of the species as the established grades of objectification, for which here as in the organic sphere nature takes the greatest care, elements can only combine in certain determined relations of weight. Yet these are only the accessory, not the essential condition of the manifestation of natural force as a chemical combination, that is, they do not belong to *it*, but to the causal conditions under which it appears. Often therefore very different forces have their place of manifestation in the same elements, combined in the same proportions of weight (as for instance starch, ligneous fibre, sugar in $C_6H_5O_5$, or, if one regards these as organic rather than chemical forces, calcareous spar, arragonite, marble, chalk in $CaO.CO_2$).

As organic bodies come into existence by generation, so inorganic bodies are produced by chemical affinity. Now, just as the sexual impulse is but the first intrusion into appearance of that Will which later stands before us in time as organism (§ 153), so affinity is nothing but the desire for manifestation of those chemical forces which, after their manifestation, are seen by us spatially as (simple or compound) bodies.

Remark.—Notwithstanding the variety of natural forces, all action in nature goes back to a unity. But this unity, which we have recognised as identical with the Will in ourselves, is not physical but metaphysical. When, therefore, natural science endeavours to reduce all forces of nature to a physical unity, we must regard this as a trespassing beyond the limits of its sphere (indicated § 25), which in our estimation can have no lasting success. It is to this endeavour to explain nature by one physical principle, that the atomic theory owes its existence, the aim of which is to interpret all processes in nature as the varied union and separation of mechanically moved atoms. We may suppose these atoms either as extensionless and so mathematically indivisible, or as extended and therefore only physically indivisible. If the first, then by no amount of such atoms, however great, could an extended body and consequently a world be produced. If atoms should on the other hand be merely physically indivisible, they must be conceived as minute bodies the cohesive power of which resists all separation, while they are only by accident, that is relatively to our body and its organs, so small, that they (unfortunately) entirely escape our perception and thus remain nothing but a mere hypothesis (with which we believe it possible to dispense). Hence is evident, that the atomic theory, in the most favourable case, would lead not to unity of force but to the reduction of the forces ruling in nature to a few (such as impenetrability, cohesion, adhesion, chemical attraction). Such a result (which after all might be easily reconciled with our system) would, however, be applicable only in a subordinate degree for interpreting natural phenomena. For the undeniably teleological constitution of nature, of which we shall shortly have to speak, will for ever mock all attempts to explain the universe by a merely mechanical operation of forces.

§ 188. As the physical forces are seized and bound to a particular place by the chemical, so again are physical and chemical forces in that mutual interpenetration which empirically speaking is called matter, temporarily fettered by the organic forces, in which the Will appears in significant gradation as plant, animal, and man. The Will, it is true, appears entire and undivided in every physical and chemical force (§ 168, 2). But while in these it manifests its being in a dull, one-sided way, and almost only in a simple and (apart from differences in degree) identical manifestation (§ 166); as organic force it expands itself, for the clearer expression and unfolding of its being, into a plurality of parts in space as organism, and into a plurality of conditions in time as life.

§ 189. The physical and chemical forces are necessarily inherent in matter (that is, in force-filled space): if I think them away, I abolish all matter; they have therefore their omnipresence and immortality in the indestructibility of matter. On the other hand organic forces cling, as it were, accidentally to matter, for they have their essence not in matter but in its form. To conserve this form, they need continually the supply of new materials, and in order not to lose matter for ever, when abandoning it in death, they require a means to perpetuate their existence beyond the individual. Hence the instincts of **nourishment and propagation**, which form the two fundamental impulses of all organic beings.

Remark.—When we reflect how Nature everywhere with a seeming indifference gives over to destruction her marvellously formed organisms, while providing with the greatest care for the preservation of the species through the strength of the procreative impulse and the abundance of seeds, we must conclude that to her the production of the individual is very easy and that of the species very difficult. How the latter, that is, how the first entrance of organic Ideas into the phenomenal world is to be represented empirically, is for philosophy a secondary question, the ventilation of which, however, being now in fashion, seems of primary importance. Since in going back in the history of our planet we come to a state in which the temperature of the earth admitted of no organic life, we must necessarily assume a first origination of the organic out of the inorganic through spontaneous generation (*generatio aequivoca*). This is in fact no more marvellous than is for instance the crystallisation of water in the air into the so regularly formed and complicated snow crystals, and, like this, is to be regarded as the entrance of Will from spacelessness into space. From the first organisms produced by spontaneous generation must have arisen by development all existing species, whether produced (according to Cuvier) independently of each other, or (according to Lamarck and Darwin) the one from the other. Many facts, in particular the "unity of type" in the formation of organisms, favour the latter theory. In no case, however, are we thereby justified in effacing the bounds, so strictly drawn by nature between species and species. And as little can we assume, with Darwin, that the production of higher out of lower species is due chiefly to external mechanical influences ("the struggle for existence"). Against his theory there are the following objections: (1) Why do we meet in nature, as also in fossils, a series of fixed grades and not a continuous chain of graduated forms, leading the one into the other? Why is it just these intermediate links and not rather the lower species which have perished in the struggle for existence? (2) The Will to life objectifies itself entire and undivided in every species of the plant and animal kingdom. Each of these therefore, the highest as the lowest, is equally perfect and equally fit for life, for all its organs cannot but correspond exactly to the aims of the Will manifested in them, since they are these aims themselves conceived as bodily parts. Hence follows, that every individual is the more perfect and the more fit for life, the nearer it approaches the type of its species, since perfection is nothing but fitness for the aims of life, and the type of the species, that is the Idea, is just that fitness—viewed as a fixed form—of all parts and functions to the respective ends of the Will, objectifying itself through the Idea. Therefore a deviation from the type of the species is never "advantageous" to the existence of an animal, unless perhaps transitorily, through adaptation to external circumstances, with the removal of which it appears as a deformity, prejudicial to the perfection of the animal, and therefore to its fitness for life.

Natural selection presupposes a selector, the struggle for existence a struggler. This is the Will to life, which, striving after deliverance, has in accommodation to external circumstances risen from grade to grade, from Idea to Idea. These transitions may have been effected in one of two ways, either by the Will springing in a favourable moment from the lower to the higher grade, or by the agency of intermediate links which, as hybrids, were dropped after having served their purpose. For nature everywhere shows itself anxious to preserve—in the inorganic realm by equivalents, in the organic by sterility—the purity of the species, that is, of the Ideas conceived empirically, and only admits of certain variations within these, which may be regarded as the Idea adapting itself to different external circumstances.

It is scarcely necessary to remark that, from our standpoint, every moral objection to the descent of man from brute disappears. For all nature is, as we saw, but a metaphysical essence, sunk through its own guilt to physical existence and working its way upward to full self-knowledge, which it reaches in man, and through which alone it attains to salvation. Thus Darwinism and Christianity, like all fundamental contradictions of natural science, religion, and philosophy, are reconciled in the system of Schopenhauer.

§ 190. As the Will to life as plant concentrates its whole being in reproduction, it has at this stage the power of transforming inorganic materials into organic. Since it finds all these in one place, it does not need the power of locomotion. As animal the Will furnishes itself, in correspondence to its more complicated aims, with voluntary movement, and, for the guidance of its steps, with an intellect, of which, when insufficient, the unconscious Will, as we saw (§ 164), vicariously takes the place. The animal intellect reaches its highest possible development (§ 115, 4) in man. Beyond him it needs no further development, since in man the Will attains to turning, to denial, to salvation, and with that to the really ultimate aim of the natural creation.

XII. On the Teleological View of Nature and its Limits

§ 191. The Will as thing-in-itself is one and harmonious. To its affirmation as world on the other hand self-conflict is essential, becoming visible in the plurality of its manifestations in time and space. Beyond the phenomenal world there is harmony, within it discord. Now not only the Will, but also the Ideas through which it is manifested, lie beyond space and time. Therefore, as their plurality is an unspatial one (§ 182), so also their contrariety is not a mutually exclusive, but rather a harmoniously co-operative one.

From this unity and harmony of the being-in-itself of Will, manifested in every organism through a particular Idea and in all existence through the totality of Ideas, is to be explained the teleological adaptation in nature, which meets us everywhere, and which, when connecting the manifestations of life in the individual organism to a unity, we call internal; and when appearing as a relation of different organisms to each other and to inorganic nature in the universal life of creation, external.

§ 192. The one Will to life, in objectifying itself entire and undivided in every living being, appears expanded in a plurality of parts in space as organism, and in a plurality of conditions in time as life. On this depends that internal adaptation, by means of which all parts of an organism show a mutual dependence, so that each organ seems both aim and means of all others, while again the organism and its life appears as the ultimate aim of all the organs. Of this we have already spoken (§ 158). Beside this we notice to our surprise an analogous phenomenon, a certain external adaptation, permeating the totality of nature, in so far as the different organic Ideas through which the Will appears in the higher grades of its objectifications, adapt themselves to a certain extent in part mutually to each other, in part to inorganic nature and its conditions, a correspondence which can only be explained by the unity of all Ideas grounded in the Will as thing-in-itself. Thus, for instance, we see the plant adapting itself to soil and climate, the animal to its element, to its prey, nay (through the teleological formation of its protective organs), to its natural enemy. Thus the eye is formed to correspond to light, the lungs to air, and just as later manifestations adjust themselves to the earlier, so we see (for instance in the adaptation of the atmosphere, of light and heat to organic life, in the obliquity of the ecliptic by which all vegetable life is conditioned, etc.) earlier manifestations anticipating the later, and forming themselves with regard to the future needs of these. For the unity of nature appearing here is a transcendent unity, for which temporal conditions and so an earlier and a later have no significance.

The teleological order of nature is, on the one side, a constitutive principle of existence, on the other hand, a regulative principle of knowledge (in organic nature perfectly reliable). It may therefore well have been this which was in Plato's mind as "the Idea of the Good," of which he says, that like the sun it is the cause on the one hand of being, on the other of knowing (Rep. vi. p. 509 B).

§ 193. To this harmony of Ideas, on the mutual correspondence and accommodation of which depends the teleological constitution of nature, appears in crying contradiction the discord in the manifestation of these same Ideas in space, time, and causality. They all, as phenomenal forms of the Will to life, possessed by the mania of existence as by a demon, force themselves with impetuosity into being, in mutually disputing matter and therefore perpetually combating, hindering, supplanting, and suppressing each other. Thus Plato's doctrine of the Idea of the Good and the unenvious goodness of the Creator is reconciled with the verdict of Heraclitus: πόλεμος πατὴρ πάντων. From this *bellum omnium contra omnes* springs in a moral respect on the one hand the evil, on the other, the suffering of the world, both of which therefore are essential to affirmation and can only be removed with it. And again in an æsthetic respect arises from it the imperfection of phenomena, especially in the organic sphere, as a result of which every phenomenon gives only an approximate expression to the Idea manifested in it, since a part of the force striving for manifestation is everywhere consumed in the combating and subduing of opposed forces. Hence the law, "that every organism only represents the Idea of which it is the image, after deduction of that part of its force, employed by it in the subdual of those lower forces which dispute matter with it."

§ 194. Thus we see, wherever the eye turns, only phenomena, not things-in-themselves; and the whole realm of nature, wherever expanded in all spheres of the heavens, shows us indeed in all its parts, the thousandfold-repeated images, εἴδωλα, ὁμοιώματα of Ideas, but not Ideas, not Will, not Being-in-itself. Thus Plato was right, when he compared us (Rep. vii. p. 514 A sq.) to prisoners, sitting chained in an underground cave and forced by their fetters to look without moving on the wall in front of them, so that they see neither the light at their back, nor the objects passing behind them, nor even themselves, but only the shadows of these objects and their own shadows on the wall before them, and take these for the real things. Is it possible for us to turn away our gaze from this wall of time, space and causality, in order to see no longer the shadows of things, no longer the images of Ideas, but the prototypes, as they are in themselves, the Ideas themselves in unspoiled form and beauty?

This question leads us to the considerations in our third part.

THE SYSTEM OF METAPHYSICS

PART III

THE METAPHYSICS OF THE BEAUTIFUL

I. Historical

§ 195. It was Plato who, animated by a metaphysical spirit, directed to Being-in-itself, turned his searching gaze on the inconstant flight of the phenomenal world, in order to find out, what amid the "flux of becoming" of Heraclitus was the Being of Parmenides, what amid the ceaseless coming into existence and perishing of things was the unchangeable and the constant. In doing so, he observed that nature, notwithstanding plurality and becoming, is yet not in itself throughout varied and changing, that on the contrary we perceive in it ever the same manifestations in different places and at different times; which, being in themselves identical, would coincide to a unity, were they not separated by space and time. Space and time, however, are a nonentity as Plato felt, and as every metaphysical mind from the first has more or less clearly felt, though the late discovery of the secret, by the demonstration of the subjective origin of space and time, was reserved for the genius of Kant. He thereby became the founder of a new era in the history of the world, of the manhood of humanity, of the period of organic thought (that is, of scientific thought carried through every department), the germs of which, sown by him, begin even now to sprout, and the fruits of which, defying all calculation, rest in the bosom of futurity. Had it been granted to Plato, undisturbed by foreign influences, to extract time, space, and causality from the world of perception, and thus to restore the identity separated by them to a unity, the becoming and developing to an unchangeable entity, he might have attained not to his, but to our Ideas, and perhaps have saved mankind some two thousand years of metaphysical error. But fate had decided otherwise as to the intellectual life of many ages, when it was pleased to throw Plato into the arms of Sokrates, whose mission, though a very meritorious one and of great importance for philosophy, was of quite another kind. Sokrates namely, without concealing the fact that he neither rightly understood nature (Plato, Phaedr. p. 230 D) nor the profound views of nature of his predecessors (Diog. Laert. II. 22), had turned away voluntarily from both, in order to direct all the power of his mind to a single subject, the action of man, a one-sidedness which, though justifiable, was fatal to philosophy. He believed to raise human action essentially, in making it dependent on fixed concepts, present to the mind as purposes. Thus his untiring activity was directed to the logical determination of ethical concepts, which as one, universal, and constant, should be realised in the plurality of actions. Now just as two crystals, in penetrating each other, mutually destroy the purity of their formation, so in Plato's vast mind the tendency towards Ideas realised in nature, which he had received from the teaching of Heraclitus and Parmenides, was combined with the Sokratic striving after concepts to be realised in the action of man. It is this blending of these outwardly similar, but inwardly fundamentally differing elements which gives the writings of Plato so enigmatical a character.

This might also explain how it was that Plato, like Ulysses, who, set down on the coast of Ithaka, did not recognise his fatherland, missed, nay spurned, the only way which might have led him to that intuition of the Ideas which had been the longing of his youth, namely the way of Art, with the highest productions of which he, as the immediate heir of an art development without equal, was so nearly connected. But the overwhelming personality of Sokrates, whose ethics ran: "τὸ ὠφέλιμον ἀγαθόν" (the useful is good) and whose æsthetic creed was "τὸ χρήσιμον καλόν" (the serviceable is beautiful (Xen. Mem. 4, 6), had fascinated him, as he may at times have felt himself and seems to express in the Symposion (p. 216 C) under the mask of Alkibiades. And to a development of Sokratic tendencies it is due, that we see him, the metaphysical genius, heir to the throne of the world-annihilating Parmenides,— busied with the construction of a State concept the realisation of which would scarcely have been of significance for the highest aims of mankind, and for love of which, guided by moral considerations, he deals in a lamentably summary way with art. The phenomenal world, he argues, is an imitation of the Idea, art is an imitation of phenomena: hence it is an imitation of an imitation, and merits no serious consideration.

§ 196. Aristotle also does not rise beyond the conception of art as an imitation of the real. But it is not so much the individual (τὰ καθ' ἕκαστον) as the universal (τὰ καθόλου) which art has to imitate, and while the historian relates what happened (τὰ γενόμενα), the task of the poet is more ambitious (σπουδαιότερον): he has to represent what, according to the nature of things, might happen (οἷα ἂν γένοιτο). This involves that not phenomena as such, but the universal and essential expressed in them, is the object of art.

Aristotle, moreover, turned his attention to the influence exerted by art on the contemplating subject. According to him it is the aim of the tragedy, by exciting fear and pity, to accomplish in us a purification from similar emotions (δι' ἐλέου καὶ φόβου περαίνουσα τὴν τῶν τοιούτων παθημάτων κάθαρσιν, Poet. 6). If we may generalise this passage, we have as Aristotle's fundamental view of art something like the following: "All of us, one more, another less (Polit. 8, 7, p. 1342 A 5 sq.), have emotions (for instance, fear and pity) and the need of giving them utterance. The satisfaction of this need in practical life is often attended by unpleasant consequences, while in art it is harmless, and in this lies (apart from subordinate aims as παιδεία, διαγωγή, instruction and amusement), the value of art."—This conception of art as a psychical Kathartikon (which one might be tempted to parody after the manner of Aristophanes) is certainly an unworthy one. Still it contains much that deserves consideration, and has arisen, as we might conjecture, through Aristotle associating wrongly two perfectly right observations. He noticed how art often calms marvellously the excitement of the mind (Polit. 8, 7, p. 1342 A 8 sq.). On the other hand he could not fail to observe that, by the contemplation of a work of art, certain emotions are stirred within us (in tragedy, for example, fear and pity). But that these æsthetic emotions differ *toto genere* from those of practical life, that their relation to these is that of the supramundane to the mundane, of the metaphysical to the physical, from seeing this Aristotle was prevented by the restriction of his view to the empirical world. Appealing to a single case (p. 1342 A 8) he co-ordinates, without being aware of the μετάβασις εἰς ἄλλο γένος, both kinds of emotions and looks merely at the difference in their practical results. Art thus becomes for him the means of procuring relief from emotion not, as in life, with subsequent suffering, but with delight (κουφίζεσθαι μεθ' ἡδονῆς), and of enjoying a harmless pleasure (χαρὰν ἀβλαβῆ) unattended by evils.

Two thousand years passed away before the need was felt of advancing beyond the æsthetic views of Aristotle.

§ 197. It was Kant who here also laid a new foundation, in going back from the comparing contemplation of beautiful objects in nature and art to the contemplating subject, in order to analyse (after the less important attempts of others) for the first time seriously and penetratingly the feeling called forth in us by the beautiful, and with it the real root of the æsthetic phenomenon. He defined the feeling for the beautiful as a delight, to which, amongst other qualities, he ascribed that of being (unlike the delight in what is pleasant or good) entirely unconnected with interest, that is without relation of any kind to the desiring faculty (the Will) of the feeling subject.

Kant, in thus defining the feeling for the beautiful as **a disinterested delight**, stated a psychological fact, the accuracy of which every one may test by self-observation. The love of the beautiful is a delight and therefore under all circumstances an emotion of the Will, but this emotion takes place without the beautiful object having any relation to the Will of the beholder, that is, any interest for his person. Nay, the impression of the beautiful fades away in proportion as any relation of the beautiful object to the desires of the subject enters his consciousness.

In this emotion of the Will without relation to the Will lies a contradiction which from the empirical standpoint is irreconcilable.

II. The Æsthetic Phenomenon considered from the Empirical Standpoint

§ 198. In the empirical, that is the individual view, subject and object are always connected by nearer or remoter relations of space, time, and causality. The consciousness of these relations is called the interest (according to its etymology from *inter-esse* "to take part in") which we take in an object.

This interest is twofold. It is called **satisfaction**, when the object is favourable to the purposes of our Will, **dissatisfaction**, when unfavourable to these. Hence it is clear that, from the empirical standpoint, pleasure is only a special kind of interest, that therefore all pleasure is an interested one, that is, dependent on the consciousness of the relations between object and subject.

§ 199. Now, since all interest which I take in an object, shows itself as the consciousness of a relation to the same, and since every relation is nothing but a connection in time, space, and causality, which, in this sense, make up the sphere of interest, it follows that a disinterested delight is only possible, so far as this connection, or at least the consciousness of it, is removed. Hence the subject of æsthetic delight is not the Will so far as it is individualised in time, space, and causality, and necessarily entangled in the net of relations, but the Will only in so far as it feels itself raised above the individuality as which it appears. Here the disinterested delight in æsthetic contemplation shows itself as a phenomenon leading beyond the natural order of things, the explanation of which accordingly devolves on metaphysics.

This will become clearer by contrasting the individual with the æsthetic contemplation of things.

III. Individual and Æsthetic Contemplation

§ 200. There are, as we saw, two standpoints from which to investigate the world by abstract thought,—the empirical and the transcendental. To these correspond exactly two alone possible methods of regarding things through perception, the individual, which is the rule, and the æsthetic, which occurs transitorily and as an exception under certain subjective and objective conditions.

§ 201. In the individual contemplation subject and object stand to each other as individual beings, belonging to the totality of empirical reality. As such they are, as we saw, always connected by nearer or remoter relations of space, time, and causality, in the consciousness of which relations, in fact, all interest consists. Æsthetic perception occurs, when, with full activity of the mind, the consciousness of these relations, and so the possibility of an interested pleasure is completely extinguished, so that both, subject as well as object, face each other lifted, as it were, above time, space, and causality, that is, above the principles of finite earthly existence. This marvellous, though not rare process is conditioned by a momentary transformation occurring in both, subject and object, which demands further examination.

§ 202. The subject in the individual mode of contemplation is the beholding individual. We know that individuality is Will, appearing as body in time, space, and causality. Thus it is, that all organs of the body are instruments of the Will, embodiments of its strivings directed to certain ends. One of these organs is the intellect (the brain). Hence from the individual standpoint it is nothing but an instrument of the Will, destined to work in the service of its aims.

Amongst all the complicated organs which nature has produced for the service of Will in the state of individuality, that is of corporisation, by far the noblest and most marvellous is the human intellect; so noble, that the fulfilment of its natural destiny, that is, its activity in the service of the individual Will, seems to us an unworthy bondage, and the more so, the more highly developed the intellect is. And how should not the human mind, which traverses all distances, measures all heights, illuminates all depths, which unrolls to us the picture of the universe, nay, in metaphysics leads even a step beyond this,—how should the mind not feel it as hard bondage, to be daily and hourly employed in furnishing the individual from whom it sprang, with motives for his actions, merely that he may find his ant's path through the whirl of existence,— how should it not feel itself like the bird, which, capable of soaring through the heavens finds itself confined to a narrow cage?

From this "penal servitude of willing" there is an eternal deliverance,—of that we are not yet speaking here,—and a transitory rest, a short hour of respite. This comes in moments of æsthetic contemplation. To this we are raised so often as, on occasions which we shall have next to consider, we succeed in leaving behind us the consciousness of our individual existence with all its trials and torments, so that the intellect faces things no longer as an instrument protecting the interests of the Will and careful only of the (real or possible) relations of things to it, but as a clear mirror, undimmed by any personal interest, as pure subject of knowing, which in complete self-devoting objectivity no longer spies out and searches for the individual relations of things, but contemplates the pure objective being of these in itself.

§ 203. But also in the contemplated object a change takes place, the moment we rise from the individual viewing of things to their æsthetic contemplation. The object we contemplate remains indeed in both cases the same. But it appears in ordinary life as an individual object, bound to us by spatial, temporal, and causal relations which, in so far as they regard our personal interest, appear in a strong light, thereby obscuring more or less the objective being of the thing. In æsthetic contemplation, on the contrary, in which every possible relation of objects to our Will vanishes from our consciousness, things are regarded, not for what they are as particular material individuals, bound to us by time, space, and causality, but for what they are in themselves, apart from time, space, and causality, that is, only so far as they are embodiments of Being-in-itself, of the Idea present in them.

§ 204. From what has been said it becomes clear, that the æsthetic phenomenon is connected with certain subjective and objective conditions, of which, as we shall see, now the former, now the latter preponderate and thus call forth their correlative. In proportion as the contemplating mind is inclined to objectivity, it will succeed easily in seeking in things no longer the individual, but the Idea. And in proportion as the contemplated object is a clear expression of the Idea manifested in it, it will succeed in taking us out of our subjective mood and raising us to æsthetic will-free contemplation.

To understand this thoroughly, we must examine more closely those subjective and objective conditions under which the æsthetic phenomenon takes place.

IV. Subjective Conditions of the Æsthetic Phenomenon

§ 205. A beautiful but often wrongly translated[1] passage of the Kâṭhaka-Upanishad (4, 1) runs as follows:

*Parâñci khâni vyatṛiṇat Svayambhûs,
Tasmât parâñ paçyati, na antarâtman.*

"Outwards the Self-existent bored the holes,
Hence men look outward, not within their souls";

that is, the intellect is, according to its nature, an external organ. Bright and clear lies before us the external world, extended in the three forms of our intellect,—dimly from within is mirrored in our consciousness the Will, expanded in the single perceptual form of time as volition, and this only as a rule, not always.

§ 206. For, as in looking upwards from a deep mine, the stars are visible to us even by day, but

---

[1] With thanks we acknowledge here the furtherance which Indian studies and, through them, one of the most important branches of philosophy have received by the incomparable Sanskrit Dictionary, which Otto Bœhtlingk and Rudolph Roth, aided by other excellent scholars, have, after five-and-twenty years' labour, shortly completed. To them we dedicate the following epigram:

*Yena samskṛitabhâshâyâ jñânam sûpâyanam kṛitam,
Advitîya-dvaya-ârabdham vande grantham anuttamam.
Sakalam jîvitam yâbhyâm Brahma-vidyâ-prakâçake
Bhâshârshabhe samâvṛittam, tâbhyâm astu namô namaḥ!*

(1877.)

no longer, when we ascend to the light;—or as, when sitting quietly, we feel the beat of the heart, the pulsation of the blood through the veins, but no longer, when we are moving about:—similarly, in the normal state of knowing is reflected in our consciousness the Will, with its ever-unsatisfied cravings, but no longer, when the intellect, raised by innate energy or by a sudden spring-tide of its powers, conceives the external world with increased clearness, so that its more energetic light chases at once all shadows of personal toil and trouble from our consciousness.

§ 207. That which is primary and radical in us is Will, what is secondary and accidental is intellect (§ 154). Hence it is that the preponderance of knowing over willing which is the condition of æsthetic contemplation, occurs only as an exception. It is attainable in the first place, as we saw, by an increase of intellectual energy, but further also by the mitigation of willing. Therefore very subjective natures who cling narrow-mindedly to their own personality, even when gifted, will not easily rise to the intuition of the beautiful. In vain the most wonderful aspects allure them, for in all they hear the inner voice of the Will crying disconsolately: "It is of no use to me!"—Well might they also seek relief from the torment of willing, well might they also seek to escape from themselves,

> *sed timor et minae*
> *Scandunt eodem quo dominus: neque*
> *Decedit aerata triremi, et*
> *Post equitem sedet atra cura.*

But where, through a happily constituted nature, by culture and education, practised renunciation and self-denial, desire has been tamed, the impetuosity of willing abated, there nature and art will easily succeed in drawing the beholder out of himself, in order to manifest themselves to him, no longer as a complexity of possible motives of willing, but in their purely conceived inner objective being, bathed in the light of beauty.

§ 208. In this sense it is not only genius (preponderance of intellect), but holiness also (denial of willing) which is favourable to æsthetic contemplation. This at least must be the meaning of the Sâñkhya-Kârikâ, when it says (v. 65) of him in whom the Will to life has turned:

> *prakritim paçyati purushaḥ,*
> *prekshakavad avasthitaḥ, susthaḥ,*

"the spirit beholds nature, spectator-like standing aloof, well-standing." Yet in the judgment of the Indians (surrounded by great examples of denial), æsthetic contemplation does not necessarily accompany holiness. Thus Sadânanda, himself an "ascetic of the first order" (*paramahaṅsa*), says in the Vedântasâra (p. 219, 1 ed. Benf.) of the delivered: *asya, jñânât pûrvaṃ vidyamânânâṃ eva âhâra-vihâra-âdînâm anuvṛittivac, çubha-vâsanânâm eva anuvṛitter bhavati, çubha-açubhayor audâsînyaṃ vâ;* "Even as for him the functions of nourishment, walking, etc. which were practised by him before knowledge, still continue to exist, so also continue in him the impressions of the beautiful, or he remains indifferent alike to the beautiful and to the not beautiful."

§ 209. Whoever has been touched by the beautiful in nature or art,—and who could here be excepted?—knows that in the enjoyment of it there lies an unearthly bliss. This, like every feeling, is an emotion of the Will. Accordingly the delight in the beautiful is not conditioned through a removal of the Will (without which neither being nor knowing is possible), but through the being raised above Will in the state of individuality, which is, as the metaphysics of morality has to show, the phenomenal form of the affirming Will and consequently the bearer of all sin and sorrow.—Here and here alone lies the point of contact between æsthetics and morality. The aim of morality is the negation of individuality, that of æsthetic intuition the temporal forgetting of it. The positive delight of æsthetic contemplation is to us a warrant, that beyond individuality there is not a painless Nothing, but a state the exuberant bliss of which cannot be compared to any earthly feeling of delight.[1]

Remark. The state of freedom from willing is threefold: (1) empirical, obtained by satiety, filled by sport or ennui, a second misery; (2) æsthetic, obtained by rapture, filled by the most expressive drama; (3) moral, obtained by renunciation, filled by active pity, which is a sorrow without pain.

V. Objective Conditions of the Æsthetic Phenomenon

§ 210. The nature of the æsthetic phenomenon consists, as has been shown, in a transitory raising of the mind above individual existence and its conditions: space, time, and causality. This can be attained in the first place, as we saw, by the contemplating subject being withdrawn by processes in himself from the consciousness of his individuality. But it may also be provoked by the contemplated object inviting, through its nature, more or less distinctly, to a forgetting of all that

---

[1] In the state of deliverance our individuality (as the bearer of sin and sorrow) is thrown off like a husk, and notwithstanding our ego continues to exist (though not in time). It is just that super-individual, blissful, godlike ego, dwelling entire and undivided in each of us (§ 168, 2), which, passing from its latent state, is manifested transitorily in æsthetic contemplation and permanently in the moral sentiment. If one asks whether in the state of deliverance a plurality of egos can co-exist, the correct answer is, that the question of unity or plurality has for the realm of Being-in-itself no meaning.

is finite in its imperfection and limitation, in which case we call the object **beautiful**. The full understanding of this word, impossible without metaphysics, will be attained in the course of our considerations.

§ 211. We know the Ideas (§§ 178-184) as the formative forces of the phenomenal world, the fixed types through which the Will gives expression to its being in all manifestations of the universe. We saw (§ 193) how these Ideas in the form of which the Will is objectified, are forced, in thrusting themselves into space, time, and causality, to struggle with each other for the conditions of existence. By this they suffer a more or less considerable loss of force, so that in no manifestation is their being fully and clearly realised. Accordingly no individual is a perfect ectype of its Idea (no horse, for instance, equals the horse-in-itself in *horsehood*): yet one approaches it more, another less.

§ 212. The less namely an Idea is, in its manifestations, thwarted, checked, stunted, overwhelmed by other manifestations, that is, the more perfectly an object embodies, by favour of external circumstances, the Idea of which it is the bearer,—the nearer to the Idea, the more ideal, the more beautiful is the object, and the easier it will be to it (apart from exceptions to be mentioned later), to draw us out of our subjectivity and raise us to the view of Being-in-itself, in awakening in us, through its approximation to the Idea, a reminiscence, though a timeless one, of the world of Ideas.—The contradiction in these words shows that they only say in the form of a simile what we shall try in the following to express directly, though we may scarcely hope to succeed perfectly in doing so.

§ 213. The æsthetic phenomenon is and remains a process within the subject. Nevertheless the feeling for the beautiful is called forth by a concurrence of subjective and objective conditions, of which, as was remarked above, now these now those preponderate and thereby call forth their correlative. Freedom from individual volition favours the conception of things as representatives of Ideas, the approximation of objects to the Ideas calls away the mind from its individual cares. Now this mutual influence is only explicable by an original kinship between object and subject. This is described mythically by Plato (Phaedr. p. 247 A sq.) as a contemplation of the Ideas taking place beyond the phenomenal world before birth, by which he expresses in terms of space what is spaceless, in terms of time what is timeless. Similar images occur in the Upanishads of the Veda; the scientific way was opened by Kant and Schopenhauer.

Independently of our intellect there exists not

this world, but the thing-in-itself, Will alone. In it is no subject, no object. For Being-in-itself is broken up into these only in so far as, entering the forms of representation, it becomes visible to itself as world. The first step is, that Will shapes itself into objective form (presupposing the subject, § 42) as the graduated series of the Ideas. In a certain sense one may say with Schopenhauer, that these are the Will, so far as it, as object, presupposes the subject, but not yet the subject's subordinate forms, space, time, and causality. For these last are the perceptual forms, not of the pure subject of knowing to which, as the subjective correlative of the Idea, we unself ourselves in æsthetic contemplation (§ 202), but of the subject, so far as it, as individual intellect, is a texture of space, time, and causality. Into these its innate forms, and so into the region of imperfection, our intellect projects the Ideas. Here they fight for space, time, and causality, that is, they fight to become a representation of my intellect. On this battle depends the imperfection of their manifestations. That which compels them to become realised indistinctly, disparately, and stuntedly, is therefore only my beholding individuality. Now the more perfectly they nevertheless manifest themselves (from causes the explanation of which, according to § 182 is impossible to us), the more easily will they remove this restraint and with it my individuality imposing it. Conversely, the more easily I tend to get rid of the consciousness of my individuality, the sooner shall I succeed in grasping intuitively through individual things the Ideas behind them, just because their existence as individual things is determined only by my own individuality.

Such difficult ways we must take to grasp approximately that which the nature of our intellect prevents us from understanding completely.

§ 214. One and the same object appears to us in quite a different light, according as we regard it individually, as an aggregate of possible relations to our Will, or æsthetically as ectype of the Idea. (Both kinds of contemplation are in reality very often blended, and it is impossible to decide where disinterested pleasure ceases and interested begins: so for instance in the admiration of the beauty of the beloved.) But æsthetic contemplation is not content with comprehending the temporal under the aspect of the eternal (*sub specie aeternitatis*), the individual thing as representative of the Idea, but it proceeds further to infer from the imperfect the perfect, to restore from the individual the Idea.

We have arrived, by the way of abstract thought, at the conviction, that every being is a manifestation of Will, which, however, hindered by external influences, nowhere attains quite clearly to objectification. But in considering for instance an animal the parts of which are imperfectly formed, we are able, starting from the metaphysical knowledge that all its organs are the objectively manifested strivings of its Will, to say how these organs should be constructed in order to conform perfectly to the aims of the here objectified Will, that is, in order to express clearly and entirely the Will-form or Idea manifested in them. What we do here by abstract reasoning, that the artist mind attains by way of intuition. The artist therefore is an unconscious metaphysician. Guided by an insight into the nature of things which fathoms deeper than all abstract knowledge, he is able to understand the "half-uttered words of nature," to infer from what she forms that which she intends to form, to anticipate from the direction she takes the end she is herself unable to reach. The instrument which accomplishes this idealising transformation of reality is Imagination. In so far as the imagination, in contradistinction to the memory, reproduces representations detached from their spatial, temporal, and causal relations (§ 118), it isolates these from their connection with reality and its control, and transforms them, fertilised by the artist's mind striving after the ideal, into the Idea itself which appears in them.

§ 215. Thus æsthetic contemplation rises from the merely disinterested view of nature to the beholding of the Ideas themselves. Few indeed are able, by this way, to rise from manifestation to the heights of Being-in-itself. Still fewer have the power of imparting what they have beheld on these heights (as it were "on the back of the heaven," ἐπὶ τῷ τοῦ οὐρανοῦ νώτῳ, *nâkasya prishṭhe*, as it is called with remarkable coincidence both by Plato, Phaedr. p. 247 C, and by the Muṇḍaka-Upanishad, 1, 2, 10). These few are the genuine artists. According as they express what they see in buildings, statuary, colour, speech, or sound, they are called architects, sculptors, painters, poets, and musicians.

This is the deep, because metaphysical, Origin of Art.

VI. On the Beautiful and the Sublime

§ 216. Like the whole world as representation, so is also the beauty inherent in it a subjective phenomenon, consisting, as has been shown, in a momentary and transient state of deliverance from the consciousness of individual willing. Only so far as this deliverance is determined by the energy with which the Will manifests itself through the Idea, can we speak of an objective beauty, existent in things themselves. Beauty in this (objective) sense may be defined as distinctness of the manifestation of the Idea, and an object is beautiful in proportion as one of the Ideas (enumerated § 183) attains a complete and unchecked visibility in it. Now since, as we know, all that exists is manifestation of the Ideas, every aspect of nature, every scene in human life may raise us to that state of æsthetic contemplation which has its root in the forgetting of our own individuality; and that alone is excluded which, by its nature, rouses desire or disgust, that is, inclination or disinclination of the Will the complete silence of which is the indispensable condition of æsthetic intuition. But apart from these exceptions, so soon as our mind is in the required state, everything in nature appears to us radiant in the light of beauty. Yet we usually call an object beautiful only, when it manifests an Idea with striking vividness, and when by the eloquence with which the metaphysical in it speaks to us, we are drawn upward to the same.

§ 217. Meanwhile it is well to bear in mind that, notwithstanding all objectivity of mood, we can never thoroughly do justice to the beauty of which creation is full, because our standpoint towards nature is always more or less restricted and one-sided. It is more especially the inadequacy of our sense organs and their specific determination (necessary to the service of the Will) which allows us a merely relative, but no absolute judgment of what is beautiful or ugly. Thus for instance we prefer the voice of the nightingale to that of the raven, because it sounds sweeter to our ear, while, apart from that, croaking is perhaps just as significant and, in so far, beautiful for the Idea of the raven, as is warbling for that of the nightingale. Again vegetable secretions in most cases affect our sense of smell agreeably and thus lead easily to an æsthetic conception of the vegetable world, while with animal secretions exactly the reverse takes place. So again we consider the swift horse, the majestic lion, the light-winged, bright-feathered bird as beautiful, toads, spiders, reptiles, and vermin on the other hand as not beautiful, because the determination of all their organs in the service of the Will (on which, as we shall see, all beauty of the organism depends) in the one instance comes within the sphere of our perception, in the other not, although it is quite as much there. And again the monkey, this wonderful embodiment of the climbing instinct, appears to us ugly, because, misled by an accidental likeness, we cannot help comparing it with man. It is due to this one-sidedness of our standpoint, that in many cases we ourselves presume to improve the Idea æsthetically, as for instance in shaving the beard. But nature did not work for eyes like ours which dwell only on the surface, when she covered the delicate and eloquent features of mouth and chin with a mass of insignificant hairs.

Remark.—From the above it is clear that, in reference to beauty, only individuals of the same species should, properly speaking, be compared with each other, not representatives of different species. Yet, since the Will attains in the scale of the Ideas to a gradually clearer manifestation (§ 180), it may certainly be said that in beauty the inorganic Ideas are surpassed by the organic, lower organisms by the higher, and all other Ideas by man.

§ 218. A special kind of the beautiful, dependent however alone on our subjectivity, is the sublime, the feeling of which arises as follows. Often in some aspect certain Ideas, though manifested very clearly, yet fail to draw us out of our individuality, because the very grandeur and power of the aspect in which consists its beauty, has in another respect a terrifying effect on our Will, in making us conscious of the littleness and weakness of our personality. Now if, in such a case, we succeed in soaring above the anxiety of the individual Will to objective contemplation, and in such a way, that our personal fear remains in the background of our consciousness, without however drawing us down from æsthetic contemplation to concern for our own ego, there arises in us the feeling of the sublime. In reality all that is beautiful is sublime, since by its elevation above all earthly wants it raises us also beyond our individual existence. But it is only when this exaltation takes place consciously (in being wrung from the interests of the troubled Will) that the everywhere identical nature of the beautiful comes, by the accidental fact of our personal resistance, to our immediate perception, and is then called by a very characteristic name the sublime. The objects which call forth in us this mood (revealing the inner essence of all that is beautiful) are called mathematically sublime, when it is their size in space and time which reminds us of the limitation of our own individuality (the starry heavens, eternity). They are called dynamically sublime, when the forces of nature (that is the Ideas) display in them an activity by the overwhelming power of which is awakened in us the feeling of danger to our own personality (a thunderstorm, a tempest, a volcano), or again, when they oppress the Will, in arousing the consciousness of being destitute of the conditions of our subsistence (a winter landscape, a desert).

Remark.—The sublime, which exhorts to the renunciation of willing with all its misery, has its exact opposite in what is alluring, so far as this, by provocation of desire, draws away from æsthetic contemplation to the sphere of individual willing. Since all that stimulates our Will removes the condition of will-free intuition, that which allures (in the sense in which we here use the word) is incapable of rousing a purely objective contemplation and is therefore to be rejected in art (painted food or drink for instance which stimulates the appetite, figures exciting lust, indecent scenes in romance, Offenbach's music). As the alluring rouses the desire, so the disgusting excites the aversion of the Will and consequently admits as little as the other of the conception of the Ideas which are manifested in it as in all that exists. By this the objections, raised by Plato in the Parmenides (p. 130 C-E), are answered.

VII. On the Beautiful in Nature

§ 219. The Ideas—in the distinct manifestation of which all beauty (in an objective sense) consists—are, as we know, nothing but those physical, chemical, and organic forces of nature through which the Will to life is manifested in all that exists. Now as the imperfection of the manifestations of the Ideas is conditioned solely by their entrance into the subjective functions of space, time, and causality, so also is the greater or less energy of their appearance a subjective phenomenon, existing only for us. We need not wonder therefore at seeing this energy and with it the beauty of natural objects connected in the first instance with a series of purely subjective conditions. To these belong before all the necessary objectivity of mind on the part of the beholder; further novelty and rareness of aspects (as in youth, in travelling, in strange natural phenomena) greatly facilitate the conception of the Ideas appearing in things. Lastly we may mention—as depending on a relation of the object to the contemplating subject and therefore belonging to these subjective conditions—the due order and fitting alternation of objects amongst themselves. This indeed furthers æsthetic contemplation in a high degree, since the contrasts point to, and thus mutually interpret, each other. (Compare for instance the monotony of the plain with the mountain landscape in which hill and dale, forest gloom and sunny flowery meadow, rigid rock and lively water alternate.)

After these subjective aids to æsthetic contemplation it is on the energy and distinctness with which the Ideas are impressed on matter, that the beauty of nature depends. This occurs, however, in different ways, according as the Ideas belong as physical and chemical to the inorganic, or as types of plants and animals to the organic sphere.

§ 220. The bodies of **inorganic** nature are, as we have seen (§§ 183. 185. 187), the chemical Ideas manifested objectively in space. These, that is the chemical elements and combinations occurring in nature, appear, wherever they fill space, with equal distinctness. Hence the energy of their action upon us—in which lies their æsthetic significance—will as a rule be the greater, the more *extensively* they occupy space. Thus the feelings inspired in us by the ocean are very different from those aroused by a specimen of its water in a glass. Each of these chemical Ideas contains in itself, as we found probable (§§ 185. 186), all physical forces, though in different degrees of intensity. Hence follows, that the æsthetic effect displayed by the physical Ideas will be the stronger, the more *intensely* they appear in the substances to which they are bound. Thus for instance the physical Idea of gravity appears more distinctly in stone than in wood, a fact of great importance, as we shall see, for the æsthetics of architecture. In inorganic nature therefore (in contrast to the organic world) it is partly by the extension, partly by the intensity of their manifestation, that the distinct appearance of the Ideas and therefore the beauty of objects is increased. Thus it is that mountains, a waterfall, a great fire affect us so powerfully, while diminished a hundredfold they would scarcely draw from us a glance. This might perhaps explain how it is that even space and time themselves, when perceived in great dimensions, dispose us to the sublime, although they are not Ideas at all but only the condition of the possibility of their phenomenal appearance. For it is just this possibility of their being filled which raises us to æsthetic contemplation.

§ 221. We saw (§§ 185. 187) that the essence of the chemical forces consists in their being an aggregate of all physical forces in gradual and characteristically determined combinations, appearing in a particular place. It is therefore ultimately always and only the physical Ideas which speak to us in the bodies as also in the corporeal changes of inorganic nature. Yet of these (the list of which, § 183, should be referred to) not all are fit to produce an æsthetic effect. Least of all perhaps heat, since this has reference not to the external objective senses but to feeling in general and by this directly to the Will, the excitement of which removes the condition of æsthetic contemplation. Among the physical Ideas which invite to will-free perception, may be named first impenetrability and gravity, the wrestling of which with each other is everywhere visible (in the heavy mountain, the sustaining earth, etc.). Rigidity takes form in the towering mountain cliffs, and that the more distinctly, the steeper their descent and the more jagged their forms. Fluidity in its vivid war with gravity appears in water, when winding as murmuring brook through the meadows, or precipitated as raging waterfall, when as stream it bears mighty ships, when it reposes as the smooth mirror of the lake, or rolls along as billow of the illimitable ocean in the ἀνήριθμον γέλασμα of Æschylos. As solidity in land, fluidity in water, so the third mode of cohesion appears in curling smoke or in the clouds driven by the wind. But above all inorganic Ideas it is that of light, together with its reflection in colour, which is not only the necessary condition of all beautiful aspects, but also by its own beauty gladdens the noblest of the sense organs.

§ 222. In **organic nature** we may define beauty by a formula of Kant's as conformity to an aim, perceived without consciousness of the aim. As everywhere else, so in the case of organisms beauty is due to a distinct appearance of the Idea. The Idea of an organism is the Will so far as it is presented as a series of spatial parts and temporal functions which co-operate for the unity of its aims. The more clearly therefore in an organism the adaptation of all its forms and movements to the aim strikes the eye, the more these are the mere embodiment of the purposes of the Will—the more expressively appears in them the Idea of the organism and the more beautiful is it. Therefore organic beauty is conformity to aim, not referred (as in anatomy and physiology) to a concept by abstract thought, but conceived intuitively, without reflection, and so without perception of an aim.

§ 223. Plants are restricted to beauty of form. In animals and men there is added the beauty of motion, called grace. As beauty in the narrower sense, that is, beauty of form, depends on the adaptation of all forms to the aims of the Will, so grace consists in the visible adaptation of movements to their aim, by virtue of which the aim in each case is attained in the shortest, simplest, and most natural way. To this law are subject not only the movements of the limbs, but all manifestations of life. Accordingly an action, a speech, a book and the like are, in an æsthetic sense, the more pleasing, the more determinedly, distinctly, and immediately is expressed in them the desired aim.

§ 224. To this is due also the greater or less beauty of industrial products, for instance household furniture, clothing, utensils, etc. These are not, properly speaking, works of art, since they serve not for the presentation of an Idea but for practical purposes. Nevertheless they have a beauty independent of their practical end, a beauty which, as such, cannot depend on anything but the distinct manifestation of an Idea. In manufactured articles, as in the whole of nature, are expressed firstly the Ideas appearing in their materials (gold, silver, silk, wool, wood, iron), yet only so far as the beauty lies in the materials, not so far as it lies in the form. The Idea manifested in the beautiful form of such objects can be no other than the Idea of man, whose will, as in every movement, every word, finds expression also in the forms of industrial products. These will therefore like bodily movements be the more beautiful, the more naively and directly they express their aim and through it the creative will of the artist. Thus it is the graceful movement of the artist hand, taking the shortest way to its end, which to-day even speaks to us from antique vases. For the beauty of Greek life, which lay in the distinct revelation of the Idea of man, extended, as to all else, so also to the activity of the craftsman and gave his productions a beauty never since reattained. This was probably what misled Plato into assuming the existence of Ideas of manufactured articles, as for instance tables and beds (Rep. x. p. 596 B), an error which was however soon recognised (Arist. Met. xi. 3, p. 1070 A 18, i. 9, p. 991 B 6).

VIII. Some Remarks on the Beautiful in Art

§ 225. Art and Metaphysics are near akin. These two and (besides morality) these alone rise above empirical existence and its petty interests. Both dwell in the contemplation of Being-in-itself, which by metaphysics is apprehended in concepts and by art in immediate intuition. For the artist looks through nature to that which is behind it, and which, though imperfectly, appears in it. This, the thing-in-itself, the Will, he seizes intuitively in its phenomenal forms, the Ideas. He "tears it out of nature" (as Albrecht Dürer says), and portrays it isolated in the work of art, the task of which is always, to make visible an Idea (not a concept), in giving it, from a particular point of view, pure and unimpeded development. To this it is due that poetry is not only, as Aristotle says, more philosophical than history, but that art in general is more instructive than reality. For while we see the Ideas in nature broken up in space, time, and causality, and thus only "through the mist of objective and subjective contingencies," the artist removes this mist, so that the true Being of things becomes perceptible, in the interpreting mirror of art, even to the duller eye. To gain this for the voluntary perception of the Idea, in which alone all beauty lies, the artist makes use of certain allurements (*lenocinia*) which flatter the senses and captivate the interest. Such are: beauty of colour in painting, that of tone in music, rhyme and metre, interesting actions and exciting complications in poetry. Spurious art plays with these means, without having anything to impart to us by them. The genuine artist uses them alone for setting in relief (as a picture by the frame) the Idea the presentation of which is the sole aim of every art. Architecture, sculpture, painting, poetry, and music (which, as we shall see, goes yet deeper) serve this end, each in its own way. Here we must restrict ourselves to showing briefly in what sense each of these tries to reproduce the Ideas and thus to reveal the inner essence of things.

§ 226. **Architecture** is only partially a fine art, in that its laborious and costly works have, in the first instance, a practical end, different from the artistic and often indeed antagonistic to it. The task therefore of the architect is to vindicate, as far as is compatible with practical requirements, the claims of art. It is only with these last that we have here to do in determining which Ideas speak to us in the beauty of a building. We leave out of sight the historical development of architecture, for our task is not to explain, how beautiful styles have arisen under the influence of necessity and technique, but if possible, to discover, why certain forms rather than others have been recognised as beautiful and in consequence retained.

Whether or not the fancy of the architect has been spurred to creation by aspects of nature, such as avenues of trees and arches of boughs, an imitation of these or of any other natural objects cannot be the aim of architecture. For why should the artist wish to imitate laboriously and inadequately what nature offers everywhere in unattainable perfection? Moreover in this case the copy would be very unlike the original, the column very unlike the tree trunk, and yet superior to it in beauty.

As little can symmetry be the aim of architecture as a fine art, for in that case the model would have a similar effect to the finished work; and again where symmetry is wanting or marred (as in ruins), the æsthetic effect would be lost, neither of which is the case. Symmetry and the mathematical clearness of proportions are certainly of great importance—firstly, in serving to isolate a building from its surroundings; further, the symmetrical arrangement of all its parts facilitates the survey of its usually huge complexity and, in placing the mind of the beholder in a due and harmonious state, makes it open to the reception of what is to be imparted. Yet all this merely proves it to be the right way in which something speaks to us, but not that something itself.

If, on the other hand, we seek the beauty of a building in the perfect adaptation of all its parts to an end, it cannot be its practical end that is here understood, since, in this sense, a building may be very appropriate to its purpose without being beautiful, or very beautiful without being appropriate. Æsthetic adaptation lies rather in the obvious determination and necessity of all details not to a practical end, but to the consistency of the whole as such, so that each single part is, as it were, required by all the rest. Therefore we ask further: what speaks to us from this whole, the significance of which is manifested in this subordination of all details? What are the Ideas appearing in it, the revelation of which as end determines the adaptation of all the parts?

Like every object in nature, a building is a manifestation of Ideas, yet only of those appearing in its materials. Thus the architrave, through its gravity, seeks the earth, while the walls, by their rigidity, oppose this tendency. Rigidity and gravity, these lowest grades of the objectification of the Will to life, the bass notes, as it were, of all nature, appear in every building in a state of tension, engaged in a continual wrestling with each other.

The more clearly this struggle comes to view, the more distinctly are revealed the Ideas battling in it, the more beautiful therefore must be the building, since beauty, here as everywhere, consists in manifestation of the Ideas (§ 216). Here lies the key which, rightly used, might suffice, not so much to explain all that architecture has produced in the varying taste of different ages—by which it is influenced more than any other art—as to throw light on the secret charm which the really beautiful works of architecture immediately exercise on our feeling, and this the more strongly (generally speaking) the greater their size. For the distinctness of the Ideas here manifested increases in general with spatial extension (§ 220). In addition to extension it is further, as we saw, by intensity that inorganic Ideas act. This is the reason why wood, easily as it assumes all forms, is not so suited for works of architecture as stone, in which these forces are more powerfully manifested. To display this revelation of gravity and rigidity, and thus render it more significant, is the architect's task. For this purpose he treats the Ideas inherent in his materials in much the same way as does the dramatist the types of humanity which he wishes to bring before us. As the latter, for instance, invents important actions, so that by conflicts and fatalities of all kinds the nature of the characters he represents may be disclosed, so the architect gives clear manifestation to the action of the forces embodied in stone by depriving them of the nearest and most immediate way to the satisfaction of their striving and compelling them, by a struggle against resistant forces, to reveal more vividly their being. Thus the architrave tends through gravity to press the earth, but is allowed to do so only circuitously through the columns in which the rigidity of the stone struggling against gravity becomes visible. This contrary striving of rigidity seems to be expressed in the upward hastening fluting, while the pressure of the architrave appears in the enlargement of the column at the capital, as perhaps also in the slight bulging ($\H{ε}ντασις$) at the first third of the height. Accordingly the column is an embodiment of rigidity striving against the weighing roof, and the columnar arrangement is the type of architectural beauty. This will be the greater, the more all parts of the building are determined by the struggle of the forces here displayed, so that there is nowhere too much, nowhere too little, every weight having its appropriate support and every support being required by the weight to be borne. Then, under the influence of light—which, reflected from huge masses of stone, attains itself to the most beautiful and varied manifestation—is revealed to our gaze the powerful yet measured striving of fearful and destructive elementary forces, here presented in majestic calm, and yet in the fullest energy of their mutual action.

If this explanation of the æsthetic effect of architecture be the right one, we must award the palm, before all others, to Greek architecture. For here in the everywhere vividly portrayed struggle of gravity and rigidity the action of the Ideas present in the material receives fullest expression, and their inner being in consequence the clearest revelation. As the Classic architraval structure displays the struggle between gravity and rigidity, so Gothic architecture shows rather the victory of rigidity over gravity. The latter, turned aside, as it were, flows from the point of the arch ineffectually through the columns to the earth, while rigidity, freeing itself more and more from every weight, tapers farther and farther aloft. Thus the Gothic style becomes a beautiful symbol of the soul, purifying itself from what is earthly and oppressive, and rising devoutly to heaven. For the rest it remains far behind the Classic in point of real æsthetic effect, though taking pains to hide this want of native energy by external ornament, borrowed from sculpture and painting.

§ 227. Architecture differs from sculpture, painting, and music in that it does not portray Ideas in a material foreign to them, but merely gives clearer expression to those Ideas inherent in its own materials. It is not therefore like the others an *imitating*, but merely an *interpreting* art. In this sense it has its analogue in the artistic arrangement of water. As in architecture rigidity is portrayed at war with gravity, so here the fluid element is seen in its action under the most diverse influences, in which the rushing waterfall may be compared to the Classic, the rising fountain to the Gothic style. In a similar way landscape gardening, as also landscape painting, helps, by tasteful grouping (§ 219), to interpret the vegetable world. For the Idea of Man, so far as this is revealed in the external form, gymnastics and dancing may be named as interpreting arts, as representing the human form in the highest development of its power, dexterity, and grace. Dancing reaches its greatest perfection in the ballet, but moral considerations seem to prevent this ever being raised to the dignity of a fine art.

§ 228. The Will, which strives in a dull and one-sided way even in inorganic forces, which sprouts and grows in the plant, and desires restlessly and eagerly in the brute, arrives at the full and distinct unfolding of its essence in the light of knowledge first in Man; so much so that, compared to him, all the rest of nature seems little more than a mere foil. Hence it is that art, though not excluding subordinate Ideas (landscape and animal painting, animal sculpture, descriptions of nature), yet finds its proper and worthiest theme in the Idea of Man, and an inexhaustible subject in the portrayal of human nature and action from every point of view.

§ 229. We distinguished in man a twofold character, that of the species and that of the individual (§ 182). Every man is, in the first place, a representative of his species, of the Idea, of the type of mankind. Approximation to this constitutes human beauty. Besides this, however, every human being has its peculiar individual character, by which is conditioned what is characteristic in the action as in the outward appearance. Both elements must be expressed in the work of art; the beautiful without the characteristic is insignificant, the characteristic without the beautiful tends to caricature.

Remark. The characteristic element is not a new principle besides the beautiful, for both are the distinct appearance of the type, in the one case of the species, in the other of the individual, which, at the highest grade of the objectification of the Will, gains, as it were, the significance of a particular Idea.

§ 230. **Sculpture** has, if not for its sole, yet for its most important task the reproduction of the Idea of Man, so far as this is revealed in the external form. This form is, in all its parts, expressive, since, as we know, the whole body is only the objectively represented Will. It is due to a presentiment of this truth, that works of plastic art have always been held in high estimation. Contrasted with the human figure, as an embodiment of the Idea of Man, the garment in which we clothe it is of little importance, since the Ideas speaking to us in its draperies are only those of its materials and very inferior in kind. Hence sculpture prefers the nude, and, where free to create, tolerates drapery only so far as it reveals rather than conceals the form. In this sense, however, it can be of great service in inviting the mind to produce spontaneously, by passing from the effect to its cause, the indicated forms and so to conceive them more fully. Sculpture has the advantage of reproducing its forms in plastic roundness and full distinctness. On the other hand, to avoid the semblance of reality and the dead life of wax figures, it renounces colouring, from which the tinting of particular parts in order to give them greater distinctness, as was customary among the ancients, is widely removed. The strength of sculpture lies therefore in the expression of the figure, while in facial expression, which demands eyes and colour, it cannot vie with painting. Now, since the individual character is before all stamped on the face, the character of the species, on the other hand, on the whole figure, sculpture has chiefly to portray the latter, even though always in a particular individual direction (as Zeus, Apollo, Hermes, Hera, Artemis, Aphrodite, etc.). Thus in sculpture the beautiful element predominates over the characteristic (§ 229), and beauty of form can be far less dispensed with in plastic works than in painting.

§ 231. **Painting** renounces the relief of plastic art and confines itself to the flat surface. As compensation it has the possibility of freer movement and richer development, as also the privilege of producing, by the charm of colour, the most splendid effects. These means allow it, in contrast to the narrow limits to which plastic art is confined, to draw all that exists within its sphere and to raise us—now by the approximation of objects to the Ideas speaking in them, now by well-calculated grouping, leading to intimate comprehension, or again by the mere detaching of the subject thrown on the canvas from reality and its interests—to that objectivity in which we see everything as beautiful, because everything merely as a reflection of the Ideas. Painting thus becomes a teacher in the æsthetic comprehension of nature, a fact of which we become aware when, on leaving a picture gallery and going into the open air, we find everything there also glorified by beauty, because we see it with objective eyes. Inexhaustible is the wealth of the domain open to the painter, yet the highest object of his choice remains the Idea of Man, so far as it is in any way accessible to the eye in external being and doing. In the reproduction of the human figure painting certainly cannot equal plastic art. Its strength—a strength attainable by no other art—lies instead in the delineation of the face, through which Will illumined by knowledge finds for the various strivings and feelings in which it is manifested, its most eloquent and beautiful expression. Nor is it alone the affirmation of the Will to life which the painter portrays in the varied scenes of human life, throughout so significant and "interesting wherever seized." In the unearthly brightness of saintly faces he tries to reproduce the reflection of that turning of the Will to denial which seems to call to us : " There is a better world."

§ 232. An action, an occurrence, a scene in life is of external significance, when it forms an important link in the causal chain governing human life (ex. the action or word of a prince). It is of internal significance, when human nature from some point of view receives clear and characteristic expression in it. From this it follows that, for the representation of the Idea of Man, not so much the outer as the inner significance of an action is of account, that consequently this, not that gives the work of art its real value. If, nevertheless, the historical painter takes his subjects by preference from outwardly significant events in history and legend, the reason is the same as that which makes the dramatist choose the heroes of his works amongst crowned heads rather than from the people, a fact of which we shall have to speak further on.

§ 233. Freer in its movements than sculpture is

painting, freer than painting is **poetry**. It becomes so at the cost of renouncing entirely the visible and the concrete, and choosing as the material for portraying Ideas (to which visibility is essential), the words of language, that is the representatives of abstract concepts. These are only suitable as a means of artistic portrayal so far as the poet succeeds by his words in setting the imagination of the hearer to play, in such a way that it creates spontaneously the image in which the Idea appears. This therefore adapts itself more intimately and appropriately to the individuality of every hearer than is possible with the plastic and pictorial arts, which impose on all alike a ready-made object or scene. This transformation of his concepts into concrete form by the imagination of the hearer the poet attains by the aid of various artifices peculiar to himself. In the first place he will, as far as possible, avoid all wide and general concepts of a very abstract nature. Again, he makes a general concept more concrete in limiting its sphere by an added epithet. Finally he facilitates the closer and more concrete apprehension of concepts by forcing the hearer to extract these from images to which he refers either in place of, or for the illustration of, the concepts. This he does by means of Allegory, by which we here understand (according to the etymology from ἄλλος and ἀγορεύειν) in general the art of expressing one thing by means of another, that is, a concept by a concrete image (to be created in the imagination of the hearer). We regard therefore all figurative expressions, metaphors, similes, parables, etc. as allegories. Thus Plato in the Phaedrus (p. 253 C sq.) makes the concept of the soul perceptible in comparing it to a charioteer and two horses (anticipating its division into intellect, conscious and unconscious Will), an allegory which, with slight differences, occurs also in Indian philosophy (*Kâṭhaka-Up.* 3, 3).—Accordingly allegory leads in poetry from the abstract to the concrete, and by this to the primary source of real knowledge. In plastic and pictorial art, on the contrary, it leads from perception to the abstract concept and so to what is inferior, because secondary. Here it appears in the form of allegorical figures by which an abstract concept or general truth is to be illustrated. Now the ultimate aim of art is the portrayal of the Idea, not of the concept. Hence in plastic and pictorial art allegorical figures, so far as they illustrate the concept, have no artistic value, but only so far as, besides this, they give clear and definite expression in some direction or other to the Idea of Man.

As further auxiliary artifices in poetry we find metre and rhyme. It cannot be denied that, even by the best poets, clearness and definite expression of thought are more or less sacrificed to these. Thus the metrical fall of the syllables and the sing-song of the rhyme are dearly bought, from which may be inferred that their value is not a low one. This value seems to lie chiefly in the fact that our ear, listening to their regular recurrence, anticipates, as regards its form, that which follows, so that this appears to be not absolutely new, but prepared for by the preceding. It thus gains a kind of legitimacy and necessity which disposes us to assent the more readily to it. Metre and rhyme serve moreover, like absence of colour in sculpture and the flat surface in painting, to keep us in mind of the fact that we have to do, not with an object of empirical reality, but with a work of art. Thus they help to sustain the objectivity of mood, necessary to æsthetic contemplation.

§ 234. So much for the auxiliaries of poetic art. Its aim, like that of all art, is the portrayal of the Ideas, above all of the Idea of man. It is true, no sphere of being is to be excluded from poetry, but in descriptions of nature the absence of definite percepts is prejudicial to it, an evil which (as Lessing has shown in the Laokoon) the art of the poet can only partially overcome. On the other hand poetry celebrates its greatest triumphs in the description of human life and action. For here, being no longer restricted like plastic and pictorial art to reproducing the external, it lays bare the whole inner organisation of the character, as does the sculptor the external form. Since man can only reveal his being in a plurality of spatial and temporal manifestations, the Idea of man cannot in consequence be so perfectly represented by sculpture and painting (restricted as these are to a single well chosen moment) as by poetry, which, by idealising reality, unites in a whole that which in life appears but fragmentarily. For poetic idealisation consists, not in representing men otherwise (better or worse) than they are in reality, in which case the poet would only give an untrue picture of life, but in bringing together in poetic representation, especially in the drama (though not necessarily, as the French used to believe), that which is in reality separated by time and space. We may often notice that the greatest poets are not very strict in observing the laws of time and space, the nothingness of which they feel by a kind of metaphysical instinct. Thus Helen and Penelope are even after twenty years still young and attractive, and Agamemnon arrives in Argos just as the taking of Troy has been announced by the fire signals. The less, however, the poet concerns himself with the merely formal conditions of reality, the more carefully will he treat its material part, as that containing the Idea. Here he will take pains to remove everything irrelevant and contradictory, by which in real life the revelation of a character is marred, since through temper, error, or other casual influences we all very often act otherwise than befits our individuality. While therefore in real life we frequently act as it were out of character, in poetry the characters must be "sustained." By this is meant that the poet must only lay stress on such features as are characteristic of the individual, so that we are compelled to create out of the few pencil strokes, with which for instance Shakespeare furnishes his characters, a definite and consistently connected personality. Here the poet is aided by the right given to him of lending to his characters beautiful and eloquent language, by which every emotion finds distinct expression, whereas in real life deepest pain and greatest joy are often dumb.

While poetry exercises and sharpens the eye for the apprehension of human nature, it becomes an excellent means of promoting our knowledge of mankind. Thus for him who studies his Shakespeare assiduously, all men by degrees will gain a certain transparency. In this respect poetry accomplishes far more than history, which, besides being full of falsifications, represents what has happened, imperfectly and with inadequate or problematical motivation. It has, moreover, as its aim the outward significance of actions for the progress of history and not their inward significance for the revelation of man: διὸ καὶ φιλοσοφώτερον καὶ σπουδαιότερον ποίησις ἱστορίας ἐστίν, as Aristotle rightly observes (Poet. 9).

§ 235. Perfect objectivity of mind is necessary to poetry as to every other art. When therefore (to name only the chief kinds of poetry) we distinguish the epic and the drama as the *objective* from the lyric as the *subjective* species, our meaning is only, that in the lyric the subject himself with his joys and sorrows is treated by the poet with the same objective contemplation as is, in the epic or the drama, the external world. That which the lyric poet describes, we all experience. But while man in his torture is dumb, a god, as Goethe says, vouchsafes to the poet the power of uttering what he suffers. That is, he alone has the power of mind to maintain, even in face of the suffering of his own Will, that objectivity of mind in which we recognised the necessary condition of all æsthetic contemplation, and which is perhaps nowhere more difficult than where it has to portray our inner being tossed by the storm of passion. This is why even the lyric poet seems not to attain this objectivity at once, but only after his mind is strengthened by contemplation of the outer world to that intuitive power which enables him to detach from himself, as an objective image, his own state of mind and so to free himself from it, as did Goethe by his songs. For this reason the lyric poet turns his gaze now on his own agitated soul, now on the surrounding external world, as may be seen in so many of Goethe's poems. It appears very distinctly, for instance, in the song

"To the Moon," where the aspect of the moon, filling wood and valley with hazy lustre, disposes the poet to a contemplative mood and so enables him to conceive objectively also his inner being. Therefore he says the moon "loosens" his soul, and likens it to a friend to whom one confides one's sorrow, to obtain relief.

To the subjective poetry of the lyric is opposed the more objective epic, which, in throwing off the fetters of metre, gained as the novel freer movement, thus adapting itself to the richer content of a more complex civilisation. Both the epic and the novel are yet to a certain extent subjective. We see indeed the events—for he alone reads Homer worthily who follows with the eye what he describes—but we do not lose sight of the narrator. In the drama the poet vanishes completely behind his work. It is thus the most objective and so the highest and most difficult species of poetry, in the original creation of which only two peoples, the Indians and the Greeks, succeeded (though in totally different ways).

The aim of the drama can be no other than to illustrate the Idea of man by placing before us a series of characters. In order to disclose these to us, the dramatist invents an important plot, powerfully affecting the interests of the persons concerned and forcing them in their passion to reveal to us their inmost being. For, as the nature of water is not displayed so long as it remains at rest in the pond, but when as brook it drives the mill, as river bears ships, when it rushes downwards as waterfall, springs upwards as fountain or splashes high in the ocean surge—so men seldom reveal their inner being in the common occurrences of daily life, but often, when some *terrible fate*, some *extraordinary wickedness*, or finally some *accidental chain of circumstances* brings about situations calling all passions of the soul into stormy play.

This conflict we see in tragedy kindled to a heat which allows of no other issue than the death of the combatants, whom, even when not bearing arms, we call characteristically enough the heroes of the piece. These the poet chooses by preference from among princes and high-placed dignitaries, for the fall from the height has a more terrifying effect, while the sufferings of the poor often arise from causes which to the rich appear trivial, and might in many cases be easily removed. But the tragic poet has to show how over this existence there sway forces which even high birth, wealth, and might are powerless to resist. So the mighty man, the king, the hero dies, but in him we often see extinguished, before life itself, the Will to life, since excess of sorrow has taught him the true lesson of the worth and meaning of this existence. Thus tragedy disposes us to the sublime (§ 218) in showing everywhere to what irremediable conflicts this existence to which we all belong, may lead, so preaching with earnest voice the turning away from willing and its unhappiness. Comedy, on the contrary (so far as it does not pursue satirical or political ends foreign to poetry), seems to encourage the affirmation of the Will to life, in leading through hindrances and intrigues of all kinds to a happy solution,—though, in doing so, it must be careful to drop the curtain at the right moment.

§ 236. **Music** is, as the name implies, the work of the Muses, the art κατ' ἐξοχήν, and indeed the whole drift of our inquiry leads us to recognise in it the summit of all art, because the most immediate expression of Being-in-itself at which all art aims. This dignity is assured to it not only by the incomparable expressiveness of its language but also by the importance of what it imparts to us by it. That which speaks to us in the sounds of music is, as has long been recognised and often repeated, the feelings, the affections and passions of the human heart. Now these are nothing but the Will mirroring itself from within in the intellect, that Will which, as we know, is the thing-in-itself, the principle of all being. Music therefore, in portraying the world of feelings of the soul, discloses at the same time the inner being of all nature. For that which, in the immediate light of knowledge, flows and surges in us as emotion, freeing itself from the soul in sighs, words, and tones, and forming itself into an objective and relief-giving image—that it is which sighs and vibrates as unconscious suffering, as unfelt feeling in all sounds and tones of creation. For that which roars in the thunder, murmurs in the water, groans in the axle of the wheel, whispers in the leaves of the tree, howls as wolf and coos as dove, is nothing but the one Will to life, animating us also: "*aitad-âtmyaṃ idaṃ sarvaṃ, tat satyaṃ, sa âtmâ, tat tvam asi, Çvetaketo!*"—" Of the essence of that is this universe, that is the Real, that is the Soul, that art thou, O Çvetaketu!" (*Chândogya-Upanishad*, vi. 8-16).

Two ways lead to the knowledge of Being-in-itself, that is Will, the external way of cognition and the internal way of feeling. All other arts take the outer way, in seizing and portraying the Will in its perceptual forms, the Ideas. Even poetry, to which the inner world is opened, can only impart what it sees there indirectly by means of cognition through concepts. Music alone sets the Ideas and the whole perceptual world aside, to take its way through the ear, past the intellect, immediately to the heart, to unfold, as an objective spectacle, its revelations directly in the feeling of the hearer, though without any suffering on his part; and again and again we wonder how this way of looking immediately and yet objectively at Being-in-itself became possible to us.

The sole theme of music is the Will in all its joy and all its sorrow. Accordingly it is pure weal and woe which speak to us in the flattering accents and the deep pathos of its sounds; whether they reproduce in short merry melodies the joyous aspiration and speedy satisfaction of the Will, the soaring of hope, the fiery striving, the rejoicings of victory and festive mirth; or whether, in melancholy sounds, deviating from the keynote and winding through varied intricacies and painful dissonances, they become an image of pain, now raging in frantic fury, now creeping along in gnawing, slow-consuming craving, or seeing in desolate and utter despair all hope of life vanish, till at last, in the return to the keynote, the greatest heartache finds rest, though it be but that of the grave.

The fundamental character of willing, by the portrayal of which music discloses the depths of the human heart and with these the inmost being of the world, consists, in small things as in great, in the Will being now at variance, now reconciled with surrounding circumstances. Let us try to understand how this alternate disunion and reconciliation of the mind with the world is portrayed by music through its agents, melody, rhythm, and harmony. The soul of a musical piece is the melody, in which is easily recognised the rising and falling of willing, the intensity of which is expressed in the dynamics of the sound. Now in empirical existence there are two elements opposed to the Will with which it must reckon and struggle, in the concord of which with it consists all satisfaction, out of the resistance of which to the wishes of the heart springs all pain. These elements are on the one side the order of the universe in space, time, and causality given *a priori*, on the other those inorganic and organic forces of nature, added *a posteriori*, which are akin to the Will and share the field with it, now favouring and furthering its efforts, now resisting it and preparing struggle and distress. Similarly in music there is opposed to that sequence of sounds which we call melody, on the one side rhythm, with its *a priori* regularity, which drives the melody striving after the repose of the keynote ever farther, allowing it no rest till the tonica, or at least a harmonic interval coincides with the accent of the rhythm. On the other hand we have harmony, akin in its nature to melody, which it accompanies in its course as the surrounding forces of nature accompany the Will, now furthering, now hindering it. To complete the parallelism, we have in the dissonances, in their painful expression allowing of no rest, a self-evident objective picture of unsurmounted hindrances and unsatisfied strivings. The consonances, on the other hand, paint that harmony of human willing with the surrounding and accompanying powers of the external world, on which in fact all satisfaction depends.

Profoundly has Schopenhauer, to whose unequalled genius we owe also these interpretations, further likened the bass and the deeper voices in music to the Ideas of inorganic nature, and the higher intermediate voices to those of the vegetable and animal world.

Not particular occurrences, not single scenes of life, are the subject of music, but willing alone, that willing which underlies and is manifested in all external being and doing, in joy, pain, longing, anguish, hope, and all other emotions of the heart. Music lifts these out of the visible world in which they find expression, and pictures them alone and independently in complete generality and yet in thoroughgoing concrete distinctness. Thus music is to the text of a song or an opera what the internal is to the external, the soul to the body. The text gives us in words some important incident, some passionate mood of mind, the music describes alone and in themselves the emotions and strivings of the Will expressed in them. Every piece of music therefore interprets as clearly the essence of the incidents which it accompanies, as music as a whole mirrors the objectified Will in all its erring and striving, in all its suffering and its satisfaction, thus disclosing and revealing the deepest mystery of being, the heart of the world, the ultimate ground of all that is finite.

§ 237. So we see music, so all art engaged in unveiling and interpreting the innermost being of this whole world. Yet it is always this world alone of which art tells us in all its forms, words, and sounds. Beyond it no artist is borne by the flight of his fancy, from it even a Dante and a Milton must borrow all colours for their pictures. True, it is not things themselves but the Ideas of things which the artist portrays. But what separates the things of this world from their Ideas, is only their empirical reality, their existence in causality, space, and time, with the consequences of such an existence. From these hindrances, originating in our own intellect, the artistic genius sets things free. By this not so much the contemplated object is changed as the method of its contemplation and through this the contemplator himself. How the phenomenon of the beautiful is explained by processes within us, by the deliverance of the beholder from himself, Schopenhauer has taught us, but it was known also before him. Ὅταν τι τῶν ἐκεῖ ὁμοίωμα ἴδωσιν, Plato says (Phaedr. p. 250 A), ἐκπλήττονται καὶ οὐκέθ' αὑτῶν γίγνονται. And Goethe also says (Faust, ii. p. 258):

"Von Schönheit ward von jeher viel gesungen,—
  Wem sie erscheint, wird aus sich selbst entrückt."

"Of beauty they have sung in every age,
  Who sees it is from bonds of self set free."

But this state of transport, in which we seem to lose ourselves, is rather a return to ourselves, a return from the strange land in which we sojourn to our true home. For it is indeed only above empirical existence—that existence which is not and ought not to be—that the beholder feels himself raised, when his ego pales as a shadow in the light of beauty, when his whole individuality is dissolved, as it were, in contemplation. This fading away of his individual existence is the source of that bliss which fills the beholder. It is a sign that the goal of our existence, that which is really positive and essential, must be sought beyond individuality. In raising us to this, the contemplation of the beautiful grants us a satisfaction without measure, not by the fulfilment of wishes, but by the temporary removal of the entire possibility of such. Yet ever and again the beholder, after being lost in contemplation, is laid again under the ban of reality. He awakes like a captive who, slumbering in his dungeon, dreamt of freedom.

Is there from this dungeon of existence an escape without return? From these bonds of empirical reality—in which we are driven from life to death, from death to new life in perpetual circuit—is there an eternal deliverance?

This question points to the last and the most important subject of our inquiry, to which we now proceed.

THE SYSTEM OF METAPHYSICS

PART IV

THE METAPHYSICS OF MORALITY

I. Preliminary

§ 238. Man has two opposed activities. The one going from the external to the internal is knowing, the other directed from within to without is acting. Knowing is twofold—abstract and perceptual. Thus we have three fundamental functions—thinking, perceiving, acting.

§ 239. These three functions are originally and essentially physical (belonging to the phenomenal world), that is, they presuppose the reality of causality, space, and time. Under this supposition thinking is empirical, and leads, as we have shown, to materialism, perceiving is individual and apprehends things according to their (nearer or remoter) spatial, temporal, and causal relations to the beholding subject, but not according to their objective Being-in-itself. Lastly, acting is egoistic, that is, affirmative of the ego or the Will to individual existence, as is clear from the following.

Acting is the passing from one state to another by means of an act of the Will. Such is only possible, if the succeeding state is preferred to the preceding; this again presupposes that by this change dissatisfaction is decreased or pleasure increased. Now space, time, and causality restrict my being, and with it the possibility of feeling pleasure and pain, to my individuality (and to what I consider as belonging to the sphere of my ego, such as family, property, honour, etc.). Consequently, pleasure and pain, from the empirical standpoint, can only be motives of action so far as they have reference to our own individuality; that is, all action is egoistic, affirmative of the individuality.

§ 240. We know that the physical order of the universe originates fundamentally in an error, since space, time, and causality, on which it is based, are not, as we naturally suppose, *aeternae veritates*, that is, an eternal and unchangeable order lying in things themselves, but only functions, originating in our intellect, in which we conceive Being-in-itself (Will, the Ideas), and so behold it as world. Hence in contrast to our inborn consciousness of the physical order of the world in space, time, and causality, stands the truer, better, more real consciousness of the metaphysical order without space, time, and causality. And in fact the whole task of metaphysics is reduced to showing how this consciousness of the metaphysical order comes to light in the three departments of thinking, perceiving, and acting, and how from these there spring, like three stems from one root, the three metaphysical phenomena of Philosophy, Art, and Morality (which last conception, if one only understands it deeply enough, coincides with that of Religion).

§ 241. Space, time, and causality are called, as the basis of the physical, that is, of the individual order of things, the **principle of individuation.** Through innate entanglement in this principle and its illusion our thinking is empirical, our perceiving individual, our acting egoistic, that is, it distinguishes between the ego and the non-ego, and so affirms the individuality. It is due to a penetration of the principle of individuation, that our thinking becomes no longer *empirical* but *transcendental*, our *perceiving* no longer *individual* but *æsthetic*, our acting no longer *will-affirming* but *will-denying*. The following scheme, rightly understood, will greatly facilitate the insight into the connection of our whole metaphysical system. Committed to memory it will at the same time serve to keep in view the consciousness of the organic unity of our philosophy, which is indispensable also to the understanding of all details.

Physics (World)	**Metaphysics (God)**
(1) Thinking: *empirical*	*transcendental*—Philosophy.
(2) Perceiving: *individual*	*æsthetic* —Art.
(3) Acting: *affirming*	*denying* —Religion.

§ 242. Explanation of this scheme. *Firstly*, we have, in the sphere of thought, the **empirical** standpoint, restricted to space, time, and causality, and culminating in materialism (§§ 7-30). Opposed to this is the transcendental standpoint, from which we demonstrated the subjectivity of space, time, and causality (§§ 47-68), deducted these from the world (§§ 69-77. 86-88), and deciphered the remainder, that is force, as Will (§§ 146-153. 159-166), thereby attaining to the last possible understanding of nature. *Secondly*, the perception of things rises from the **individual** view which regards them as a totality of spatial, temporal, and causal relations to the beholding subject (§§ 198-201), to æsthetic intuition. This penetrates and sets aside these relations, seizes the true inner being of that which is here manifested, that is the Idea (§§ 202-224), and embodies it in works of art (§§ 225-236). Now it is this same twofold nature of consciousness which appears *thirdly and lastly* in the actions of man as two tendencies—opposed as magnetic poles—of the Will manifested in them. For opposed to the natural and egoistic actions, affirming the Will to life, are certain actions which, often externally not distinguishable from the first and blended with them, yet show inwardly a diametrically opposed striving. This is, according to different standpoints, defined as good, moral, holy, Christian, etc., but is more fittingly described as a denying of the Will to individual existence. For the only explanation of these actions is that the actor always sacrifices in them to a certain extent his own individual and limited existence by expanding his ego beyond the bounds of his individuality, recognising his own self in others, and thus breaking through the barriers of space, time, and causality in a *practical* respect as does the artist in an *intuitive* and the philosopher in an *abstract* way.

§ 243. According to this parallelism, which will find its further elucidation in the sequel, the denial of the Will to life and with it all virtue and holiness depends on nothing but a penetration of the principle of individuation (§ 241), consequently on knowledge alone. But this knowledge is of a quite peculiar kind and related in a metaphysical sense to the doctrine of the subjectivity of space, time, and causality, as is in an empirical sense intuitive understanding to abstract knowledge. Now, just as no physical abstract doctrine can ever replace the physical intuitive knowledge of the world, so our metaphysical abstract teaching (irrefutable as it is) would scarcely succeed in producing that metaphysical intuitive understanding on which moral action depends. Nay, we shall be compelled farther on to recognise that the metaphysical knowledge of the a-priority of space, time, and causality, which, as contradictory to the nature of our own intellect, was in abstract form only attainable in the most intricate ways, is in the intuitive form in which it underlies moral phenomena no longer an intellectual act at all. For intellect is nothing but a texture of space, time, and causality, all of which are here suspended. Thus the moral phenomenon is a deeper rooted process, a partial or total transformation of the Will itself, which, in moral actions, turns itself as it were away from the world and its order. To us only, since we have no intellectual form in which to conceive it, and must therefore of necessity clothe it in the heterogeneous forms of affirmation, this turning of the Will to denial appears as an unconscious removal of these, as an intuitive breaking through the phenomenal forms of affirmation, space, time, and causality. In this point, to which our consideration will repeatedly recur, lies the real difficulty—unparalleled in any other science—of the metaphysics of morality. The deeds of denial, though occurring daily before our eyes, are to our intellect, as a mere organ of affirmation, as little conceivable in their real essence as is the freedom (absence of causality) in which they have their root. Hence our attempt to portray these in the forms of our understanding must remain imperfect in like manner, as does the image of a corporeal object on a plane surface, the proportions of which are indeed accurately depicted, but in a distortion regulated according to the laws of perspective.

§ 244. **Order of procedure.** The Will is, as thing-in-itself, exempt from causality and consequently free (§ 168,$_3$). Hence with regard to individual existence two ways are equally open to it. The one is the **willing** of individual existence which, as the affirmation of the Will to life, viewed through the forms of our intellect, appears as the world, extended infinitely in space and time and regulated throughout, in small things as in great, by causality. The other way is the **not-willing** of this same individual existence, the manifestation of which, as the denial of the Will to life, lies beyond the forms of our understanding and remains therefore wholly barred and inconceivable. Therefore we know the denial of the Will to life only in so far as it breaks through this world of affirmation in moral actions, actions which, for that very reason, are at variance with the natural order of things and its laws originating in the intellect. They gleam through the darkness of existence as the light of another—of a better world. But we have no eyes to catch this light save by its reflection in morality. Hence we must restrict ourselves to showing, by the aid of experience, both affirmation and denial in the deeds of men, thus making the last step honestly possible to an intellect like ours. To this end we have to prove beforehand, that to the affirming Will existence, to existence the present is assured (immortality of the soul); secondly, that necessity, as the mere phenomenal form of freedom, does not release us from the responsibility for what we commit or omit (freedom of the Will). This being done, we must take into consideration this world as the stage of the affirmation of the Will to life, to understand how on the one side all wickedness, on the other all evil of which the world is full, spring necessarily from egoism, which, as we shall see, is the fundamental form of affirmation and inseparably bound up with it. Consequently a salvation from moral and physical evil is only possible through a complete transformation of our being, consisting in a turning of the Will. In this change of the Will we shall recognise, in accordance with the fundamental doctrines of Christian and Indian religion, the real moral goal and the ultimate aim of this existence. The nature of this turning of the Will to denial, the ways it takes and the principle manifested in it will be the subject of the last questions which we have to raise and—so far as the nature of our intellect admits of it—to answer.

II. On the Immortality of the Soul

§ 245. The immortality of the soul, this truth dearer to men than any other, stands and falls with the fundamental dogma of Kant (§ 92). From Kant's doctrine follows the immortality of the soul, from the immortality of the soul the doctrine of Kant.

§ 246. We showed already above (§§ 155-157) how the immortality of the soul is the inevitable consequence of the a-priority of space, time, and causality. Whoever therefore has followed our considerations, will not misunderstand us if, for the sake of imprinting this important truth and its proofs in the memory, we throw it into the form of a syllogism.

>Time exists only in our consciousness.
>Beginning and end are only in time.
>———
>Consequently beginning and end exist only in our consciousness:

that is, they belong only to the form in which our intellect sees things, but not to things as they are in themselves. Thus from the ideality of time follows immortality.

§ 247. Conversely, whoever clings, from whatever

grounds, to the immortality of the soul, must acknowledge transcendental Idealism as a necessary consequence of his belief. For, questioned from the empirical standpoint, nature asserts not immortality but exactly the reverse. Openly and naively she preaches in her unmistakable language the truth that man by generation comes from nothing to existence and by death returns from existence to nothing. If therefore the belief in immortality is to be maintained at all, we must necessarily deny to the assertions of nature objective and absolute validity. Now to do so, we obtain a scientific right alone by Kant's doctrine that nature is only manifestation and not thing-in-itself, that consequently the truth of her assertions is merely subjective—valid for intellects like our own—and relative.

§ 248. We shall arrive at a more intimate understanding of immortality than is possible by way of abstract conclusions, in proportion as we are able to understand the profound saying of Schopenhauer, that life is assured to the Will, and the present assured to life.

1. The Will, in the state of affirmation, has to life as which it is manifested, not a merely accidental relation, as to a thing which it may take or not take, but is necessarily bound up with it. For life is in fact nothing else but the Will itself, as it is portrayed in the higher grades of its objectification in the forms

of our intellect. Thus life is the visibility of the Will to life, accompanying it as the shadow the body, and, like the shadow, showing itself, wherever the light of the intellect shines. Where therefore there is Will to life, there also is life, so long as the forms of our intellect, that is, so long as time, space, and matter exist, consequently to all eternity. Aeons indeed may pass away in the life of nature in which no organic or living being exists, but in these there is no intellect, therefore no time, therefore no world. They are only an empty scheme of the empirical view of things. Therefore Schopenhauer says with truth,—life is assured to the Will; or as an Indian verse says (*Ashṭâvakragîtâ*, 10, 3):

Yatra yatra bhavet trishṇâ, saṃsâraṃ viddhi tatra vai.

"Know that wherever there is desire, there in truth is also the *saṃsâra*."

2. But further. We, it is true, divide time into the infinite past, the infinite future, and the extensionless present, separating them. But in reality there is no past, no future, and there never will be one. Both are mere abstractions; the sole form of existence is the present. Perishable as it is, it can yet never be lost. Step by step it accompanies existence as its never-failing phenomenal form. Since then to-day it is still to-day, and this truth will never lose its validity, we may assert, as a result of the most immediate observation—an observation

irrefutable and to be experienced every moment—the tenet of Schopenhauer : **the present is assured to life**.

§ 249. The immortality of the soul is the timelessness of our inmost being, the Will. It is therefore, properly speaking, no real continuance of life beyond death, but an **indestructibility without continuance in time**. In vain we torment ourselves to realise perceptually this abstract and, in an empirical sense, contradictory concept, for it sets aside these very forms of the intellect through which alone perceptual knowledge is possible. If therefore we would bring the conception of immortality nearer and make it more intelligible, we must resolve on doing violence to truth and, just as the soul itself has been conceived as substance, that is, in the form of space, so we must view its immortality through the spectacles of time. These presupposed, immortality appears as the **transmigration of souls**, a myth removed from the truth only in so far as it views in the form of time what is timeless. Hence it is met with not only as a primitive belief perhaps of all peoples, but has also been for the wisest of all time a subject of wondering meditation. In the Bible even there are traces of it, though these are scanty and uncertain (Ps. xc. 3 ; St. Matth. xi. 14, xvi. 14 ; St. John ix. 2). Its real home is India, where from of old it has been the basis of belief, and has an incredibly great practical influence. To the Indian this whole world appears as the *saṃsâra* (§ 176), that is, the transmigration-circuit of souls. These pass from one body into another, to receive punishment and reward for the deeds of a former life from all eternity to all eternity, unless one attains to perfect knowledge (*samyag-darçanam*), in which case his soul leaves the cycle of empirical existence to enter *nirvâṇam*, which is home, rest, bliss.

§ 250. If we could resolve to adopt this conception of immortality as a transmigration of souls— figurative it is true, yet nearer to the truth than any other—we might perhaps answer the question as to the continuance of our individuality thus, that our individuality does indeed endure beyond death, but only so long as the affirmation of the Will of which it is the expression. Animals, with the exception of the highest, have only the character of their species, no individual character (§§ 182. 229). In proportion as in animals the entire empirical manifestation finds its full explanation in the Idea of the species (and all varieties in the adaptation of this Idea to the various external circumstances, §§ 182. 189), in the same proportion is the single animal a mere ectype of the Idea. In the eternity of the Idea, therefore, the brute has its immortality. The phenomenon of Man, on the other hand, cannot be explained only by the character of the species, since this in him is supplemented by an individual character (equally innate and manifested in the whole life). Hence this character is, as much as the Idea of the species, a principle of the explanation of the phenomenon, must lie therefore behind it, and is consequently not dissolved with the dissolution of the phenomenon.

Individuality is the innate character of the Will. Life is its expansion in the light of intellect, through which is attained either an approach to denial or a hardening in affirmation. Both are the very fruit of life; for as this we have to consider that modification of willing which the individual takes over with it from life to death. Now if Schopenhauer's hypothesis is right, that the (individually determined) Will is, as the radical element in us, inherited from the father, the intellect as the secondary from the mother, the riddle of generation (that most mysterious point in the empirical order of things) is solved. The Will, united in the father with an intellect which does not suffice for the renunciation of willing (and with it of generation), seeks a new intellect, which the mother gives it, that is, the Will hastens from generation to generation to an ever new expansion of its being in the light of another intellect, until, attaining perfect self-knowledge, it freely denies itself and enters salvation. The following verse of Goethe's might be interpreted as a description of this process:

> Alles Vergängliche
> Ist nur ein Gleichnis (is phenomenal, not the thing-in-itself);
> Das Unzulängliche
> Hier (in denial) wird's Ereignis (denial is, so to say, the only real process in the phenomenal world);
> Das Unbeschreibliche (for thinking which we have no intellectual form),
> Hier ist es gethan (practically accomplished);
> Das Ewig-Weibliche (the intellect always inherited from the mother)
> Zieht uns hinan (to salvation).

Against this rôle which generation seems to play in the plan of salvation, it might be objected that, in the case of generation being by accidental hindrances prevented, or in so far as it terminates in the woman, an advance to salvation is cut off to the Will. But such objections merely prove that we have here to do with a transcendent process, the connection of which is partly revealed to, partly hidden from the empirical view of things, restricted as this is to the surface of nature,—in the same way as threads, wound into a ball, when seen from without, now allow of their inner connection being traced, now run inextricably into each other.

III. On the Freedom of the Will

§ 251. The contrast between the empirical and the transcendental standpoints runs, as a continuous contradiction between the two methods of consideration, through our whole system. But it appears nowhere so clearly as at that point where, turning our gaze within, we perceive through the veil of the phenomenal world, here becoming more transparent (§ 148), Being-in-itself as the Will. Here this great antinomy which solves all the riddles of existence, which includes and reconciles all other contrasts— the contrast between phenomena and the thing-in-itself was, long before the time of Kant and Schopenhauer, thrust on the thinking mind, and led to the old controversy whether man's Will is free or whether it is in all its manifestations necessarily determined by motives and consequently not free—a question which, in a limited but specially important sphere, acknowledges as possible and investigates that contrast which Kant and Schopenhauer were called upon to extend to the whole of existence. Thus their philosophy is heralded (as the sun by the dawn) by the question as to the freedom of the Will which, centuries before their time, in the philosophical as in the theological domain, occupied, tormented, and set at variance the minds of men.

§ 252. To be necessary means nothing more

than to follow from a given cause. Every change in nature therefore is necessary, since every change can only occur so far as it forms a link in the chain of causality. This does not exclude its being in other respects the opposite of necessary, that is accidental. For to be accidental means merely not to follow from a given cause. Accordingly every occurrence in the world is both necessary and accidental; necessary with regard to the concatenation of causes from which it springs, accidental in respect to every other causal series with which it meets in space and time without however being determined by it. Accident or chance, therefore, is every intersection of two independent causal series which, meeting in space and time, unite to form a new event.

Remark. Thus it is necessarily caused by motives that some one passes a house at a certain time. And it is just as necessarily determined by causes, that at the same moment a tile is loosened from the roof and falls. But the unfortunate coincidence of the two events is a chance.

§ 253. As chance is the negation of a particular causal connection, so freedom (in the sense in which we here use the word) is the negation of all causality. Accordingly the question as to the freedom of the Will signifies this: Are the actions in which man's Will is manifested, the necessary and inevitable product of the character and of the motives influencing it, or does the natural law of causality here suffer an exception, so that to a certain man in a given case (that is under the influence of a particular motive) two contrary actions are possible? Is it for instance equally possible to a man, arriving at a point where the road diverges, to go to the right or to the left? That a man, apart from physical impossibilities, can do what he will, of that there is no doubt. But whether he can also will otherwise than he wills, whether in a given case from that which he wills and accordingly does, he could as easily will and so as easily do the opposite,—whether for instance in the above case where, if he will, he may go to the right, or if he will, to the left, he could just as easily will to go to the right as to the left—that is the question.

§ 254. Whatever enters and can enter the domain of our understanding, consequently whatever exists (§ 76), is subject to the constraint of causality, because this is an innate form of our intellect, from which we cannot under any circumstances escape. Now the action of man belongs like everything else to that sum total of empirical reality which is dependent on the intellect. It follows therefore that our actions must be throughout the necessary product of those inner tendencies or springs of action (as we may call them) forming the empirical character, and of the motives which, from without, call these into play. Accordingly if these two factors were only fully known to us, the future action of a man might (as Kant says) be predicted with the certainty of an eclipse. This will appear less paradoxical, if we reflect that the deeds of a man are only the visibility of his Will, that is, merely the reflection of his innate character in the intellect woven of space, time, and causality. What in itself is Will, appears in space as body, in time as life, in causality as those actions constituting the course of life. Actions, therefore, can never turn out other than is the Will of which they are the mere visibility. That is, they must necessarily proceed as they are and not otherwise from the quality of the Will which is stimulated to manifestation by outward motives.

§ 255. The doctrine of determinism is a corollary of the law of causality, and consequently a simple application of a principle established *a priori*, that is before all experience, to a case which certainly, of all possible cases, is the nearest. This being so, it is strange that not only the ordinary mind can in no wise reconcile itself to this doctrine, but that even acute and profound thinkers (such as Spinoza, Priestley, Voltaire) have succeeded only after long resistance in acknowledging this truth, a truth demonstrable *a priori* (that is with mathematical certainty). But they all probably experienced what each of us experiences as regards the freedom of the

Will. If we look through the apparatus of our intellect, that is, outwards at our actions, we see them springing with necessity as effects from the motives which, as causes, determine the Will. So soon, however, as we direct our attention inwards to the only point where (according to § 148 and with the there given restriction) it is granted to us to set aside the forms of our intellect and seize the thing-in-itself as the Will within us, we are overcome again by the consciousness—a consciousness yielding to no logical argument—that our Will is free. Free not merely so far as we can do what we will, but also so far as it depends on ourselves alone at every moment and under every circumstance to will thus or also otherwise. Therefore no criminal even would (save for the sake of appearance and without believing his own words) allege the necessity of his deeds as an excuse for them. And again no proof of determinism will ever be valid and overwhelming enough to prevent the freedom of the Will being again and again proclaimed as a fact of inner consciousness. This consciousness of the freedom of our Will, which signifies nothing less than the ever-open path to salvation, cannot possibly be explained (as by Schopenhauer) as a self-delusion, due to the intellect becoming acquainted with the resolutions of the Will first in their execution and before that considering contrary decisions equally possible. For if this were so, in the course of life—the intellect having become acquainted with the Will it serves—that consciousness of freedom would disappear. We must rather admit that in this duality of our consciousness of the necessity and freedom of our action is expressed the great contrast between phenomena and the thing-in-itself, which, as we shall see, has a far-reaching moral significance. This significance appears at this point—the most important of all—so clearly that it made itself felt even to the ordinary mind untouched by philosophy. Accordingly we might call that conviction of the freedom of the Will an innate chapter of metaphysics, implanted, as indispensable, in every man.

§ 256. There are thus three great transcendental truths mutually requiring, supporting, and supplementing each other:

1. All that belongs to the phenomenal world lies in the bonds of space, time, and causality; the thing-in-itself—proved as Will—is, on the other hand, free from these intellectual forms in which the world is built up.

2. If I look outwards, I see everything through the medium of space, time, and causality. If I look within, I perceive, under certain restrictions, that which exists independently of these intellectual forms—the Will as Being-in-itself, beyond which there is no being.

3. If I look outwards at my deeds, I see that

they all, being necessitated by motives, must without exception be as they are and not otherwise. If I look inwards, I find myself free and equally capable of willing an action or its opposite. In this consciousness of freedom is rooted the responsibility for what I do or leave undone, the nature of which can under certain circumstances give me qualms of conscience, not to be reasoned away by any subtlety of *a priori* deduction.

Remark.—If after all these explanations some one still asks: "Am I then really free in my action or am I not?" The exact answer is: "You are not, for your action is the necessary product of factors which as causes precede in time, and consequently belong, in the moment of action, to the past, are therefore no longer in your hand and yet inexorably determine the present. You are not free. That is just as certain, as it is certain that this table stands before you, just as certain, but also not more certain. And so, just as this table in space and time has only empirical reality, but as thing-in-itself is at the same time spaceless and timeless (however inconceivable it may be), so your action is only determined phenomenally by causality, as regards its inner nature on the contrary it is at the same time exempt from causality that is free (inconceivable as it may be). Hence you are nevertheless free."

§ 257. Thus every man has for himself and in his inmost being the knot which joins two worlds, the moral diversity of which will be the further subject of our inquiry. For the contrast between *phenomena* and the *thing-in-itself* is finally nothing but that between the *affirmation* and the *denial* of the Will to life. For as space, time, and causality on the one hand separate phenomena from the thing-in-itself, so also on the other they divide affirmation from denial. They are indeed only the forms of affirmation on which individual existence, and with it all sin—not indeed depends (for then the intellect would be the sinful element) but yet seems for our conception to depend, so that every act of denial appears as a practical breaking through of these forms, as an unconscious passing beyond them.— Here already it becomes clear that only the deeds of affirmation are *necessary*, while those of denial on the other hand are *free*, and that an action will contain just so much freedom, that is, exemption from causality and consequently incomprehensibility, as it contains denial, that is, morality. Since, however, the works of denial appear on the stage of this world, they must of necessity enter its forms and so be manifested in the hue of affirmation. Therefore they also, though belonging to a world order of eternal freedom, must nevertheless, seen through the spectacles of causality, appear to our understanding as in a certain sense necessary and determined by motives. This occurs in a way, it is true, which at once distinguishes them from the deeds of affirmation, springing from the opposite tendency of the Will, and which will next be the subject of our investigation.

IV. The Pagan and the Christian Standpoints, or the Affirmation and the Denial of the Will to Life

§ 258. Opposed to the standpoint of affirmation or the *Pagan* is the standpoint of denial or the *Christian*. It is true, the conceptions Paganism and Christianity are not used here in the ordinary and historical sense, but in a somewhat different one, to be gathered from the further course of our inquiry. We shall not, however, forgo these names in a book designed, in the first place, for Western readers. For firstly, in setting forth the doctrine of the denial of the Will, we must attach it to the historical form in which we have received it, and this for our part of the world is Christianity. Again it is of importance to point out to our theology with all energy the way she must take for her safety, the way she sooner or later will take, though momentarily she delays breaking her earthen vessels, not knowing that their contents, in the process of elimination of foreign matter, have crystallised and need no longer any tradition as covering.

Remark. The eternal saving doctrine of denial appears in Christianity as the giving up of one's own sinful will to a holy will conceived as **personal.** This is an anthropomorphic conception, irreconcilable with science, and has the further objection that it leads away from the main purpose and (what is worse) favours eudæmonism. On the other hand we cannot hope to find a form more capable of deeply moving the soul, one more conducive to the spirit of genuine religion, than that of the Bible. Therefore for the people also in the future it will still have currency as exoteric teaching:—ἐκείνοις δὲ τοῖς ἔξω ἐν παραβολαῖς τὰ πάντα γίνεται (St. Mark iv. 11);—enough, if by means of science we succeed in leading the thinking portion of mankind, not as hitherto away from the thing, but rather more deeply into it, namely from exoteric to esoteric Christianity, which is the metaphysics of Schopenhauer.

§ 259. We have reduced all becoming and all being in nature to an operating, all operating to a willing, and have denoted the principle of this willing, which shows itself in various forms in conscious and unconscious, animate and inanimate nature, by the word **Will**. In doing so we found that the Will, which is the thing-in-itself and with that the ultimate principle of all being, is unknown to us as it is in itself. We know it only from a particular side, namely so far, as in willing or affirming individual existence, Will is objectified as this universe in the phenomenal forms of affirmation, time, space, and causality.

Now it is in some way conceivable even *a priori*, that Will—since as thing-in-itself it is not subject to causality, and consequently lies outside the sphere of all constraint—should be capable not only of a **willing**, but also of its reverse, namely, of a **not-willing**. That is, it is originally equally possible to it *to will* individual existence, that is, *to affirm* it, and consequently to appear in space, time, and causality,—or on the contrary *not to will* it, that is, *to deny* it. We are, however, prevented once for all by the nature of our intellect from understanding whether, and in what way, there is opposed to the realm of willing or affirmation, which is this infinite world, a realm of not-willing or denial. For since with the forms of our intellect individuation, and with it affirmation is necessarily established, such a realm of denial can never be manifested in these forms, can consequently never be the object of an understanding like ours.—Nay, for this realm of denial (βασιλεία τῶν οὐρανῶν) there seemed indeed no place left after Copernicus by his discovery had taken away the heaven. Infinite space, infinite time, and the unending chain of causality, these principles of material, individual, sinful existence, filled everything—till a stronger than he came, who in his turn took away space, time, and causality, in proving them to be the subjective forms of perception, thus making room for another order of things than ours.

§ 260. From what has been said it follows undoubtedly, that theology, to exist at all as a science, must base herself on Kant's doctrine. This she will do the more speedily, the sooner, at a time when she is most closely pressed by historical criticism and natural science, she remembers her real advantage.—Unlike theology philosophy considers it her task to analyse what is given by nature, to reduce it to its ultimate elements and there to stop. We might, therefore, at the point which our inquiry has reached, content ourselves with stating that the existence of a realm of denial, opposed to that of nature, is not impossible, so that of a denial of the Will there would be no further question, but that nature itself here offers a series of phenomena absolutely inexplicable by the natural principle of the affirmation of the Will to life. In investigating, namely, by aid of the surest experience, the action of man, which is in general, like the rest of nature, an expression of the affirmation of the Will to life, we meet a series of actions which are in the natural order of things inconceivable, being diametrically opposed to this world and its laws, contradicting these in every sense and, as it were, totally unhinging them. These phenomena, which can only be conceived as a breaking through of denial into the sphere of affirmation, are the deeds of genuine morality. They are preached, as the Gospel of a better world, daily before our eyes in a way which cannot be gainsaid. They are, in the truest and strictest sense of the word, miracles, which occur around us ever anew, and if all other miracles fall to the ground, these will remain,—and they are sufficient.

The deeds of morality are miracles because (strange as it sounds) they are impossible and yet real. This is the contradiction they bear in them, this is the difficult problem which they lay on the thinking mind. To this it is due that moral investigations, as the most important, are also the most difficult in the whole range of philosophy. In order not to err here we must take into consideration the totality of action possible to man. For this purpose it is necessary to classify the same according to some principle which will guarantee the completeness of our procedure. Such a principle we have now to seek.

§ 261. Legislation, the aim of which is protection from wrong, is concerned with one thing alone —that certain actions should be done and certain others left undone. As to the causes from which this doing or this leaving undone springs, it is indifferent, for that lies outside its province.—The standpoint of morality is exactly the reverse. For it external action is only of significance so far as it is the symptom of something internal, of the moral disposition from which it springs. To determine, therefore, the worth or worthlessness of an action morality looks not at the outward result, but solely at the intention, at the aim pursued with this. According to their aims, therefore, we have to establish our classification of actions.

There are two things and two alone which can determine that manifestation of our Will which we call action—either the wish to further well-being or the intention to cause ill. Now, on the other hand, this intended well-being or ill, which as aim underlies all actions small or great, refers necessarily either to our own selves or to others. Accordingly every act possible to man pursues as aim either one's own well-being or another's ill, or one's own ill or another's ill. This being so, all human actions may be divided into four classes to one of which every action must inevitably belong. These four classes go back to as many possible main springs of action which, as we shall see, determine the moral merit or demerit of actions, so far as two of them are based on the affirmation, two on the denial of the Will to life, as shown by the following scheme.

Aims: Springs of action:

1. Another's ill— *malice*
2. One's own well-being } — *egoism* } **Affirmation** (Paganism).
3. Another's well-being } — *compassion*
4. One's own ill— *asceticism* } **Denial** (Christianity).

Since action can have no aims other than these here enumerated, these four springs of action mentioned above are the sole possible ones. Yet they may be still further reduced to two, since, as we shall see, all malice originates in egoism, and every act of compassion contains as its essence an act of asceticism. Thus the totality of human action appears as the expression of two opposed currents, one *egoistic, affirming, mundane*, the other *ascetic, denying, supramundane*, which in reality are often indistinguishably blended, the clear and strict separation of which, however, and their reduction to two opposed principles, is the highest, as it is the last, task of our philosophy.

V. Egoism
as the General and Necessary Phenomenal Form of the Affirmation of the Will to Life

§ 262. The affirmation of the Will to life is its existence in space, time, and causality. Such an existence is necessarily and inevitably an egoistic one, so that egoism is proved to be the general phenomenal form of the affirmation of the Will.

Proof: Every existence which as body occupies a particular space, and as life fills a particular time, is of necessity a limited one. For however great may be the space and time in which it is, there still remains sufficient space and time in which it is not, because, as we have proved (§§ 7. 9), space and time are infinite. This limitation of every existence involves its having on this side the limit ego, beyond it non-ego. It is exactly the consciousness of this distinction between ego and non-ego which makes egoism. Thus it is necessarily bound up with the forms of affirmation, space, and time.

From this proposition follow two conclusions of the greatest importance for the metaphysics of morality.

1. If egoism is the general phenomenal form of the affirmation of the Will to life, it follows that all deeds springing from egoism (or malice, which proceeds, as we are about to show, from it) contradict the world order of affirmation, reach beyond it, and bear witness to another order of things than ours.
2. The egoism of affirmation is, as we shall further understand, the inexhaustible source of all that is bad and evil. It is consequently the only and radical sin in us. If now it is necessarily bound up with empirical existence, it, and with it sin, can only be removed by the removal of empirical existence itself. Now since existence is assured to the Will (§ 248), such a removal is not attainable by renouncing life but by renouncing the Will to life.

§ 263. All empirical existence, from the stone to man, is properly speaking egoistic, for all that exists distinguishes between ego and non-ego. Thus even inorganic bodies: the boulder which, in crashing downwards, shatters whatever lies in its path; the machine, in crushing what obstructs its motion; the ball when, in piercing the body, it leaves behind the sharply-defined traces of its ego. But we speak of egoism in its narrower sense only in the case of that existence which distinguishes, not by its mere action, but with consciousness, between ego and non-ego, that is of animal and human nature. Meanwhile the brute even is not aware of its egoism *in abstracto*. It knows it only subjectively, not objectively (§ 115,$_4$), and thus not with full consciousness. This last appears only in man, and with it comes the knowledge of the sinfulness of existence itself, on which is based the possibility of a conversion of the Will to denial.

§ 264. Besides egoism, which aims at one's own good, we have named above, as the second spring of affirmation, malice, the ultimate aim of which consists in occasioning another's suffering. Here the pain of another is not, as in the case of egoism, means to an end, namely our own welfare, but is itself end and immediate satisfaction. One might therefore be tempted to refer malice to the influence of supernatural demoniacal powers, but that it can be psychologically demonstrated as merely the manifestation of a very high degree of egoism, which therefore remains as the only spring of affirmation, as the necessary phenomenal form of which we have recognised it.—All willing namely involves a not having, consequently a wanting, consequently a suffering. Hence follows, that to a more intense willing there corresponds a severer suffering, that accordingly there increases, with the degree of egoism in general, the degree of the suffering attached to existence. Now the extreme egoist sees around him others who cling less vehemently to existence and its delights, who are less afflicted by egoism and accordingly suffer less than himself. The mere sight of them is for him an injury, in that it reminds him of his own privation, and makes it, by contrast, first really perceptible and painful. From this arises an ill-feeling towards them which, so long as they are happy, is manifested as envy and, when some evil overtakes them, as malicious pleasure in their misfortune,—two very familiar sensations, since scarcely any one of us is quite free from them. Now from this pleasure which delights in another's misfortune, it is but a small step to real malice, which spontaneously causes another's suffering to find in the sight of it alleviation of its own torment. For malice always springs from severe personal suffering, whether arising, as we have shown, from excess of egoism or from heavy misfortunes. One should therefore never forget, in seeing a malicious act, that he who perpetrates it, **must be very unhappy**, and that the surest way of giving him in his inmost heart a wholesome wound is to recompense his evil with good. For he too, however deeply entangled in affirmation, is **a man**, and in every man slumbers the spirit of denial, and there is none in whom it may not be awakened. This cannot be done by preaching morality (which as a rule is but turned to ridicule) but by practising it. For love is a fire which kindles wherever it reaches and can melt, if only hot enough, even stone and iron.

R e m a r k.—Like malice, re ve n g e, which is closely akin to it, pursues as ultimate aim another's suffering. But it is far more pardonable, because here it is not a high degree of egoism, but injury inflicted by others which drives us to cool the heat of our own suffering by the aspect of the torments of him who is guilty of it. Hence revenge is often overcome in the very moment of execution by pity, which with malice is not so easily the case, because malice is rooted in egoism which excludes pity as its opposite pole.—Very different from revenge is punishment; the aim of the one is to injure, of the other to better, and therefore to benefit, like the physician whose hand we bless even when it cuts, even when it burns. —Of this we shall speak further on.

§ 265. As from causality springs the necessity of all our action, so from space and time arises the egoism in which it is rooted. As little therefore as we can imagine a free action, that is one not determined by motives, so little is it possible to conceive, from the empirical standpoint, of another spring of action than that of egoism. This goes so far that even the actions of pure morality, in which is manifested the denial of the Will to life, that is, the removal of natural egoism, appear, merely in order to be comprehended by the forms of our intellect, as both, necessary (§ 257) and egoistic. But the egoism of these deeds is no longer an individual one, but one expanding the ego over the totality of being. Its real nature is thus totally removed, so that it remains merely as a form of comprehension, inherent in the intellect and therefore irremovable, in which we here even range what presupposes its removal. Of this seeming or moral egoism, clad in which the otherwise inconceivable deeds of denial appear, we shall speak later. At present it is with **real or individual egoism**, as the natural form of all empirical existence, that we have to do. Here we shall show how from it, in which, as we have seen, all deeds of malice are involved, on the one hand all that is bad, on the other all that is evil springs with necessity.

VI. The Egoism of Affirmation as the Source of the Bad

§ 266. The two fundamental strivings of that egoism which has reached organic existence, even when embodied in man, are nourishment and propagation. These, considered in the second part of this book (§§ 162. 189) from the physical, are now reviewed from the moral side.

1. We saw that the body is nothing but the objectified Will to life, manifested in space, so that instead of affirmation of the Will we might also say affirmation of the body. The affirmation of the body is only possible through nourishment; that is, we cannot affirm our own existence otherwise than by denying continually the existence of others (plants and animals). If we would not ourselves perish, we must resolve to inflict on other beings, no less vehemently desirous of life than we, and as much the aim of their own existence as we are of ours, that which, if done to ourselves, we should regard as the greatest wrong. Here it becomes clear that sinfulness is bound up with existence itself and can consequently be removed only with its removal.

2. All existence in time comes sooner or later to an end. Time itself is alone infinite. But the Will to life, of which each of us is an embodiment, aims not at existence at a certain time but at existence absolutely, therefore—since time is merely the phenomenal form of this existence—at existence in all time. From this springs that instinct to prolong existence beyond one's own life which is manifested in generation. By this is tied ever anew the knot

of existence. And it is not only by the feeling of life here reaching its climax, but also by the consequences attending it, and still more by the consciousness of guilt accompanying it, that generation proves itself the sharpest expression of willing, the focus of the affirmation of the Will to life. To the Will affirming itself in generation the gates of salvation are opened anew in the child, while it becomes for its parents, by the sacrifices it imposes on them, a means of discipline to denial. This is the meaning of the paradoxical scripture text (1 Tim. ii. 15): σωθήσεται διὰ τῆς τεκνογονίας (applicable not only to the woman but also to the man).

If even existence, sustaining itself by nourishment and propagation, is a sin, much more so is the augmentation of these tendencies beyond what is natural and necessary. From this spring gluttony, unchastity, avarice and the like, vices, not only directly repudiated by our moral feeling (the voice of denial within us), but condemned also by nature herself (the principle of affirmation) and visited by her on the offender.

Remark.—It is because the body is the mere visibility of affirmation that we are ashamed of it, and especially of those parts which are the expression of the focus of affirmation, although only after innocence (which is the mere unconsciousness of guilt) has given place to the "knowledge of good and evil," and therewith to the consciousness that corporeal existence itself is sin (Gen. ii. 25; iii. 7). On the contrary we are not ashamed of the face, from which glances the possibility of salvation,—and yet nobody likes to be gazed at long and attentively.

§ 267. Of actions which ought not to be there are two possible kinds, so far as these refer either to another than the doer or to the doer himself. In the latter case such actions may, as has been shown, be very reprehensible (owing to their expressing always a high degree of affirmation), but they are not properly speaking wrong. For the conception of wrong involves the suffering of it at the hands of others, because against one's own will: *volenti non fit injuria*. The name of wrong must therefore be reserved for those actions in which the degree of affirmation of one's own egoism goes so far as to break from its own sphere into that of another, in order to deny it.

Remark.—For the same reason there can be no such thing as duties towards ourselves. For all duty (even that of parents to their children) rests on an express or tacit contract according to which I freely undertake to perform certain things. If I do not fulfil these, I do wrong, unless the other releases me from my obligations. Now if I am that other myself, no release is necessary. Thus it becomes clear that the conceptions wrong, right, and duty can have a meaning only in reference to others.

§ 268. Every ego commands a certain circuit. This is called the sphere of egoism. Thus inorganic bodies possess the place they occupy in space. Like these the egoism of plants is confined to a particular spot. Yet even they greedily stretch their roots downwards, their branches upwards. The brute loosened from the soil, manifests its egoism over a narrower or a wider range. But first in man is associated with superior force the conception of property and consequently the capability of possessing. He declares all other beings in nature as without rights and possessions, as things for his use. Accordingly men have appropriated the whole earth and divided it amongst themselves—nor would they scruple to divide the moon, if they could only reach it.

§ 269. Every man's egoism has a threefold range. It extends firstly to *what he is*, secondly to *what he has*, thirdly to *what he represents*. Accordingly in man we can distinguish three spheres of egoism, under which may be ranged all that is valuable in life, all aims of earthly desire. This threefold division therefore forms the basis of the doctrine of happiness that is eudæmonology, or as we might more appropriately call it, egoismology, as Schopenhauer,—descending from the height of his Christian view of the world to the standpoint of ancient Pagan ethics,—lays it down in his "Aphorismen zur Lebensweisheit."

First Sphere of Egoism: *what one is*

In the first place every one has a primary right to his own body and his own life, as also to the (intellectual and physical) forces of his body and the work produced by them.—Here already it becomes clear, that suicide, though in a high degree reprehensible (as we shall show later), cannot (apart from eventual obligations from which a man withdraws himself by it) be properly called wrong.

Second Sphere of Egoism: *what one has*

Next to his own body and life, every one extends his egoism over a larger or smaller circle of objects which he calls his own. It may be disputed whether the right of property rests on the first seizure, or on the cultivation of a thing. In reality the two are for the most part blended, since seizure as a rule demands work, and the cultivation of a thing is frequently restricted to the taking possession of what nature offers.

Third Sphere of Egoism: *what one represents*

Besides body and life, goods and chattels, there is still a third thing which we call ours. This is the opinion which others have of us, on which depend honour, rank, and fame. Ideal as are these possessions, based on the mere opinion which others have of us, they become of importance through the close relations of men to each other, which make us in so many ways dependent on others. Hence it is that ambition for rank and fame is so powerful a spur even of nobler natures. Honour again, which has not to be acquired but merely preserved, is held so precious that with its loss (as the saying is) all is lost. The striving to gain by outward demeanour the favourable opinion of others, in order to shine in their estimation, on which one relies rather than on his own judgment of himself, is called **vanity**. The exact reverse of it is **pride**, which is the firm conviction of one's own worth, joined to a certain indifference to the opinion of others about it, and is quite compatible with real **humility**, which is the knowledge of the nothingness of existence applied to ourselves, and is with right regarded as a Christian virtue akin to denial.

Remark.—Honour is further divided into **commercial honour**, relating to integrity in business and conduct; **professional honour**, having reference to fitness for, and faithfulness in, duty in an entrusted post; and **sexual honour**, which refers to the relations of the sexes and is for the female sex especially of great importance.—A ludicrous species is **knightly honour**, so far as it seeks not to deserve the esteem of others through seemly behaviour, but rather to gain it by defiance, with force, weapon in hand. It thus thinks to coerce the opinion of others, while it is in fact its freedom from constraint which is the prerequisite of the recognition given as honour.

§ 270. **Wrong** is the invasion of the territory of another's egoism. It is therefore threefold, according as it occurs in one of the three spheres of egoism:

1. Wrong to the body, whether by injury of it (cannibalism, murder, mutilation, wounding, torturing of every kind), or by unlawful appropriation of its powers (slavery, forced service, withholding of pay).
2. Wrong to property (robbery, theft, fraud).
3. Wrong to honour (insult, slander).

The respect due to the sphere of another's egoism rests to a great extent on convention. For this reason also the conception of wrong as an invasion of this sphere is a conventional one. Therefore according to the time, the country, and the personal views of the doer, an act must pass as a proof of generosity and self-sacrifice which, under other circumstances, would be accounted a grave crime. For moral judgment, which looks not at the deed but at the spirit manifested in it, must take as standard not what is wrong, but what in each single case was regarded as such.

There are two means of doing wrong: force and cunning. The latter is more contemptible because it involves a confession of one's own weakness, also, perhaps, because it always rests on reflection and is conditioned by intellectual superiority, which should rather lead to the removal of iniquity. Considered from the moral standpoint, however, both, force and cunning, when standing in the service of wrong, are equally reprehensible. It is just as wrong to injure our neighbour's body by open assault as by poison, his property by robbery as by theft, his honour by open insult as by evil-speaking behind his back.

§ 271. All wrong consists in the seeking of one's own good at the cost of another and rests consequently upon egoism. From egoism, which can at times turn to malice (§ 264), all that is bad in the world springs, according to the law of causality, with necessity.

Now it is clear that what is reprehensible when, in accidentally interfering with another's interests, it produces on the one hand what is bad, on the other what is evil, remains equally reprehensible even when no such interference takes place. Thus sin lies not in the deeds through which, by aid of casual circumstances (motives), it is manifested, but in egoism, and therefore in our natural existence itself. This namely is throughout nothing but the embodiment of the Will to life, as it affirms itself in one more, in another less vehemently. The intensity of this affirmation admits of an infinite number of degrees which together form a graduated scale of moral worth or worthlessness, from the freezing-point of absolute egoism to the boiling-point at which our ego evaporates in self-denying love to others. Each of us occupies by nature a fixed point on this scale, movable by no arbitrary influence, by which the innate character is indicated. This character develops in actions at the instance of motives the occurrence of which is determined by chance, and on which it may for instance sometimes depend that a certain character, that is, a certain degree of vehemence of affirmation, takes, in the one case, the form of a peaceful and regular life amid one's fellow-citizens, in the other that of a criminal career. A poetical illustration of this truth may be found in many novels. It strikes us still more directly when, in studying the faces of famous criminals, we find them to our surprise very like those of ordinary men.

The doctrine that sin is innate is one of the deepest truths of Holy Scripture. Even in the Old Testament, the original spirit of which it contradicts (§ 177), we see it gushing forth here and there like a living spring amid stony ground (for instance Gen. vi. 5, viii. 21; Ps. li. 7), while in Christianity it expands to a lake, enabling us to cross to the opposite shore of salvation. Οἶδα γάρ, says the Apostle (Rom. vii. 18), ὅτι οὐκ οἰκεῖ ἐν ἐμοί, τοῦτ' ἔστιν ἐν τῇ σαρκί μου, ἀγαθόν. These words, which we may appropriate in their entirety to ourselves, signify firstly, that the (empirical) ego is identical with the body which we have demonstrated as its objectity (§ 156), secondly, that that which ought not to be, is our ego, our empirical existence itself.

From our considerations on the ultimate root of human nature, as also from the passages of scripture cited, which may have arisen from similar considerations, it follows inevitably that sin can never be extirpated by a change of works, which are merely its outward symptoms, but alone by a change of the inmost basis of existence, through a transformation of the egoistic Will itself. In the feeling of this truth the Psalmist already prays (li. 12): "Create in me a clean heart, O God, and renew (*chaddêsch*) a right spirit within me!"—If in these words he considers the prayed-for transformation of his heart as one not dependent on his own action, we must also in this agree with him.

Before, however, we can follow the train of these thoughts, we have to look at the egoism of affirmation from the reverse side, to convince ourselves that from it proceeds, as on the one hand the badness, so on the other the infinite suffering of the world, with equal necessity.

VII. The Egoism of Affirmation as the Source of Evil

§ 272. The doctrine of the nothingness of existence and of the suffering of the world takes a prominent place in the thought systems of the sublime masters Buddha and Schopenhauer. For it is, according to them, suffering, whether felt as our own or known as that of another, which is the cause of that turning away of the Will from life, in which we shall recognise, in harmony with the greatest among men, the ultimate goal, the highest destination of our existence. A deeper reflection, however, shows that this motivation of self-denial by the suffering inseparable from existence belongs merely to the attempts to represent, through the medium of the intellect, what is for it irrepresentable.—The turning of the Will is a process belonging to the order of things-in-themselves; therefore it does not admit the application of the law of causality. Consequently to speak of a motive for this change of Will is inadmissible (even if it be called a quietive). Moreover the denial of the Will, if we see in it merely an escape from the sorrows of existence, would not be distinguished, save in the more suitable choice of means, from suicide, from which (as will later become clear) it is fundamentally different (since suicide according to § 248 is an endeavour which misses its aim). And further it would come under the general conception of the striving after happiness and thus fall completely in the sphere of affirmation, the exclusion of which is just what is essential in it.—We shall see later how the supposed causation of self-denial by suffering belongs merely to the hue of affirmation clad in which the deeds of denial must appear, if they are to be in any way conceivable to us.—Here we have merely to show how the **nothingness** as also the **suffering** of existence is necessarily based on the affirmation of the Will to life and can therefore only be removed with it (for where there is denial, there, as will later become clear, the whole possibility of suffering has vanished), even though the removal of suffering cannot be considered as the real aim of denial without misrepresenting it.

§ 273. The affirmation of the Will to life is willing as it becomes visible in **space, time, and causality** as world. We have now to show how in and with these primary elements of existence all its sufferings are inevitably bound up.

Every existence in **space and time** is a limited one, consequently, however great it may be, it is yet, in comparison with the infinity of space and time, infinitely little and in so far **nothing**. We realise this nothingness of existence more clearly than ever, when drawing near the temporal limits of our existence, that is, death. Then, looking back on life, we first understand in their deepest sense the words with which on his lips Buddha died: "**All is without permanence.**"

On the other hand our existence is subject to the constraint of **causality**, from which springs the necessary predetermination of all our doing as of all our suffering, so that we can escape neither the one nor the other. As therefore space and time condition the nothingness of our earthly existence, so causality determines its hopelessness.

This existence is essentially a willing. It is important to understand how all suffering is only possible under the assumption of willing, nay, consists solely in this, while on the contrary, as will appear later, not-willing, which constitutes denial, can be as little touched by suffering as the sunbeam by the storm-wind. Thus, with the Indians, we might recommend the denial of the Will as the surest remedy for the ills of existence, but that it could be foretold with certainty, that, for those who seek it as such, it is as little to be found, as is darkness by lighted candles.

Every single act of willing has an aim. Willing in general is without aim: " All is vanity,"—

H^{a}bêl h^{a}bâlîm ! âmar Koheleth,
H^{a}bêl h^{a}bâlîm, hakkol hâbel!

as it is preached with untranslatable pathos by the Hebrew sage.

This aimlessness of willing is manifest in all nature, from the course of the planets—revolving without rest and goal in unwearying labour round their fixed star—up to man. Look for instance at the plant; slowly and laboriously its life develops from seed to leaf and stalk, from leaf to blossom, from blossom to fruit, to cease with what it began—with the seed. As the plant, so the animal, so man. In the first third of his existence he lives to obtain a living; laboriously he prepares himself for a calling. In the second third he thinks of propagation; he founds a family. And in the third he can observe how his offspring start again from the beginning with the same comedy, while he, dying to enjoyment and work, feels himself more and more set aside and excluded from the circle of flourishing life. This is the wormwood which remains to men, when they have drained the cup of life to the dregs. The philosopher alone (in the sense in which each may be one) stirs the draught—and drinks healing.

Willing, the visibility of which is life, rolls impetuously between two alternating states. From desiring it hastens to attaining, from attaining to new desiring. Now all desiring involves a want and consequently a suffering. All attainment on the other hand proves disappointment, so far as the end gained does not allow us to rest there without the feeling of emptiness, stagnation, dissatisfaction.—

> So tauml' ich von Begierde zu Genuss,
> Und im Genuss verschmacht' ich nach Begierde.
>
> Thus reel I from desiring to enjoying,
> And in enjoying languish for desire.

Between the pain of working and the ennui of

repose we are tossed hither and thither, and it is wisdom to prefer to possessing—striving, to enjoyment—labour and sorrow (Ps. xc. 10).

§ 274. The Sânkhya system distinguishes three kinds of suffering, *âdhi-âtmika, âdhi-bhautika, âdhi-daivika,*—caused by ourselves, by others, or by fate: a classification we may adopt, though not quite in the sense of the schoolmen.

The first class of sufferings (*âdhi-âtmika*) springs from ourselves (*âtman*). We saw already how individual existence as such is an inexhaustible source of suffering.

The second class (*âdhi-bhautika*) includes the sufferings which the various beings (*bhûtâni*) in which the Will manifests itself as plurality, decree to each other through the mutual interference of their egoistic tendencies. From this springs that perpetual war and struggle of beings against each other, which assumes through all civilisation and humanity, through state, legislation, education, and the like, only another and milder form, but remains essentially the same.

So far as all suffering comes either from within or from without, it might be collectively assigned to one or the other of these two categories. Yet the Indian may be right in distinguishing besides these a third class of sufferings (*âdhi-daivika*), springing neither from the nature of our individual existence, nor from the deliberate selfishness and wickedness of others, but decreed to us by the gods (*deva*), or by fate (*daiva*), that is, by chance. For not alone in the fate tragedies of the ancients (as for instance the "King Œdipus" of Sophokles), but also in daily life we may see often enough how from the best intentions which others may cherish towards us, from the most active preparations we make for our own happiness, through chance, error, and misunderstanding of all kinds, the greatest misfortune arises. Thus every existence, even the happiest, seems continually beset by mischievous powers which threaten every moment to assert their claims on it. Hence Schopenhauer says rightly, that all earthly happiness walks on undermined ground.

§ 275. Calm and unbiassed reflections like these may serve as a standard for estimating the value of an existence such as ours, and for furnishing in a question, the candid and competent reply to which must rest on the individual experience of each, a general and abstract rule, such as philosophical inquiry demands. Now, if we would turn from these to immediate experience, to see how almost everywhere it shows us want, misery, and wretchedness as the fundamental type of this existence, if, looking from our own perhaps bearable lot as from an oasis in the surrounding illimitable desert, we would fix our eyes on the fate of men in less favoured circumstances and in less settled times and countries, to let pass before our imagination the countless pictures of misery, famine and plague, battlefields, hospitals, prisons, and torture, or if we would but cast a glance at the dark alleys and narrow houses of our cities, and again a glance at the palaces and villas of the rich, to see everywhere discord, ill-will, vice, with grief and misery in their train,—then indeed we might chime in with the melodious wail of Sophokles:

> μὴ φῦναι τὸν ἅπαντα νι-
> κᾷ λόγον· τὸ δ', ἐπεὶ φανῇ,
> βῆναι κεῖθεν ὅθεν περ ἥ-
> κει, πολὺ δεύτερον, ὡς τάχιστα,[1] —

nay, we might with Shakespeare raise the impious question:

> *Whether 'tis nobler in the mind to suffer*
> *The slings and arrows of outrageous fortune;—*
> *Or to take arms against a sea of troubles,*
> *And by opposing, end them?—*

—did there not sound to us from another region a voice of unearthly strength, yet unspeakably mild and consoling: "In the world ye shall have tribulation; but be of good cheer,—I have overcome the world!"—

---

[1] Not to be born is of all the best; but by far the next best is, if one is born, to return thither whence he came as quickly as possible.

Who thus speaks, is the Will to life who overcame the world by overcoming himself;—who thus speaks, that art thou, —— so soon as thou wilt.

VIII. Temporal Measures against the Badness and Evil springing from Egoism

§ 276. All wrong consists, as we saw, in an invasion of the sphere of another's egoism, whether injuring the person, the property, or the honour of our neighbour. Wrong is the origin of right. Every man namely is allowed to protect himself, to repel the intrusion of another into the sphere of his own affirmation of the Will, even if this should involve an invasion of the Will-sphere of the aggressor, an injury to the injurer. This warding off of wrong is the right which is everybody's due by nature. Therefore if there were no wrong, we should as little speak of right, as of light, if darkness were unknown to us. Like wrong, the warding off of it which is called right, may be exercised in two ways: first by force, secondly by cunning. Here may be answered the question, in how far there can be a right to lie.

§ 277. In the natural state of things every one is free to injure others to the utmost. At the same time he must, on his part, expect injury from everybody else.—Very soon probably men came to the

T

conviction that, under such circumstances, the pleasure of doing wrong was as a whole far outweighed by the pain of suffering it. They thus agreed to purchase, by renouncing the practice of wrong, freedom from suffering it, and to maintain this principle with united force against the egoistic desires of the individual. Such a union of men is called the **state**. It is in its nature an **institution for protection against wrong**. This does not exclude the possibility, that such a common authority, superior to all resistance of the individual, when once in existence, might in a wider sense be, and as a fact is, employed for the representation and furtherance of other common interests.

Remark. The task of the state as a protective institution is threefold: (1) protection from without, (2) protection from within, (3) protection against the protector.

First Task of the State: protection from without.

The maxim of the right of the stronger, abolished now within every civilised state, is still the only one valid between state and state, from which we may judge how immature our race still is. For it may be foretold with certainty that the time will come when war will be looked back upon as a long past atrocious barbarity of a dark age.

Second Task of the State: protection from within.

To be an egoist is, humanly speaking, allowed, so long as one's egoism is not of such a degree as to injure others. Accordingly what the state considers as its task is the repression, not of the egoism of its subjects, but of such manifestations of it as are hurtful to their fellow-men. The state fulfils this task by opposing to the motives for doing wrong a series of stronger motives for not doing it, in the form of threatened punishment. The penal code is therefore merely a register of counter-motives against crime, and the criminal law of a state is restricted to the deterring from crime by punishment, not to the expiation of it: for the very reason, that it lies quite beyond the capacity of a judge to try the heart and reins, and so determine the real worth or worthlessness of a deed.—This justification of the right of punishment first set forth by Plato, is comprised by Schopenhauer briefly and well in the words of Seneca (*de ira* i, 19, 7): "*Nemo prudens punit, quia peccatum est, sed ne peccetur.*"

Third Task of the State: protection against the protector.

The omnipotence of the state, laid in the hands of an individual, may easily lead to abuse. Hence arises, on the one hand, the necessity of setting certain constitutional limits to it, on the other, the justification for placing the ruler, by means of property, honour and the like, so high above the rest, that his egoism, paralysed by the immediate satisfaction of all its wishes, cannot break out to the detriment of his subjects. On the egoism of the ruler depends also the advantage which a hereditary monarchy has over other forms of government. By means of it the well-being of the royal family is indissolubly linked with, and in a certain sense dependent on, the welfare of the land. An elective monarchy, on the other hand, though it has the advantage of placing in every case the ablest in the highest position, seems to be less recommended by experience, in that it furthers the temptation to enrich one's own house, to found a family power and the like, thereby leading, as history has shown, to the ruin of the country.

§ 278. In and with the state there is a second and important means for accustoming egoism to the limits necessary to make life as a community tolerable. This is **education**, which (apart from preparing us for a calling) pursues two aims, firstly *the culture of the intellect*, secondly *the culture of the Will*.—(1) On the intellectual side the aim of education can only be to acquaint the pupil with the true nature of the world and life, in giving him the benefit of the experience which others have made before him, in order to spare him his own perhaps bitter experience.—(2) On the other hand the task of education is to cultivate the Will. Yet on this its influence is a limited one. Every influence namely takes place by way of causality through motives. These already presuppose, in order to operate, a particular quality of Will. Hence follows, that a real change of the Will, a transformation of its innate character (consisting in a certain degree of intensity of affirmation) is not possible by means of education. Virtue, therefore, in the moral sense, cannot be taught: *velle non discitur*, as the teacher of Nero said. Nevertheless the value of education for the culture of the Will is incalculably great, since it often rests on this alone, whether a certain man takes the precipitous path of vice and crime, or accustoms himself to earn, by peaceable and honourable activity in the regular relations of life, that satisfaction of his egoism which answers to its innate demands. —This aim education accomplishes in determining the Will, the transformation of which lies outside its province, to take, by means of well-chosen motives, a harmless way to its satisfaction. On this path it keeps it by example, instruction, and restraint, until it becomes habit or second nature. Thus it is by building on the indolence of human nature, that education makes out of evil-natured characters tolerably good men.

§ 279. In spite of right, law, and state, our egoism would often grate harshly against that of our fellow-men and make existence an uncomfortable one, if it were not admitted as a principle, inculcated by education, that each of us, so far as is possible, and so long as no serious interests are at stake, should disavow his own egoism and appear to be wholly at the service of the egoism of another. This hypocrisy—universally practised, seen through by every intelligent mind, and, because the intention of deception is absent, permissible—is politeness.— Of that denial of the Will in favour of another the attainment of which is the highest, as it is the hardest, moral task, politeness makes a semblance—to delight the eye. Yet it is after all a prescribed course of action, a dug canal which, it is true, leads uphill from the stream of Will, and can therefore never be filled by it,—so long as it follows the natural laws of egoism attracting, like gravity, earthwards. But to the operation of supernatural forces is due the removal of these natural laws, in a way of which we shall immediately have to speak, as also the gradual transmutation of that which as politeness is mere semblance and hypocrisy into hearty good-will and sincere love of our neighbour.

Thus politeness is indeed no virtue, as the Chinese believe, but yet a way-mark to virtue, which the Will may or may not follow, and meanwhile a valuable surrogate of it.

IX. Legality and Morality

§ 280. Let us assume that it were possible, whether by religious menace, or by temporal precautions against egoism, to suppress all excess of it to such a degree that injustice should be completely banished from the earth. Such a condition of perfect legality would outwardly resemble an order of things in which right sprang unfailingly from morality. Yet inwardly both would be fundamentally different, and whatever civilisation might gain through legality without morality, the eternal aims of our existence would not be in the least furthered by it. For all such efforts to banish evil from the world by means of police, justice, and superstition, can only be compared to a medical treatment which removes the symptoms of the disease while leaving the latter untouched. At most we might perhaps succeed in checking the manifestation of egoism in life, but never in suppressing egoism itself. All such outside influences must as such necessarily take the way of causality. There is no possibility of influencing a man otherwise than by furnishing him (whether through threats and promises, or by instruction and example) with motives for his action. These are in their nature nothing but intellectual images. As such they enter the sphere of knowledge, which they may enlighten, correct, transform, and from which they may, according as they are applied, impel the Will to manifestation in very diverse directions. At the Will, however, they find their natural limits; and just as rays of light, reflected from bodies, make these visible without changing their nature, so motives, in breaking against the Will, bring its inner being to manifestation in actions, though in no way capable of modifying in the slightest degree the kernel of our being, that is, our innate intensity of the affirmation of the Will to life. From this inborn determination of our Will proceed, as the mere reflection of it in space, time, and causality, all deeds as necessarily as from the tree its fruits. They have therefore in a moral sense no further significance than this, that they are the visibility of our Will. From this truth, which is entirely scriptural (St. Matth. xii. 33-35), it follows inexorably, that even actions which are good, conformable to law, that is, legal actions are in a moral sense quite as worthless and reprehensible as bad ones, so long as, like these, they spring from the soil of our natural existence, which, as we have shown, is nothing but affirmation of the Will to life, that is egoism and consequently sin. Briefly and forcibly this conclusion is expressed in the words of St. John (iii. 6): τὸ γεγεννημένον ἐκ τῆς σαρκὸς σάρξ ἐστιν.—Disheartening as may be these considerations for all those whose horizon does not extend beyond natural existence in space, time, and causality, so little will they discourage us if we are animated by religion, that is, by the consciousness that the better part of our being, that our original Self is to be sought not in this world at all but beyond it, not in our natural existence but in that which lies behind it and which persists even after its dissolution. Hence these principles, gained from the observation and investigation of the facts, little popular as they are, form nevertheless the foundation of the two great religions of mankind, of the Christian, which maintains the worthlessness of good works, and of the Indian, which even asserts their condemnability, as the following glance at both confirms.

§ 281. In **Biblical theology** there corresponds to the difference between legality and morality that between *justification by the law* and *justification by faith*, which is generally speaking the distinction between the Old and New Testaments. The law of the Old Testament accompanies its commands and prohibitions with threat of punishment and promise of reward. It addresses itself accordingly to the egoism of man, for which alone punishment and reward have significance. Thus the law, if fulfilled, would have as consequence legality without morality.—The insufficiency of this ethical standpoint, felt only here and there in the Old Testament, appears everywhere distinctly in the New (though the latter is in other respects far from being free from lapses into eudæmonism). Christ points (St. Matth. v. 20-30) with the greatest emphasis from the outward deed to its inward root, and lays stress on purity of heart and mind. The fourth Evangelist puts into his mouth (St. John iii. 3) the summons to a new birth which springs ἄνωθεν, from above, that is, not from physical but from metaphysical influences. St. Paul contrasts with justification by works justification by faith χωρὶς ἔργων νόμου, with which is bound up a renewal of the whole man, and from which virtuous works proceed with necessity. What faith is, we shall have to ask further on. Here, however, we may denote it as that which has as its inevitable result morality. It is impossible that faith in this sense can consist in a mere holding as true certain external facts.

Deeper, purer, more developed, we meet the same contrasts on the soil of **Indian theology**. Thus Çankara (in the survey of the Vedânta doctrine with which he prefaces his commentary on the *Brihad-âraṇyaka-upanishad*) distinguishes two portions of the Veda, the section on works (*karma-kâṇḍa*) and the section on knowledge (*jñâna-kâṇḍa*), which are analogous to the twofold division of the Bible. On their connection Çañkara expresses himself essentially as follows. The deepest reason why the world is "imposed" on the soul, is the ignorance (*ajñânam*) of the latter, "which has as characteristic the illusion peculiar to it from nature of being both actor and enjoyer" (*kartritva-bhoktritva-svarûpa-abhimâna-lakshaṇam*[1]), that is, expressed in our language, of being individual, so that at bottom ignorance is the same as that which we call entanglement in the principle of individuation (§ 241). From this ignorance springs "the wish to attain what is desirable, to avoid what is undesirable" (*ishṭa-anishṭa-prâpti-parihâra-icchâ*) or, as we should say, egoism. From this again proceed all works, good as well as bad, without distinction. These require for their expiation a repeated imposition of the world on the soul, that is, a renewed course of life, and they too determine the quality of the same. Now for him who is animated by the egoistic desire

[1] Compare with our literal translation of these epithets that of Frank: "*quae designatur per cupidinem et arrogantiam, qua agens et fruens in propriam fertur naturae formam,*" or that of Röer: "*which by its nature prides itself in the feelings of self, dominion and possession,*" and ask how the profound philosophical views of the Indians can strike root with us, so long as one is referred to translations of this kind.

after welfare, is designed the section of the Veda on works. This teaches the means by which for the succeeding birth a better state may be secured in the *Saṃsâra*. A preponderance of sinfulness leads downwards into the bodies of animals and plants. Obedience to the laws of Scripture raises to the world of the fathers, to that of the gods, to that of Brahman. Equilibrium of virtue and vice leads again to human existence. Thus by works may be acquired a higher rank in the cycle of transmigrating souls, but they are unable to lead beyond these to an eternal union with the *Brahman*. This is possible by knowledge (*jñânam*) alone, which is taught in the knowledge section, that is, in the Upanishads. Knowledge in the Indian system corresponds to what by Christianity is called faith. Its result is annihilation of works, cessation of transmigration, and eternal deliverance. And while even in the New Testament it is still said of the dead that die in the Lord: τὰ δὲ ἔργα αὐτῶν ἀκολουθεῖ μετ' αὐτῶν (Rev. xiv. 13), a wonderful and oft-quoted verse of the Veda says:

Bhidyate hridaya-granthiç, chidyante sarva-saṃçayâḥ,
Kshîyante ca asya karmâṇi, tasmin drishṭe para-avare.

—" Of him who sees that which is the highest and the lowest—the knot of the heart breaks—all his doubts are solved—and his works become nothing" (*Muṇḍaka-upanishad*, ii. 2, 8).

§ 282. At the turning-point which our inquiry has reached, we shall briefly summarise its chief results.

1. The Will is, in an empirical sense, not free: as the tree so its fruits, as the man so his deeds. These all, being called forth by motives the occurrence of which is determined by chance, spring from the inner character with inexorable necessity.
2. This inner character is Will, and affirming Will, the nature of which, as we have shown, is egoism. This, as the kernel of our natural existence, animates us all with greater or less intensity, and from it proceed not only all vice and crime, but also honest work and the moderate enjoyment of a legitimate course of life. If therefore anything in us is sinful and condemnable, it is our whole natural existence.
3. From this it follows incontestably, that moral improvement is not possible by a change in our actions, but, if at all, then only by a change of the Will which forms the basis of our existence, by a transformation of the innate character, a new birth of the whole natural man.
4. Such a transformation depends neither on an external influence by others nor on self-determined resolutions of improvement. For all

motives have their limits in the inborn character. They may develop it in actions and so reveal it, but they can never change it. — This (and no more) is the bearing of Schopenhauer's doctrine that the innate character is constant and invariable.

To these empirical facts and the cheerless prospect they reveal, is opposed the claim of religion which urges moral improvement, and addresses itself in doing so to ourselves—is opposed the voice of conscience which, unperplexed by all these reflections, pronounces its inexorable verdict of condemnation on wickedness—is opposed experience itself, which, in spite of all deductions of empirical knowledge, shows instances of sudden and total change of Will, as also of a gradual progress towards good, of an increasing purification of our inner character in the course of life.—These phenomena, which will occupy us further, cannot be explained from the principles of natural being, above set forth by us, from the unfree nature of the Will and the invariability of the character. Thus it seems as if we were drawn to good by a power lying outside of ourselves, and stretching from the world beyond into this. Yet every one feels that good would no longer be good if effected in us by another than ourselves. Accordingly our moral improvement is in a certain sense entirely independent of ourselves, and again in a certain sense entirely our own work.

In the affirmation of the Will, of which our natural existence, as also this infinite world, is the embodiment, this power of change does not lie. But affirmation is only a part of us, is only the one pole of our being, the opposite pole of which lies in eternity and is yet near and attainable in the inmost heart of each of us. Here is the point where necessity and free-will, the work of grace and improvement by one's own power, Augustine and Pelagius join hands, where the strife of ages finds final reconciliation in the philosophy of Schopenhauer.

These hints will become more intelligible, if we now proceed to consider the denial of the Will to life, by determining firstly, at the hand of experience, its nature, by showing further the ways leading to it, and lastly by investigating the new principle manifested in it.

X. On the Nature of the Denial of the Will to Life

§ 283. Above we divided all actions possible to man into four classes, according to their four fundamental tendencies, so far as all, without exception, aim either at the well-being of one's self or the well-being of others, or at the ill of one's self or the ill of others. We then showed how egoism, striving after the well-being of self, is the fundamental type and the indispensable phenomenal form of the affirmation of the Will to life. We saw further how it is this egoism, arising at times to malice, which occasions harm to another without benefit to one's self. Thus all deeds in which is expressed the affirmation of the Will to life, are reduced to egoism. Besides it no other spring of action for the Will in the affirming state is even imaginable. This was deduced above (§ 262) from the limitation of existence in space and time, but it may also be directly perceived in the following way. All ill is a restraint of willing, all well-being is an unrestrained willing. Now affirmation is in its entire nature nothing but willing. Hence it lies in its inmost nature to be a continual struggle against the restraints of willing, consequently an unceasing striving after one's own well-being.

But strangely, nay, marvellously, the surest experience offers a series of actions the ultimate aim of which is not the good of self but partly that of another at the cost of one's own, partly even one's own ill, sought voluntarily and purposely without further object. In the sphere of these actions is included all that we call kindness of heart, morality, virtue, and holiness. These stand in contradiction to the entire natural order of things, based as it is on egoism. For such actions, when genuine, show everywhere a more or less high degree of renunciation, resignation, and denial of self and its interests. This it is indeed which gives them that more than earthly value which appeals so directly to our feeling. Accordingly we have to recognise, as the principle of these actions, a removal of affirmation in which all sinfulness consists, a **denial of the Will to life**. This expression, though objectionable and liable to misunderstanding by reason of its seeming negativeness, must be retained, since it alone denotes that which, as a universal and essential characteristic, distinguishes these actions from all others. For the rest it goes back to no less an authority than Jesus Christ Himself, who says: "He that will come after me, let him deny himself, ἀπαρνησάσθω ἑαυτόν" (St. Matth. xvi. 24).

We have now to show how such an act of self-renunciation forms the essence of every moral action.

§ 284. All actions, consequently those of morality also, relate either to the doer himself or to another. In the first case all egoistic actions, aiming at the well-being of self, are excluded from the sphere of morality. They may be *prudent* (adapted to a particular end), nay, even *wise* (adapted to the welfare of our whole existence), but *good* they cannot be called. For the motive of self-love underlies them, and this, as every one feels, robs an action of its moral worth. Thus of these deeds relating to one's self, only those can be called moral which pursue, by an act of renunciation, the ill of self as aim, that is ascetic actions, the moral significance of which will appear later on. Here we turn from these, the self-denying character of which is beyond question, in the first place to those actions which have as ultimate aim the good of another. We shall see in the case of these also, that, what lends them moral worth and assures them our recognition and admiration, is always an act of self-renunciation, of denial of the Will to life.

§ 285. A deed the ultimate aim of which is the furtherance of another's welfare, contains as a rule two elements—the one *eudæmonistic*, so far as the other's happiness is furthered by it, the second *ascetic*, so far as this furthering of another's happiness is for the doer associated, in every case, with greater or less sacrifice—that is, so far as he, in order to promote another's welfare, curtails and denies his own. Now the question is, whether both these elements are essential to a good deed, and if not, which of the two constitutes its real essence and gives it its moral worth.

Let us suppose the eudæmonistic element were wanting. Suppose a sacrifice, made with the best intentions, fails through accidental circumstances in its object, and, instead of furthering our neighbour's good, causes exactly the reverse. Such a deed would nevertheless, for our feeling, retain its full worth. Conversely let us suppose that a kindness, though highly beneficial in its effects, yet fails in the ascetic element, whether through its being associated with no renunciation on the part of the doer, or through its having as cause some egoistic motive—ambition, vanity, hope of reward here or hereafter, in short, any kind of striving after one's own good,—such an action, in proportion as we discovered its real egoistic spring, would immediately and inevitably lose all moral merit in our eyes. For, in fact, all good works undertaken with an egoistic view in the background, *have their reward* (St. Matth. vi. 2), and only such deeds have not their reward which are practised without any hope or wish of reward, without any idea of a possible recompense. For they are accompanied by what the Indian regards as the requisite of morality and expresses in the beautiful compound, *iha-amutra-phala-bhoga-virâga*, that is, "renunciation of the enjoyment of reward here and hereafter."

From these considerations it follows indisputably, that what we recognise as worthy and admirable in a moral action, not seldom with the feeling of personal shame and, as it were, reluctantly, is nothing but its ascetic element——that is, that act of self-renunciation, of denial of our own Will which is manifested in it.

This denial of the Will has three degrees. Either it goes only so far, that we forbear injuring another, in that, even where we might, we will not further our own good at the cost of his. Or it may determine us to make some sacrifice of ourselves, that another in his need may be helped. Or lastly, it takes as its ultimate aim the renunciation of self with no other object than that of combating the striving after well-being and happiness implanted in each of us by nature, because we recognise that it is sinful and ought not to be. Corresponding to these we have, as the three alone possible virtues, justice, love, and asceticism. They are the three steps by which, in gradual ascent, the way leads to the denial of the Will. But thither there is yet another way, without steps, rough and steep. Both of these we have now to examine.

XI. The Two Ways to Denial

§ 286. All of us, so long as we continue to thrust ourselves by birth into this world of suffering, find ourselves in a state of affirmation, that is of sin. But we are all also called to enter into salvation through the strait gate of denial. Thither lead two paths, one of which each of us will sooner or later take, one smooth and pleasant—the way of virtue; the other hard and terrible—the way of suffering. True, in both cases the great guide to salvation is suffering, which is, as we showed, essential to this existence, and the object of which is, to point away from it to what is better. But the difference is, that in the first case it is the **known suffering of another** which, as we shall now show, becomes, as compassion, the source of all virtue. In the other, on the contrary, it is the **felt suffering of ourselves** which breaks at last even the hardest Will and leads into the arms of salvation.—Thus that eternal compassion which never forsakes any one of us, speaks to us first gently by the medium of the intellect, then harshly and terribly in attacking the Will within us, that is ourselves.

§ 287. Before considering more closely these two ways to the denial of the Will, the one through another's, the other through our own suffering, it is of great importance to understand the following consideration, which, though repeatedly hinted at, can only here be developed as a whole.

To the physical order of things is opposed a metaphysical order, to the realm of affirmation a realm of denial, which yet remains completely closed and incomprehensible to the intellect framed as it is of space, time, and causality. Our intellect is only the mirror of willing, which (being in itself no intellectual phenomenon, no object of knowledge) is expanded by the intellect in its forms, space, time, and causality, and so becomes visible as world. In this sense intellect is the νοῦς of Anaxagoras which creates the world ever anew in each of us, and which determines the teleological constitution of things (§§ 158. 192). It is also in the truest sense the light with the origin of which begins, according to Genesis, the creation of the world. It is, however, but a natural light, designed for the manifestation of willing, that is, for the investigation of Nature, but destitute of all organs for the comprehension and conception of the Supernatural. Hence we can denote and describe this only as non-willing, denial of the Will, *nirvânam* (that is extinction), heaven (the infinite void of space), thus by purely negative expressions. And yet denial must rather be the really positive and existent, in comparison with which this great and glorious world is a mere dream, a shadow, a breath, a nothing.

The realm of denial is inconceivable to us, because we are forced, by reason of these very intellectual forms of space, time, and causality, to exclude it from the sphere of what, from our standpoint, we call being. Similarly the deeds of denial, springing from, and bearing witness to, this realm, though taking place daily before our eyes, are nevertheless in their real essence inconceivable. This is the meaning of Jesus, when He compares the spirit of denial manifested in such deeds—that is, the Holy Spirit who accomplishes in us the turning of the Will, the new birth—to the wind, the sound of which we hear but cannot tell whence it cometh and whither it goeth. These deeds are inconceivable, because, as free, they lie beyond causality, as non-egoistic, beyond space and time, to which our understanding is irrevocably bound. Meanwhile these deeds of denial, while breaking through the natural order of things, rank at the same time as integral parts of it. Like all occurrences in this world they are a possible object of knowledge, and must as such appear clad in the livery of the prince of this world, in form and hue of affirmation, that is in space, time, and causality. This takes place in the following singular way.

The universal phenomenal form of all affirming actions is this, that they proceed with necessity from the inner character and from the motives influencing it from without. The inner character is always egoism; the motive always a suffering, for this alone (§ 239) impels to that change of our condition which we call action; the action occurs always with necessity. These three elements, egoism, suffering, necessity, are the phenomenal form of affirming actions. Now it is just in this phenomenal form that deeds of denial also appear, because this form is based on our intellect, from which we cannot escape. Thus it is that the deeds in which the Will denies itself, though belonging to a sphere where eternal freedom reigns, appear under the aspect of necessity. Hence they seem further to be the product of egoism as character, and of suffering as motive. Yet this egoism is no longer an individual one, restricted to the sphere of the empirical and limited ego, but one which expands itself over our neighbour, over our fellow-creatures, and lastly over all being. And corresponding to this it is no longer individual suffering, but the suffering of others, appropriated by compassion, which he who denies himself makes his own. For it is not as a vicarious and atoning sacrifice, as Jewish realism believed, but because he knows himself one with all that exists, that the Holy One (and all who resemble Him) bears the sorrows (Isa. liii. 4), that He bears the sins of the world (St. John i. 29).

As far as the heavens are from the earth, so far are these deeds of denial from those of affirmation, and this difference proclaims itself at once in the inner heart. So soon, however, as we dissect an act of self-renunciation under the lamp of the intellect, it seems in it also to be egoism which, fleeing from suffering, performs the moral act with necessity.

This conception of holiness as an egoism which recognises itself in others, is, as we showed, an inadequate one. Yet it is the deepest comprehension of these supernatural deeds, attainable by the plummet of our intellect. We owe it to the profound thought of Indian sages, whose works are full of it, and from whom Schopenhauer has adopted it. Briefly and simply it runs in the words of Manu (12, 91):

sarvabhûteshu ca âtmânaṃ, sarvabhûtâni ca âtmani samaṃ paçyan, âtmayâjî svârâjyam adhigacchati.

"Recognising himself in all beings and all beings in his own self, he, kindling the sacrifice to self alone, enters into absolute freedom."

§ 288. From the above it follows that the turning of the Will to denial can in no wise be regarded as an (egoistic) flight from the sufferings of existence; though indeed denial, as the way to not willing, is certainly the true panacea of willing as well as of all its hindrances, that is of all suffering; and although the constitution of the world, so full of suffering, whether known in others or felt in ourselves, if it does not produce the turning of the Will (for it is not subject to causality), yet, for our conception, seems to produce it. With this reservation that we have here to describe what is in its nature indescribable, that therefore our description of it is in a certain sense figurative, we turn to consider the two ways to denial, of which the first is virtue, the second suffering.

§ 289. By the first way the Will attains the turning to salvation in making, through the medium of knowledge, the sufferings of others its own, thus averting itself (apparently egoistically) from existence and its sorrows. The appropriation of another's suffering by knowledge is called **compassion.** It is in the (practical not poetical) sense in which it is here used an empirically inexplicable, because essentially metaphysical, phenomenon. For the compassionate man, in recognising himself in the sufferer and accordingly making his pains his own, removes practically and unconsciously the barriers of space fixed between ego and non-ego, just as the philosopher removes them by abstract knowledge, the artist by immediate intuition.

From compassion as an egoism expanded by transcendental knowledge spring, as we shall show, the three alone possible virtues of justice, love, and asceticism, though, however, only for the intellectual or external conception which drags everything down to that sphere of willing, of affirmation, of egoism, alone accessible to it. In reality on the contrary, and viewed from within, all virtue is a not-willing and has its root in the ascetic soil of denial, to tread which is meanwhile forbidden us by the nature of our intellect. Thus it is that the purest and highest of all virtues, that of asceticism, is the least intelligible.

First Step to Denial: *Justice*

§ 290. He is just who does no wrong to another, in that he refrains from breaking into the sphere of another's Will (§ 270), in giving, in respect of body, property, honour, to every one his own (*suum cuique*). This behaviour may proceed from two very different causes. Either it arises from egoism, so far as the just man forbears doing wrong from fear of awkward results to himself, whether temporal punishment, loss of good name, or retribution hereafter, or from pure indolence, habit, or vanity. This kind of justice (δικαιοσύνη πάνδημος) has no moral worth. Opposed to it is a justice of a different origin (δικαιοσύνη οὐρανία)—a justice which does no wrong to another, because it will not have him injured, and this, because it anticipates the pain which would befall the other by the infliction of wrong; consequently it has its origin in compassion. Compassion is accordingly the moving spring of all genuine justice, even when just action proceeds not from the immediate emotion of the heart, but, as oftenest, from the once accepted, inviolable principle, under no circumstances to take from another what is his due. For this principle itself springs ultimately from compassion, by which it is fed, as the reservoir out of which we draw at need, is fed by the scanty and intermittent spring. Meanwhile our consciousness repudiates an injustice, even when he against whom it is directed does not suffer under it, whether because he does not feel or because he never learns his loss. This shows clearly that the ultimate basis of moral justice appears only to our affirmation-fettered comprehension as compassion: in reality it is the, to us unintelligible, asceticism of denial.

Second Step to Denial: *Love*

§ 291. There are three kinds of love, which philosophy has to discriminate, even though in reality they often merge in, and blend with, each other: (1) sexual love (ἔρως), to be conceived as the love to the limbs of our own body, and closely akin to maternal love, which is likewise dependent on instinct; (2) love of friends (φιλία), which makes sacrifices and, as the case may be, accepts them, and which rests moreover on the egoistic needs of communication, amusement, consolation, advice, etc.; (3) the love of our neighbour (ἀγάπη), which is stimulated by *compassion* (the reverse and negative complement of which is *joy in another's joy*) to aid the sufferer, without distinction of person, a love extending to all that suffers, therefore, of course, to animals also.

This last kind alone is a moral phenomenon, akin to the denial of the Will. Conjugal love, parental love, and the love of friends are such only, so far as they contain the ascetic element. This is indeed always more or less the case, in spite of their being primarily rooted completely in egoism. For in a wonderful way we find this world of affirmation dashed with an element of denial without which it could scarcely exist. It resembles that element of fire snatched by the world-forming Prometheus from another sphere, a small portion of which serves to sustain the world, while the whole would consume it.

With justice, which renounces the seeking of personal well-being at the cost of another, love ranks as a higher step to denial, so far as love furthers another's good at the cost of its own. While the just man recognises himself in the other only so far as is necessary not to injure him, he who is possessed by love goes a step farther. He breaks through the barriers of his individuality, fixed by nature, in order to treat the other as himself (ἀγαπήσεις τὸν πλησίον σου ὡς σεαυτόν), just because he sees in the other only himself again. Thus he stretches this recognition of his ego in his fellowmen farther and farther, until it even extends to those who are hostile to himself (ἀγαπᾶτε τοὺς ἐχθροὺς ὑμῶν), until he gives to him who demands his cloak his coat also, nay, gives up his life for his enemies. Here the love of the neighbour passes into complete denial of self,—here the second virtue is absorbed in the third and highest.

Third Step to Denial: *Asceticism*

§ 292. Asceticism is related to the other virtues as is to the repentance of single transgressions the consciousness of the sinfulness of our whole existence. Like all that is highest, it is the most exposed to misunderstanding and abuse, and can only be called genuine where it appears as the continuation, as the intensification of justice and love. Hence it is only under this condition, that it is admitted in Scripture (1 Cor. xiii. 3). Its connection with the lower steps to denial is, according to the external view of our knowledge, the following. Compassion, from which all true virtue (for our conception) flows, may reach a degree at which the recognition of one's own ego in another embraces all that lives, so that a man now lives in and for others as formerly he lived in and for himself. But continually, so long as he is in the body, the saint is in danger of being drawn down from the heights of this knowledge to the illusion of individuation. For he sees, as the Apostle says (Rom. vii. 23), "another law in his members warring against the law of his mind." Thus the never quite conquered sinfulness of corporeal existence drives him, in perpetual struggle "to mortify the members of the body" (Col. iii. 5) "and its deeds" (Rom. viii. 13), "to crucify the flesh with the affections and lusts" (Gal. v. 24). From this in fact asceticism, in all its manifold forms, proceeds, from mere abstinence of every kind up to the most fantastic feats of Indian ascetics. These last, filled with the consciousness, that with the annihilation of willing disappears at the same time that hindrance of willing which is called pain, devise for the body the most exquisite tortures, in order to attain by these, and to confirm ever anew, the certainty, that the soul has freed itself from the body, the Will from affirmation. There are, however, as we shall see, other means of ascertaining this. Hence we do not wish the Indian form of asceticism to become ours, but we hope that the spirit which prompted it, may be also found among us.

For just as it is the final aim to deny not life, but rather **the Will to life**, so also it is no kind of **external work** which marks the ascetic, but the **inner spirit alone**. This is what is essential and identical everywhere in the denial of the Will. Deeds are merely its external symptoms and may therefore be very varied. So, for instance, asceticism may be manifested in the poverty which will not enjoy while others starve, in fasting and maceration which, in order to work against the affirmation of the Will, weaken the body as its manifestation. Again it may take the form of chastity which out of compassion for that which is to be begotten, and in order not to perpetuate the state of sin, abstains from generation, or solitude to which the ascetic withdraws, in order to flee from the world and its lusts. These all, so far as they spring from a genuine ascetic spirit, are great and admirable.

But this very spirit, originating in the consciousness of the sinful nature of our existence, may also be manifested in quite another way, nay, it may be recognised, wherever, in things small or great, is manifested a striving against one's own nature without an egoistic motive. Accordingly, so far as this condition is fulfilled, not only he is an ascetic who becomes voluntarily poor, but he also who, instead of using his wealth for his own gratification, applies it to the alleviation of another's suffering, or to enterprises in the service of humanity. Nor is the observer of perfect chastity alone an ascetic, but he also who in self-denying labour sacrifices himself for his family; again not merely he who through all kinds of mortification weakens the body, but also he who in devotion to the calling which is his lot, fulfils his duty without regard to his own welfare, even to the sacrifice of his own personality. He therefore who desires to take the highest road, will find the opportunity for doing so in the position he fills, whatever it be. In this sense the Code of Manu already says (11, 235):

brâhmaṇasya tapo jñânaṃ, tapaḥ kshatrasya rakshaṇaṃ, vaiçyasya tu tapo vârtâ, tapaḥ çûdrasya sevanaṃ.

"The asceticism of the learned class is knowledge, the asceticism of the military class is protection, the asceticism of the merchant class is labour, the asceticism of the çûdra class is service."

Hence it is not our work that we must change, but rather the spirit from which it springs. It is not to idle quietism that we must flee, rather must we persevere in the battle of life, conscious that the labour of existence is laid upon us to purify us from egoism and the sinfulness arising from it. For the rest we may with the Brahmans take upon us hard and painful penances, or with Buddha restrict the claims of asceticism to poverty and chastity; with John the Baptist we may eat locusts and wild honey, or with Jesus drink wine and take part in mirthful feasts; with the countless martyrs of all creeds we may die for our convictions, or (what is harder) live for them, as did Schopenhauer. The question is not **what** we do, but **how** we do it. Thus we shall not ask with the Philippian gaoler (Acts xvi. 30), "What must I do to be saved?" but rather, "How, in what spirit, shall I live and work?" The answer is in the Bible words (1 Cor. x. 31): Εἴτε οὖν ἐσθίετε εἴτε πίνετε εἴτε τι ποιεῖτε, πάντα εἰς δόξαν θεοῦ ποιεῖτε. As an interpretation of the mythical part of this the following çloka may serve:

tasmâd asaktaḥ satataṃ kâryaṃ karma samâcara,
asakto hi âcaran karma param âpnoti pûrushaḥ!

"Fulfil therefore at all times the duty incumbent on thee without attachment (to existence); for he who does his duty without attachment, that man attains what is highest" (*Bhagavadgîtâ*, 3, 19; cf. 9, 27).

But one point more we shall mention which may perhaps throw some light on the fundamental dogma of Christianity. The saint, to whom true knowledge has arisen, knows himself as the entire Will to life (§ 168, 2). Accordingly he is filled with the consciousness that he removes the sufferings of the whole world in removing his ego, which he knows is the bearer of these. And this consciousness indeed does not lie, for the saint, in removing and delivering the Will in himself, has removed and delivered this whole world. For him who is lightened by transcendental knowledge, there remains of it nothing but an unsubstantial phantom, a shadow-play without reality (§ 174). To us alone it will not seem so, just because we are still on the empirical standpoint of affirmation, and only so far as transcendental knowledge awakes in us, can we take part in his deliverance. Thus might be understood the doctrine of Christianity, that Christ in His person has saved the world, but that we are not therefore saved, until we appropriate Christ's work in faith. Faith is, as will later become clear, precisely that transcendental knowledge.

§ 293. Happy he who takes to denial the smooth path of virtue through justice, love, and asceticism. He is spared that second and terrible way which leads thither by one's own suffering. Many are those who have to take this way, and often we may observe how a very egoistic Will, clinging vehemently to life, is transformed by the breaking over it of some great calamity, whether it be long confinement to a sick-bed, the bitter loss of what was dear, or, as with the criminal before execution, the near approach of death. This is the way of suffering, called by Schopenhauer δεύτερος πλοῦς, which is the harder to men, the more vehement the Will which is to be broken. For all suffering is only a hindered willing. The more vehement this willing, the more intensely is felt its hindrance, the heavier therefore the suffering. Where, on the contrary, the willing of life has turned to not willing of it, there, with the removal of willing, is removed also the possibility of its hindrance, consequently the possibility of suffering. And when the body freed from willing lasts for a while like the rolling of the potter's wheel after the vessel is finished, even physical pain will be felt only as a faint echo.

§ 294. Retrospect. Having established the nature of the denial of the Will and considered the two ways leading to it, we shall try, by summarising what has been said on the unknowable root of morality and our inadequate representation of it, to advance in this difficult question to the utmost attainable clearness.

Approaching our task from without we distinguished first (§ 261) two aims of morality: another's well-being and our own ill, and corresponding to these two moving springs: compassion and asceticism. Further, however, we saw *on the one side* that every moral deed is in its nature an ascetic one (§ 285). *On the other hand* we were forced to derive, as the other virtues, so also asceticism (if we would not give up the understanding of it) from compassion, in recognising in it a struggling against the natural hindrance of compassion, that is, against individuation (§ 292). Thus we see the two moving springs of morality unexpectedly coinciding and standing in relation to each other as the external to the internal, or perhaps as soul to body. For like these they are in themselves an identity which, considered from two opposite standpoints, appears as twofold.

Regarded from within all morality is denial, its moving spring is always an ascetic one, its aim always the ill of self. But one's own ill as aim of an action may be expressed perhaps in words, but to think it with concepts or to imagine it in any other way is impossible. For since all being is willing (that is affirmation) we should here have to conceive the activity of a non-existent. For doing this, however, we have no intellectual faculty, since the intellect is an organ of affirmation springing from, and calculated for, it alone.

Thus we are restricted to the external consideration of the mystery of morality, in which not-willing appears as willing, denial as a peculiar kind of affirmation. For here in the distorting mirror of our intellect moral deeds like all others appear as an (egoistic) flight from suffering; and what distinguishes them from the works of affirmation is not a change of the Will (which retains its egoistic determination) but a change of knowledge. This is attainable *by the first way* in recognising one's self, as teach the Indians, in all living beings, in feeling their suffering as compassion, and in assisting its alleviation by deeds of virtue. Or it may be attained *by the second way*, in gaining by one's own personal sorrow a knowledge of the nothingness and the suffering of existence, so that one seems to prefer to the state of being that not-being which is only attainable by denial.—Again and again we reached points where we became clearly aware of the inadequacy of this whole conception. Of such a kind is also what follows.

§ 295. If suffering, rather than the mysterious transformation of the inner being, were the true and sufficient cause of denial, then it would only need the necessary degree of suffering, in order to bring the Will always and infallibly to the turn. On the contrary experience shows, that suffering may lead to an entirely different end, one which, far from being denial, is rather a high degree of affirmation. This last refuge of the Will to life, broken by no suffering, is **suicide**. In it we see that self-conflict which is essential to the Will in the state of affirmation (§ 191) in its highest and most terrible struggle, in that the individual, taking arms against himself, destroys himself. What drives a man to suicide is always excess of suffering (suicide through insanity is not suicide). Now all suffering is a hindering of willing, and is, as we saw, the more strongly felt, the more vehement the willing. It must be felt in a very high degree to outweigh the love of life implanted in us. Hence it is that suicide always betokens a high degree of the affirmation of the Will. It is condemnable for this reason alone, that the suicide flees from the suffering which should lead him to denial. We know that he flees in vain, since life is assured to the Will to life (§ 248). Where there is Will, there also is life, because it is only its visibility, given us as a boon for the attainment of self-knowledge and through that, of denial. Of this boon the suicide robs himself, in taking from his Will its visibility, that is, life which might have led to salvation. Hence the deep compassion which seizes us in every such case.

§ 296. Hard sounds the word **denial**. Yet the Saviour who first used it says again: "My yoke is easy and my burden is light," and only to us it seems otherwise so long as we are full of affirmation. To be healed from this, life is granted us, the teachings of which no theory can replace. Only in the course of life comes the right acquaintance with the nature of affirmation, and with it the possibility of a turning away from it. Hence in youth we do not so easily reconcile ourselves to the Christian call to denial. Not so farther on. In old age, when the true worth of life has been taught by life itself, then, oftener perhaps than it appears, the dying away of the body is met by a dying away of the Will. This it is which gives the face of the old man that contemplative serenity, so different from the expression on other aged faces on which the Will, unbroken by existence, and looking back on vanishing life, stamps a quite peculiar disappointment.— And so death draws near. He has, as the Indians say, two faces. The one is fearful and terrible. He shows it to those who, when the capacity for living fails, are yet full of the craving for life. His other face is friendly and kind. He shows it to those in whom the Will has turned. Thus the apostle saw him when, at the end of a life course without compare, he was in doubt only as to whether he should die or live for others (Phil. i. 21-24). In the hour of death is decided, as Schopenhauer says, whether a man falls back into the bosom of nature to new life, new suffering and death, or whether he belongs to these no longer, but enters the realm of denial, called in the Bible βασιλεία τῶν οὐρανῶν, by the Indians *Nirvânam*, which expression denotes "extinction" and at the same time "bliss." True, it is an extinction, but only of the intellect and with it of this infinite world of which intellect is the bearer. But even the Pagan poet asks in deep presentiment:

τίς οἶδεν, εἰ τὸ ζῆν μέν ἐστι κατθανεῖν,
τὸ κατθανεῖν δὲ ζῆν;

and the Christian buries the children as soon as they are born with Christ by baptism into death (Rom. vi. 4), well knowing that from the highest standpoint this life of sin is **death**, the dying with Christ on the other hand, the entrance into real and eternal **life**.

XII. On the Principle of Denial

§ 297. There still remains a last question, the satisfactory answer to which lies, it is true, less in our power than that of any other.—By what means is wrought in the Will, the fundamental character of which is the clinging to life, that mighty transformation and turning away from life which is, as we saw, the source of all virtue and holiness, and which is appointed, as last and highest aim, to each of us?—

Causality is only the phenomenal form of the affirmation of the Will, while the Will itself lies outside of it, and is consequently free. Hence the only possible explanation of this process lies in this freedom of the Will which is just what makes it impossible to give a cause for its turning. But freedom in this sense is a purely negative concept, and if anything is positive, it is certainly that of which we are here speaking.

Christianity teaches that that transformation and new birth of the inner man as which it describes the turning of the Will, is wrought by faith. The question is, what is to be understood by this? The definition of faith as ἐλπιζομένων ὑπόστασις, πραγμάτων ἔλεγχος οὐ βλεπομένων (Heb. xi. 1) is a purely verbal one, and amounts finally to a being convinced without sufficient grounds. In vain we look around for another and non-mythical explanation of this very real condition which the Christian religion calls faith. Only so much is clear that faith is (1) the sufficient cause of morality and, nevertheless, (2) an intellectual phenomenon of a kind indeed specifically distinct from empirical knowledge.

Indian theology takes us a step farther in this direction, in defining empirical knowledge summarily as ignorance (*avidyâ*) and opposing to it (§ 281) the principle of denial as knowledge (*vidyâ*). By this is understood the metaphysical knowledge of the unity of being from which flows naturally the annihilation of the individual state, as also virtue and morality, since these are only a recognising of our own ego in others. We acknowledged that this doctrine (in the sense of which the concept of πίστις may be interpreted to the people) contains the deepest conception of denial attainable by us. But even this remains, as we saw, coloured over with the hue of affirmation, in so far as it derives the works of denial from compassion, that is, from egoism expanded by knowledge which, stimulated by the suffering of the world as motive, produces the phenomena of virtue and holiness with necessity. But it is in fact not the willing but the not-willing of life, not egoism but the exact reverse of it which shines forth in the deeds of denial. To think and to conceive this, however, is not granted us because, as it seems, denial would in that case sink to a speculation of egoism. And so we see spread over the most important of all questions, a veil which no mortal hand shall ever lift.

§ 298. If we may give to the most significant of all objects the most significative name, if it is meet to leave to the obscurest thing the obscurest word, it is this **principle of denial** and nothing else which we might designate by the name of **God.** Yet under this name nothing less is to be understood than a personal, consequently limited, consequently egoistic, consequently sinful being. If one tries to understand (which seldom happens) what personality really means, one will be inclined to regard the conception of the Being of beings as personality almost as blasphemy. It is far rather a supernatural power, a world-turning principle, a something which no eye sees, no name denotes, no concept reaches nor ever can reach. And this Being in the last and profoundest sense are we ourselves. For it is we of whom a hymn of the Ṛigveda (10, 90) sings that one part of our being constitutes this universe and three parts are immortal in the heavens. From the metaphysical substratum of our being, which lies beyond existence in the bosom of the divine, spring forth, in proportion as we become aware of the aberration of our existence, those creative elementary forces which, changing the unchangeable, lead from the death-darkness of sin by virtue and holiness to the light of denial. In this sense, rejecting all synergism, we may say in the words of scripture: Θεὸς γάρ ἐστιν ὁ ἐνεργῶν ἐν ὑμῖν καὶ τὸ θέλειν καὶ τὸ ἐνεργεῖν (Phil. ii. 13).

As for Christianity, so for us also God is the principle of salvation, which, as the Holy Ghost, makes itself felt daily and hourly in our heart. Nay, we might with the Bible view go yet a step farther and conceive God at the same time as the principle of creation, if we would resolve (figuratively speaking) to place the Fall before the creation of the world. In this case the creation of the world would be the expansion of affirmation in space, time, and causality, and consequently the making of it visible, in which in fact lies the first step to salvation.

§ 299. Let us turn back from these high-soaring and daring speculations to experience, to interpret which is the beginning and end of our task; and even as we behold the sun by its reflection, so let us grasp the divine by its traces in experience, and confine ourselves to that. These traces we shall find nowhere but in our inner being, where they appear in both spheres, in that of willing and in that of knowing.

In our Will the divine is manifested as that power which accomplishes its turning to denial. This turning may take place suddenly, but it may also be brought about by a gradual transformation of the heart. Such contradicts, it is true, the invariability of the empirical character. But this means nothing more than that we have no intellectual form by which to conceive it. Again of the overwhelming strength of this power of turning we can form no conception. For a force which would be strong enough to stop the earth in its course and to set it in motion in the opposite direction, must be called weak in comparison to the power of the Holy Ghost. In the former case it would be a question of a merely physical change, though a great one, but here we speak of a turning of the Will to life, of which this whole universe, with all its suns and planets, is the mere phenomenon, and which yet dwells whole and undivided in each one of us, and in each one of us will turn to salvation.

The second trace of the divine in us concerns knowledge. Here it shows itself as that inner voice which sits in judgment, even against our will, on the good and bad deeds, as well of others as of ourselves. It is manifested as that indignation which seizes us at the sight of each wicked deed, and as the admiration, often mingled with shame, which is involuntarily drawn from us by a noble action.—But our own doing also has in this voice its judge. It sounds in the anguish of conscience which, after a committed crime, seizes the criminal and has often enough driven him into the arms of temporal justice. And it comes over us after good actions, performed often with heavy personal sacrifice, as that satisfaction with which no attainment of selfish ends, no possession of earthly happiness can compare— as the peace of God which passeth all understanding.

CONCLUSION

§ 300. If in conclusion we look back on our whole metaphysical structure, it appears to us as a granitic mountain which, on the firm rocky ground of experience towering high and higher, terminates in three summits.—We reached the first of these summits when, in the metaphysics of nature, we attained to the conviction of the unity of all being and recognised how the one Will to life was spread at our feet as the infinite variety of the world. The second summit we climbed in the metaphysics of the beautiful. Above us we saw the world of the Ideas in eternal splendour, beneath us their imperfect shadows in nature. But there still remained in the metaphysics of morality, the third summit, highest of all. Here, if anywhere, we might hope to cast a glance into the eternal realm from which this whole world proceeds as the place of probation and healing. With effort we have climbed this utmost summit of human knowledge and find it—wrapped in clouds; so that painfully groping we scarce find a footing at the very spot where we are nearest the region of light.

Higher no wing can bear us,—here ends the path, losing itself in mist, but not hopelessly. And so we may be content if, gazing upward from this highest summit of the finite, we perceive through the thinning cloud-veil the eternal stars, clearly enough to lighten our way through the night of existence.

> *Na tatra sûryo bhâti, na candra-târakaṃ*
> *Na imâ vidyuto bhânti, kuto 'yam agniḥ.—*
> *Tam eva bhântam anubhâti sarvaṃ,*
> *Tasya bhâsâ sarvam idaṃ vibhâti.*

"There shines not the sun, nor moon, nor stars, neither these lightnings, much less earthly fire. After Him, the Shining One, all things shine, by His light is lighted this whole world" (*Kâṭhaka-upanishad*, v. 15).

ON THE

PHILOSOPHY OF THE VEDÂNTA

IN ITS RELATIONS
TO OCCIDENTAL METAPHYSICS

AN ADDRESS

delivered before the Bombay Branch of the Royal Asiatic Society,
Saturday, the 25th February 1893

BY

DR. PAUL DEUSSEN

PROFESSOR OF PHILOSOPHY IN THE UNIVERSITY OF KIEL, GERMANY

REPRINTED FROM THE ORIGINAL EDITION
BOMBAY, 1893

TO

ALL MY INDIAN FRIENDS

WHOSE KINDNESS

HAS MADE MY JOURNEY THROUGH INDIA

FROM NOVEMBER 1892 TILL MARCH 1893

IN ALL PARTS OF THE PENINSULA

SO DELIGHTFUL, INSTRUCTIVE, AND HEART-ELEVATING

I DEDICATE THESE FEW PAGES

IN RECOMMENDING THEM TO THEIR

SERIOUS CONSIDERATION

P. D.

FAREWELL TO INDIA.

O sun of India, what have we committed,
    That we must leave thee and thy children now,
Thy giant trees, thy flowers, so well befitted
    To thy blue heaven's never-frowning brow?

And you, our Indian friends, whose hearty feeling
    Deep sympathy with you has fast obtained—
From Ceylon to Peshawar and Darjeeling,
    Are you now lost to us, so soon as gained?

Farewell! Now Space and Time, in separating
    Our bodies, will create a cruel wall;
Until forgetful darkness overshading,
    Like Himalayan fog, bedims you all.

Did we but dream of your brown lovely faces,
    Of your dark eyes, and gently-touching hands?
Was it a dream that left such tender traces,
    Accompanying us to foreign lands?

O yes, a dream is all that we are living,
    And India be a dream in this great dream:
A dream, repose and recreation giving,
    Under a paler heaven's fainter beam.

But what are Time and Space, whose rough intrusion
    Will separate what is so near allied!
Are they not taught to be a mere illusion?
    May we not be against them fortified?

O yes, this thought shall be our consolation,
    When we are severed soon by land and sea!
Your sun and ours is one! no separation!
    Keep friendship, friends, let it eternal be.

COLOMBO, 16*th March* 1893.

THE PHILOSOPHY OF THE VEDÂNTA

On my journey through India I have noticed with satisfaction, that in philosophy till now our brothers in the East have maintained a very good tradition, better, perhaps, than the more active but less contemplative branches of the great Indo-Aryan family in Europe, where Empirism, Realism, and their natural consequence, Materialism, grow from day to day more exuberantly, whilst metaphysics, the very centre and heart of serious philosophy, is supported only by a few, who have learnt to brave the spirit of the age.

In India the influence of this perverted and perversive spirit of our age has not yet overthrown in religion and philosophy the good traditions of the great ancient time. It is true that most of the ancient *darçana's* even in India find only an historical interest; followers of the Sânkhya-System occur rarely; Nyâya is cultivated mostly as an intellectual sport and exercise, like grammar or mathematics, —but the Vedânta is, now as in the ancient time, living in the mind and heart of every thoughtful Hindoo. It is true that even here, in the sanctuary of Vedantic metaphysics, the realistic tendencies, natural to man, have penetrated, producing the misinterpreting variations of Çankara's Advaita, known under the names Viçishtâdvaita, Dvaita,

Çuddhâdvaita of Râmânuja, Mâdhva, Vallabha,—but India till now has not yet been seduced by their voices, and of hundred Vedântins (I have it from a well-informed man, who is himself a zealous adversary of Çañkara and follower of Râmânuja) fifteen perhaps adhere to Râmânuja, five to Mâdhva, five to Vallabha, and seventy-five to Çañkarâchârya.

This fact may be for poor India in so many misfortunes a great consolation; for the eternal interests are higher than the temporary; and the system of the Vedânta, as founded on the Upanishads and Vedânta Sûtras and accomplished by Çañkara's commentaries on them,—equal in rank to Plato and Kant—is one of the most valuable products of the genius of mankind in its search for the eternal truth—as I propose to show now by a short sketch of Çañkara's Advaita and comparison of its principal doctrines with the best that occidental philosophy has produced till now.

Taking the Upanishads, as Çañkara does, for revealed truth with absolute authority, it was not an easy task to build out of their materials a consistent philosophical system, for the Upanishads are in Theology, Kosmology and Psychology full of the hardest contradictions. Thus in many passages the nature of Brahman is painted out in various and luxuriant colours, and again we read, that the nature of Brahman is quite unattainable to human words, to human understanding;—thus we meet sometimes longer reports explaining how the world has been created by Brahman, and again we are told that there is no world besides Brahman, and all variety of things is mere error and illusion;—thus we have fanciful descriptions of the Saṃsâra, the way of the wandering soul up to heaven and back to earth, and again we read, that there is no Saṃsâra, no variety of souls at all, but only one Âtman, who is fully and totally residing in every being.

Çaṅkara in these difficulties created by the nature of his materials, in face of so many contradictory doctrines which he was not allowed to decline and yet could not admit altogether,—has found a wonderful way out, which deserves the attention, perhaps the imitation, of the Christian dogmatists in their embarrassments. He constructs out of the materials of the Upanishads two systems, one esoteric, philosophical (called by him *nirguṇâ vidyâ*, sometimes *pâramârthikâ avasthâ*), containing the metaphysical truth for the few, rare in all times and countries, who are able to understand it; and another exoteric, theological (*saguṇâ vidyâ, vyâvahâriki avasthâ*), for the general public, who want images, not abstract truth;—worship, not meditation.

I shall now point out briefly the two systems, esoteric and exoteric, in pursuing and confronting them through the four chief parts, which Çaṅkara's system contains, and every complete philosophical system must contain:—

I. Theology, the doctrine of God or of the philosophical principle.

II. Kosmology, the doctrine of the world.

III. Psychology, the doctrine of the soul.

IV. Eschatology, the doctrine of the last things, the things after death.

I. Theology.

The Upanishads teem with fanciful and contradictory descriptions of the nature of Brahman. He is the all-pervading âkâça, is the purusha in the sun, the purusha in the eye; his head is the heaven, his eyes are sun and moon, his breath is the wind, his footstool the earth; he is infinitely great as soul of the universe and infinitely small as the soul in us; he is in particular the *îçvara*, the personal God, distributing justly reward and punishment according to the deeds of man. All these numerous descriptions are collected by Çañkara under the wide mantle of the exoteric theology, the *saguṇâ vidyâ* of Brahman, consisting of numerous "vidyâs" adapted for approaching the eternal being not by the way of knowledge but by the way of worshipping, and having each its particular fruits. Mark, that also the conception of God as a personal being, an *îçvara*, is merely exoteric and does not give us an adequate knowledge of the Âtman;—and indeed, when we consider what personality is, how narrow in its limitations, how closely connected with egoism, the counterpart of godly essence, who would think so low of God as to impute to Him personality?

In the sharpest contrast to these exoteric vidyâs stands the esoteric, *nirguṇâ vidyâ* of the Âtman; and its fundamental tenet is the absolute inaccessibility of God to human thoughts and words;

यतो वाचो निवर्तन्ते
अप्राप्य मनसा सह ॥

and again:

अविज्ञातं विजानताम्
विज्ञातमविजानताम् ॥

and the celebrated formula occurring so often in Brihad-âranyaka-Upanishad; *neti ! neti !* viz., whatever attempt you make to know the Âtman, whatever description you give of him, I always say: *na iti, na iti*, it is not so, it is not so! Therefore the wise Bâhva, when asked by the king Vâshkali to explain the Brahman, kept silence. And when the king repeated his request again and again, the rishi broke out into the answer: "I tell it you, but you don't understand it; *çânto 'yam âtmâ*, this Âtmâ is silence!" We know it now by the Kantian philosophy, that the answer of Bâhva was correct, we know it, that the very organisation of our intellect (which is bound once for ever to its innate forms of perception, space, time, and causality) excludes us from a knowledge of the spaceless, timeless, godly reality for ever and ever. And yet the Âtman, the only godly being, is not unattainable to us, is even not far from us, for we have it fully and totally in ourselves as our own metaphysical entity; and here, when returning from the outside and apparent world to the deepest secrets of our own nature, we may come to God, not by knowledge, but by *anubhava*, by absorption into our own self. There is a great difference between knowledge, in which subject and object are distinct from each other, and anubhava, where subject and object coincide in the same. He who by anubhava comes to the great intelligence, "*aham brahma asmi*," obtains a state called by Çankara *Samrâdhanam*, accomplished satisfaction; and indeed, what might he desire, who feels and knows himself as the sum and totality of all existence!

II. Kosmology.

Here again we meet the distinction of exoteric and esoteric doctrine, though not so clearly severed by Çankara as in other parts of his system.

The exoteric Kosmology according to the natural but erroneous realism (*avidyâ*) in which we are born, considers this world as the reality, and can express its entire dependency on Brahman only by the mythical way of a creation of the world by Brahman. Thus a temporal creation of the world, even as in the Christian documents, is also taught in various and well-known passages of the Upanishads. But such a creation of the material world by an immaterial cause, performed in a certain point of time after an eternity elapsed uselessly, is not only against the demands of human reason and natural science, but also against another important doctrine of the Vedânta, which teaches and must teach us (as we shall see hereafter) the "beginninglessness of the migration of souls," *saṃsârasya anâditvam*. Here the expedient of Çankara is very clever and worthy of imitation. Instead of the temporary creation once for ever of the Upanishads, he teaches that the world in great periods is created and reabsorbed by Brahman (referring to the misunderstood verse of the Rigveda: सूर्याचन्द्रमसौ धाता यथापूर्वमकल्पयत्); this mutual creation and reabsorption lasts from eternity, and no creation can be allowed by our system to be a first one, and that for good reasons, as we shall see just now.—If we ask: *Why* has God created the world? the answers to this question are generally very unsatisfactory. For His own glorification? How may we attribute to Him so much vanity!—For His particular amusement? But He was an eternity without this toy!—For love of mankind? How can He love a thing before it exists, and how can it be called love, to create millions for misery and eternal pain?—The Vedânta has a better answer. The never-ceasing new-creation of the world is a moral necessity connected with the central and most precious doctrine of the exoteric Vedânta, the doctrine of Saṃsâra.

Man, says Çañkara, is like a plant. He grows, flourishes, and at the end he dies: but not totally. For as the plant, when dying, leaves behind it the seed, of which, according to its quality, a new plant grows,—so man, when dying, leaves his *karma*, the good and bad works of his life, which must be rewarded and punished in another life after this. No life can be the first, for it is the fruit of previous actions, nor the last, for its actions must be expiated in a next following life. So the Saṃsâra is without beginning and without end, and the new creation of the world after every absorption into Brahman is a moral necessity. I need not point out, in particular here in India, the high value of this doctrine of Saṃsâra as a consolation in the distresses, as a moral agent in the temptations of life,—I have to say here only, that the Saṃsâra, though not the absolute truth, is a mythical representative of a truth which in itself is unattainable to our intellect; mythical is this theory of metempsychosis only in so far as it invests in the forms of space and time what really is spaceless and timeless, and therefore beyond the reach of our understanding. So the Saṃsâra is just so far from the truth, as the *saguṇâ vidyâ* is from the *nirguṇâ vidyâ*; it is the eternal truth itself, but (since we cannot conceive it otherwise) the truth in an allegorical form, adapted to our human understanding.

And this is the character of the whole exoteric Vedânta, whilst the esoteric doctrine tries to find out the philosophical, the absolute truth.

And so we come to the esoteric Kosmology, whose simple doctrine is this, that in reality there is no manifold world, but only Brahman, and that what we consider as the world, is a mere illusion (*mâyâ*) similar to a *mrigatrishnikâ* which disappears when we approach it, and not more to be feared than the rope which we took in the darkness for a serpent. There are, as you see, many similes in the Vedânta, to illustrate the illusive character of this world, but the best of them is, perhaps, when Çankara compares our life to a long dream;—a man whilst dreaming does not doubt of the reality of the dream, but this reality disappears in the moment of awakening, to give place to a truer reality which we were not aware of whilst dreaming. The life a dream! this has been the thought of many wise men from Pindar and Sophokles to Shakespeare and Calderon de la Barca, but nobody has better explained this idea than Çankara. And, indeed, the moment when we die may be to nothing so similar as to the awakening from a long and heavy dream; it may be, that then heaven and earth are blown away like the nightly phantoms of the dream, and what then may stand before us? or rather in us? Brahman, the eternal reality which was hidden to us till then by this dream of life!—This world is mâyâ, is illusion, is not the very reality, that is the deepest thought of the esoteric Vedânta, attained not by calculating *tarka* but by *anubhava*, by returning from this variegated world to the deep recess of our own self (*Âtman*). Do so, if you can, and you will get aware of a reality very different from empirical reality, a timeless, spaceless, changeless reality, and you will feel and experience that whatever is outside of this only true reality is mere appearance, is mâyâ, is a dream!—This was the way the Indian thinkers went, and by a similar way, shown by Parmenides, Plato came to the same truth, when knowing and teaching that this world is a world of shadows, and that the reality is not in these shadows, but behind them. The accord here of Platonism and Vedantism is wonderful, but both have grasped this great metaphysical truth by intuition; their tenet is true, but they are not able to prove it, and in so far they are defective. And here a great light and assistance to the Indian and the Greek thinker comes from the philosophy of Kant, who went quite another way, not the Vedantic and Platonic way of intuition, but the way of abstract reasoning and scientific proof. The great work of Kant is an analysis of the human mind, not in the superficial way of Locke, but going to the very bottom of it. And in doing so, Kant found, to the surprise of the world and of himself, that three essential elements of this outside world, viz. space, time, and causality, are not, as we naturally believe, eternal fundamentals of an objective reality, but merely subjective innate perceptual forms of our own intellect. This has been proved by Kant and by his great disciple Schopenhauer with mathematical evidence, and I have given these proofs (the base of all scientific metaphysics) in the shortest and clearest form in my *Elemente der Metaphysik*—a book which I am resolved now to get translated into English, for the benefit, not of the Europeans (who may learn German), but of my brothers in India, who will be greatly astonished to find in Germany the scientific substruction of their own philosophy, of the Advaita Vedânta! For Kant has demonstrated that space, time, and causality are not objective realities, but only subjective forms of our intellect, and the unavoidable conclusion is this, that the world, as far as it is extended in space, running on in time, ruled throughout by causality, in so far is merely a representation of my mind and nothing beyond it. You see the concordance of Indian, Greek, and German metaphysics; the world is mâyâ, is illusion, says *Çaṅkara ;*—it is a world of shadows, not of realities, says *Plato ;*—it is "appearance only, not the thing in itself," says *Kant.* Here we have the same doctrine in three different parts of the world, but the scientific proofs of it are not in Çaṅkara, not in Plato, but only in Kant.

III. PSYCHOLOGY.

Here we convert the order and begin with the esoteric Psychology, because it is closely connected with the esoteric Kosmology and its fundamental doctrine: the world is *mâyâ.* All is illusive, with one exception, with the exception of my own Self, of my Âtman. My Âtman cannot be illusive, as Çaṅkara shows, anticipating the "*cogito, ergo sum*" of Descartes,—for he who would deny it, even in denying it, witnesses its reality. But what is the relation between my individual soul, the Jîva-Âtman, and the highest soul, the Parama-Âtman or Brahman? Here Çaṅkara, like a prophet, foresees the deviations of Râmânuja, Mâdhva and Vallabha, and refutes them in showing that the Jîva cannot be a part of Brahman (Râmânuja), because Brahman is without parts (for it is timeless and spaceless, and all parts are either successions in time or co-ordinations in space,—as we may supply),—neither a different thing from Brahman (Mâdhva), for Brahman is *ekam eva advitîyam,* as we may experience by *anubhava,* nor a metamorphosis of Brahman (Vallabha), for

Brahman is unchangeable (for, as we know now by Kant, it is not subject to causality). The conclusion is, that the Jîva, being neither a part nor a different thing, nor a variation of Brahman, must be the Paramâtman fully and totally himself, a conclusion made equally by the Vedântin Çankara, by the Platonic Plotinos, and by the Kantian Schopenhauer. But Çankara in his conclusions goes perhaps further than any of them. If really our soul, says he, is not a part of Brahman but Brahman himself, then all the attributes of Brahman,—all-pervadingness, eternity, almightiness (scientifically spoken: exemption of space, time, causality) are ours; *aham brahma asmi*, I am Brahman, and consequently I am all-pervading (spaceless), eternal (timeless), almighty (not limited in my doing by causality). But these godly qualities are hidden in me, says Çankara, as the fire is hidden in the wood, and will appear only after the final deliverance.

What is the cause of this concealment of my godly nature? The Upâdhi's, answers Çankara, and with this answer we pass from the esoteric to the exoteric psychology. The Upâdhi's are manas and indriya's, prâna with its five branches, sûkshmam çarîram,—in short, the whole psychological apparatus, which together with a factor changeable from birth to birth, with my karman, accompanies my Âtman in all its ways of migration, without infecting its godly nature, as the crystal is not infected by the colour painted over it. But whence originate these Upâdhi's? They form of course part of the *mâyâ*, the great world-illusion, and like *mâyâ* they are based on our innate *avidyâ* or ignorance, a merely negative power and yet strong enough to keep us from our godly existence. But now, from where comes this *avidyâ*, this primal cause of ignorance, sin, and misery? Here all philosophers in India and Greece and everywhere have been defective, until Kant came to show us that the whole question is inadmissible. You ask for the cause of *avidyâ*, but it has no cause; for causality goes only so far as this world of the Saṃsâra goes, connecting each link of it with another, but never beyond Saṃsâra and its fundamental characteristic, the *avidyâ*. In inquiring after a cause of *avidyâ* with *mâyâ*, Saṃsâra and Upâdhi's, you abuse, as Kant may teach us, your innate mental organ of causality to penetrate into a region for which it is not made, and where it is no more available. The fact is, that we are here in ignorance, sin, and misery, and that we know the way out of them, but the question of a cause for them is senseless.

IV. Eschatology.

And now a few words about this way out of the Saṃsâra, and first about the exoteric theory of it. In the ancient time of the hymns there was no idea of Saṃsâra, but only rewards in heaven and (somewhat later) punishments in a dark region (*padam gabhîram*), the precursor of the later hells. Then the deep theory of Saṃsâra came up, teaching rewards and punishment in the form of a new birth on earth. The Vedânta combines both theories, and so it has a double expiation, first in heaven and hell, and then again in a new existence on the earth. This double expiation is different (1) for performers of good works, going the *pitriyâna;* (2) for worshippers of the saguṇam brahma, going the *devayâna;* (3) for wicked deeds, leading to what is obscurely hinted at in the Upanishads as the *tṛitîyam sthânam*, the third place. (1) The *pitriyâna* leads through a succession of dark spheres to the moon, there to enjoy the fruit of the good works, and, after their consumption, back to an earthly existence. (2) The *devayâna* leads through a set of brighter spheres to Brahman, without returning to the earth (तेषां न पुनरावृत्तिः) But this Brahman is only sagunam brahma, the object of worshipping, and its true worshippers, though entering into this sagunam brahma without returning, have to wait in it until they get *moksha* by obtaining *samyagdarçanam*, the full knowledge of the nirgunam brahma. (3) The *tritîyam sthânam*, including the later theories of hells, teaches punishment in them, and again punishment by returning to earth in the form of lower castes, animals, and plants. All these various and fantastical ways of Samsâra are considered as true, quite as true as this world is, but not more. For the whole world and the whole way of Samsâra is valid and true for those only who are in the *avidyâ*, not for those who have overcome it, as we have now to show.

The esoteric Vedânta does not admit the reality of the world nor of the Samsâra, for the only reality is Brahman, grasped in ourselves as our own Âtman. The knowledge of this Âtman, the great intelligence: "*aham brahma asmi*," does not produce *moksha* (deliverance), but is *moksha* itself. Then we obtain what the Upanishads say:

भिद्यते हृदयग्रन्थिः
छिद्यन्ते सर्वसंशयाः ।
चीयन्ते चास्य कर्माणि
तस्मिन् दृष्टे परावरे ॥

When seeing Brahma as the highest and the lowest

everywhere, all knots of our heart, all sorrows are split, all doubts vanish, and our works become nothing. Certainly no man can live without doing works, and so also the *Jivanmukta;* but he knows, that all these works are illusive, as this whole world is, and therefore they do not adhere to him nor produce for him a new life after death. —And what kind of works may such a man do?—People have often reproached the Vedânta with being defective in morals, and, indeed, the Indian genius is too contemplative to speak much of works; but the fact is nevertheless, that the highest and purest morality is the immediate consequence of the Vedânta. The Gospels fix quite correctly as the highest law of morality: "love your neighbour as yourselves." But why should I do so, since by the order of nature I feel pain and pleasure only in myself, not in my neighbour? The answer is not in the Bible (this venerable book being not yet quite free from Semitic realism), but it is in the Veda, is in the great formula, "*tat tvam asi,*" which gives in three words metaphysics and morals altogether. You shall love your neighbour as yourselves,—because you are your neighbour, and mere illusion makes you believe, that your neighbour is something different from yourselves. Or in the words of the Bhagavadgîtâh: he, who knows himself in everything and everything in himself, will not injure himself by himself, *na hinasti âtmanâ âtmânam.* This is the sum and tenor of all morality, and this is the standpoint of a man knowing himself as Brahman. He feels himself as everything, — so he will not desire anything, for he has whatever can be had; —he feels himself as everything, — so he will not injure anything, for nobody injures himself. He lives in the world, is surrounded by its illusions but not deceived by them: like the man suffering from *timira*, who sees two moons but knows that there is one only, so the Jîvan-mukta sees the manifold world and cannot get rid of seeing it, but he knows, that there is only one being, Brahman, the Âtman, his own Self, and he verifies it by his deeds of pure disinterested morality. And so he expects his end, as the potter expects the end of the twirling of his wheel, after the vessel is ready. And then, for him, when death comes, no more Saṃsâra : न तस्य प्राणा उत्क्रामन्ति । ब्रह्म एव सन् ब्रह्म अप्येति He enters into Brahman, like the streams into the ocean :

यथा नद्यः स्यन्दमानाः समुद्रे
अस्तं गच्छन्ति नामरूपे विहाय ।
तथा विद्वान् नामरूपाद्विमुक्तः
परात्परं पुरुषमुपैति दिव्यम् ॥

he leaves behind him *nâma* and *rûpam*, he leaves behind him *individuality*, but he does not leave behind him his *Âtman*, his Self. It is not the falling of the drop into the infinite ocean, it is the whole ocean, becoming free from the fetters of ice, returning from its frozen state to that what it is really and has never ceased to be, to its own all-pervading, eternal, almighty nature.

And so the Vedânta, in its unfalsified form, is the strongest support of pure morality, is the greatest consolation in the sufferings of life and death,—Indians, keep to it!

THE END.

WORKS BY THE SAME AUTHOR.

Commentatio de Platonis Sophistae Compositione ac doctrina, 1869. (Marcus, Bonn. 1 Mark, 25 Pf.)

Die Elemente der Metaphysik, 2nd Ed., 1890. (Brockhaus, Leipzig. 4 Mark.)

Das System des Vedânta, 1883. (Brockhaus, Leipzig. 12 Mark.)

Die Sûtra's des Vedânta, mit dem Commentare des Çañkara, 1887. (Brockhaus, Leipzig. 16 Mark.)

Der Kategorische Imperativ, Vortrag, 1891. (Toeche, Kiel. ½ Mark.)

IN THE PRESS.

Allgemeine Geschichte der Philosophie, mit besonderer Berücksichtigung der Religionen. Erster Teil: Einleitung und Philosophie des Veda bis auf die Upanishad's (Leipzig, Brockhaus).

Die Upanishad's des Veda, übersetzt und mit Einleitungen versehen (Leipzig, Brockhaus).

BOOKS ON PHILOSOPHY.

CRITIQUE OF PURE REASON. By IMMANUEL KANT. Translated by F. MAX MÜLLER. With Introduction by LUDWIG NOIRÉ. 2 Vols. 8vo. 16s each.

    Vol. I. HISTORICAL INTRODUCTION.
    Vol. II. CRITIQUE OF PURE REASON.

KANT'S CRITICAL PHILOSOPHY FOR ENGLISH READERS. By J. P. MAHAFFY, D.D., Professor of Ancient History in the University of Dublin, and JOHN H. BERNARD, B.D., Fellow of Trinity College, Dublin. 2 Vols. Crown 8vo. Vol. I. 7s. 6d. Vol. II. 6s.

    Vol. I. THE KRITIK OF PURE REASON EXPLAINED AND DEFENDED.
    Vol. II. THE PROLEGOMENA. Translated with Notes and Appendices.

FIRST AND FUNDAMENTAL TRUTHS: being a Treatise on Metaphysics. By JAMES M'COSH, D.D. Extra Crown 8vo. 9s.

MORAL AND METAPHYSICAL PHILOSOPHY. By F. D. MAURICE, M.A., late Professor of Moral Philosophy in the University of Cambridge. New Edition. 2 Vols. 8vo. 16s.

    Vol. I. ANCIENT PHILOSOPHY AND THE FIRST TO THE THIRTEENTH CENTURIES.
    Vol. II. FOURTEENTH CENTURY AND THE FRENCH REVOLUTION, WITH A GLIMPSE INTO THE NINETEENTH CENTURY.

A HISTORY OF PHILOSOPHY. With special reference to the Formation and Development of its Problems and Conceptions. By Dr. W. WINDELBAND, Professor of Philosophy in the University of Strasburg. Authorised Translation by JAMES H. TUFTS, Ph.D., Assistant Professor of Philosophy in the University of Chicago. 8vo. 21s. net.

    TIMES.—"A text-book of metaphysics, which has been well thumbed in the original since its publication in 1892, and will probably be equally popular in its well-executed English version."

GENETIC PHILOSOPHY. By President DAVID J. HILL, of the University of Rochester, U.S.A. 7s. net.

    ** In this book the author deals with the following subjects: *The Genesis of Matter; the Genesis of Life; the Genesis of Consciousness; the Genesis of Feeling; the Genesis of Thought; the Genesis of Will; the Genesis of Art; the Genesis of Morality; the Genesis of Religion; the Genesis of Science.*

    TIMES.—"A treatise in which more practical problems of philosophical research are handled, and handled ably."

    GLASGOW HERALD.—"A well-written and suggestive book."

MACMILLAN AND CO., LONDON.

BOOKS ON PSYCHOLOGY AND ETHICS

THE PRINCIPLES OF PSYCHOLOGY. By WILLIAM JAMES, Professor of Psychology in Harvard University. 2 Vols. 8vo. 25s. net.

TIMES.—"An important, and in some respects a novel contribution to the literature of philosophical speculation. The novelty consists in this, that Professor James stands equally aloof from the two schools which have divided philosophy between them since the dawn of Speculation. . . . This conception of a psychological propaedeutic for the metaphysic of the future is undoubtedly a fruitful one, though it exposes its author to the combined attack of the two schools which have hitherto divided the field of philosophy between them."

HANDBOOK OF PSYCHOLOGY. PART I. SENSES AND INTELLECT. By JAMES MARK BALDWIN, M.A., LL.D., Professor in Princeton College. Second Edition, Revised. 8vo. 8s. 6d. net.

HANDBOOK OF PSYCHOLOGY. PART II. FEELING AND WILL. By JAMES MARK BALDWIN, M.A., Ph.D., Professor in Princeton College. 8vo. 8s. 6d. net.

NATURE.—"Well arranged, carefully thought out, clearly and tersely written, it will be welcomed in this country as it has been welcomed in America. That it views psychology from a standpoint somewhat different from that which Mr. Sully takes up in his *Outlines* will render it none the less acceptable to English students."

ELEMENTS OF PSYCHOLOGY. By JAMES MARK BALDWIN, Professor in Princeton College. Crown 8vo. 7s. 6d.

OUTLINES OF PSYCHOLOGY. By HARALD HÖFFDING, Professor at the University of Copenhagen. Translated by M. E. LOWNDES. Crown 8vo. 6s.

THE ELEMENTS OF THE PSYCHOLOGY OF COGNITION. By Rev. ROBERT JARDINE, D.Sc. Third Edition, Revised. Crown 8vo. 6s. 6d.

PSYCHOLOGY. By JAMES McCOSH, D.D. Crown 8vo. Part I., 6s. 6d. Part II., 6s. 6d.

        I. THE COGNITIVE POWERS.
        II. THE MOTIVE POWERS.

HANDBOOK OF MORAL PHILOSOPHY. By HENRY CALDERWOOD, LL.D., Professor of Moral Philosophy in the University of Edinburgh. Third Edition (Twentieth Thousand), largely rewritten. Crown 8vo. 6s.

THE METHODS OF ETHICS. By HENRY SIDGWICK, LL.D., D.C.L., Knightbridge Professor of Moral Philosophy in the University of Cambridge. Fifth Edition. 8vo. 14s.

OUTLINES OF THE HISTORY OF ETHICS, for English Readers. By Prof. H. SIDGWICK. Third Edition, Revised. Crown 8vo. 3s. 6d.

MACMILLAN AND CO., LONDON.

BOOKS ON LOGIC.

FORMAL LOGIC, Studies and Exercises in. Including a Generalisation of Logical Processes in their Application to Complex Inferences. By JOHN NEVILLE KEYNES, M.A. Second Edition, Revised and Enlarged. Crown 8vo. 10s. 6d.

A TEXT-BOOK OF DEDUCTIVE LOGIC FOR THE USE OF STUDENTS. By P. K. RAY, D.Sc., Professor of Logic and Philosophy, Presidency College, Calcutta. New Edition. Globe 8vo. 4s. 6d.

By W. STANLEY JEVONS, F.R.S.
Late Professor of Political Economy in University College.

PRIMER OF LOGIC. Pott 8vo. 1s.

ELEMENTARY LESSONS IN LOGIC, Deductive and Inductive, with Copious Questions and Examples, and a Vocabulary of Logical Terms. Fcap. 8vo. 3s. 6d.

STUDIES IN DEDUCTIVE LOGIC. Second Edition. Crown 8vo. 6s.

THE PRINCIPLES OF SCIENCE. A Treatise on Logic and Scientific Method. New and Revised Edition. Crown 8vo. 12s. 6d.

PURE LOGIC: AND OTHER MINOR WORKS. Edited by R. ADAMSON, M.A., LL.D., Professor of Logic at Owens College, Manchester, and HARRIET A. JEVONS. With a Preface by Prof. ADAMSON. 8vo. 10s. 6d.

By JOHN VENN, F.R.S.

THE LOGIC OF CHANCE. An Essay on the Foundations and Province of the Theory of Probability, with special Reference to its Logical Bearings and its application to Moral and Social Science. Third Edition, Rewritten and greatly Enlarged. Crown 8vo. 10s. 6d.

SYMBOLIC LOGIC. Crown 8vo. 10s. 6d.

THE PRINCIPLES OF EMPIRICAL OR INDUCTIVE LOGIC. 8vo. 18s.

MACMILLAN AND CO., LONDON.

NATURE SERIES.

Crown 8vo.

POPULAR LECTURES AND ADDRESSES. By Lord KELVIN, P.R.S. In three Vols. Vol. I. Constitution of Matter. Illustrated. 7s. 6d. Vol. II. Geology and General Physics. 7s. 6d. Vol. III. Papers on Navigation. 7s. 6d.

THE TRANSIT OF VENUS. By Prof. G. FORBES. With Illustrations. 3s. 6d.

HOW TO DRAW A STRAIGHT LINE: A Lecture on Linkages. By A. B. KEMPE, B.A. Illustrated. 1s. 6d.

ON LIGHT. The Burnett Lectures. By Sir GEORGE GABRIEL STOKES, M.P., F.R.S. Three Courses. I. On the Nature of Light. II. On Light as a Means of Investigation. III. On Beneficial Effects of Light. 7s. 6d.

LIGHT: A Series of Simple, Entertaining, and Useful Experiments. By A. M. MAYER and C. BARNARD. Illustrated. 2s. 6d.

POLARISATION OF LIGHT. By W. SPOTTISWOODE, LL.D. Illustrated. 3s. 6d.

SOUND: A Series of Simple, Entertaining, and Inexpensive Experiments. By A. M. MAYER. 3s. 6d.

MODERN VIEWS OF ELECTRICITY. By Prof. O. J. LODGE, LL.D. Illustrated. 6s. 6d.

A CENTURY OF ELECTRICITY. By T. C. MENDENHALL. 4s. 6d.

THE CHEMISTRY OF THE SECONDARY BATTERIES OF PLANTÉ AND FAURE. By J. H. GLADSTONE and A. TRIBE. 2s. 6d.

THE CHEMISTRY OF PHOTOGRAPHY. By Prof. R. MELDOLA, F.R.S. Illustrated. 6s.

CHARLES DARWIN. Memorial Notices reprinted from *Nature*. By THOMAS H. HUXLEY, F.R.S.; G. J. ROMANES, F.R.S.; Sir ARCHIBALD GEIKIE, F.R.S.; and W. T. DYER, F.R.S. 2s. 6d.

THE SCIENTIFIC EVIDENCES OF ORGANIC EVOLUTION. By GEORGE J. ROMANES, M.D., LL.D. 2s. 6d.

ARE THE EFFECTS OF USE AND DISUSE INHERITED? An Examination of the View held by Spencer and Darwin. By W. PLATT BALL. 3s. 6d.

EXPERIMENTAL EVOLUTION. By H. DE VARIGNY. 5s.

TIMBER, AND SOME OF ITS DISEASES. By Prof. H. M. WARD, M.A. Illustrated. 6s.

ON THE COLOURS OF FLOWERS. By GRANT ALLEN. Illustrated. 3s. 6d.

FLOWERS, FRUITS, AND LEAVES. By Sir JOHN LUBBOCK. Illustrated. 4s. 6d.

ON BRITISH WILD FLOWERS, considered in Relation to Insects. By Sir JOHN LUBBOCK, M.P., F.R.S. Illustrated. 4s. 6d.

THE ORIGIN AND METAMORPHOSES OF INSECTS. By Sir JOHN LUBBOCK. With Illustrations. 3s. 6d.

THE APODIDÆ. A Morphological Study. By HENRY MEYNERS BERNARD, M.A., Cantab. With 71 Illustrations. 7s. 6d.

THE RIGHTHAND-LEFTHANDEDNESS. By Sir D. WILSON. Illustrated. 4s. 6d.

SEEING AND THINKING. By Prof. W. K. CLIFFORD, F.R.S. Diagrams. 3s. 6d.

MACMILLAN AND CO., LONDON.

THE EVERSLEY SERIES.

Globe 8vo. Cloth, 5s. per Volume.

CHARLES KINGSLEY'S NOVELS AND POEMS.
WESTWARD HO! 2 Vols. HYPATIA. 2 Vols. YEAST. 1 Vol. ALTON LOCKE. 2 Vols. TWO YEARS AGO. 2 Vols. HEREWARD THE WAKE. 2 Vols. POEMS. 2 Vols.

JOHN MORLEY'S COLLECTED WORKS. In Eleven
Vols. I. VOLTAIRE. II. III. ROUSSEAU. IV. V. DIDEROT AND THE ENCYCLOPÆDISTS. VI. ON COMPROMISE. VII.-IX. MISCELLANIES. X. BURKE. XI. STUDIES IN LITERATURE.

DEAN CHURCH'S MISCELLANEOUS WRITINGS.
Collected Edition. Six Vols. I. MISCELLANEOUS ESSAYS. II. DANTE: and other Essays. III. ST. ANSELM. IV. SPENSER. V. BACON. VI. THE OXFORD MOVEMENT—Twelve Years, 1833-1845.

EMERSON'S COLLECTED WORKS. Six Vols. With
Introduction by JOHN MORLEY. I. MISCELLANIES. II. ESSAYS. III. POEMS. IV. ENGLISH TRAITS, AND REPRESENTATIVE MEN. V. THE CONDUCT OF LIFE, AND SOCIETY AND SOLITUDE. VI. LETTERS, AND SOCIAL AIMS.

CHARLES LAMB'S COLLECTED WORKS. Edited,
with Introduction and Notes, by the Rev. Canon AINGER, M.A. Six Vols. I. THE ESSAYS OF ELIA. II. POEMS, PLAYS, AND MISCELLANEOUS ESSAYS. III. MRS. LEICESTER'S SCHOOL, and other Writings in Prose and Verse. IV. TALES FROM SHAKESPEARE. By CHARLES and MARY LAMB. V. and VI. THE LETTERS OF CHARLES LAMB.

LIFE OF CHARLES LAMB. By ALFRED AINGER.

THE POETICAL WORKS OF JOHN MILTON.
Edited, with Memoir, Introductions, Notes, by DAVID MASSON, M.A., LL.D. In three Vols. I. THE MINOR POEMS. II. PARADISE LOST. III. PARADISE REGAINED, AND SAMSON AGONISTES.

THE COLLECTED WORKS OF THOMAS HENRY
HUXLEY, F.R.S. Vol. I. METHOD AND RESULTS. Vol. II. DARWINIANA. Vol. III. SCIENCE AND EDUCATION. Vol. IV. SCIENCE AND HEBREW TRADITION. Vol. V. SCIENCE AND CHRISTIAN TRADITION. Vol. VI. HUME, WITH HELPS TO THE STUDY OF BERKELEY. Vol. VII. MAN'S PLACE IN NATURE, AND OTHER ANTHROPOLOGICAL ESSAYS. Vol. VIII. DISCOURSES, BIOLOGICAL AND GEOLOGICAL. Vol. IX. EVOLUTION AND ETHICS, AND OTHER ESSAYS.

MACMILLAN AND CO., LONDON.

THE EVERSLEY SERIES.

Globe 8vo. Cloth, 5s. per Volume.

THE WORKS OF THOMAS GRAY, IN PROSE AND VERSE. Edited by EDMUND GOSSE. Four Vols.

RECORDS OF TENNYSON, RUSKIN, AND BROWNING. By ANNE THACKERAY RITCHIE.

STRAY STUDIES FROM ENGLAND AND ITALY. By J. R. GREEN.

FRENCH POETS AND NOVELISTS. By HENRY JAMES.

PARTIAL PORTRAITS. By HENRY JAMES.

LETTERS OF JAMES SMETHAM. With an Introductory Memoir. Edited by SARAH SMETHAM and WM. DAVIES. With a Portrait.

LITERARY WORKS OF JAMES SMETHAM. Edited by W. DAVIES.

ESSAYS BY GEORGE BRIMLEY. Third Edition.

LETTERS OF JOHN KEATS. Edited by SIDNEY COLVIN.

THE CHOICE OF BOOKS, AND OTHER LITERARY PIECES. By FREDERIC HARRISON.

SCIENCE AND A FUTURE LIFE, AND OTHER ESSAYS. By F. W. H. MYERS, M.A.

THE WORKS OF R. H. HUTTON. CRITICISMS ON CONTEMPORARY THOUGHT AND THINKERS (Two Vols.). LITERARY ESSAYS. THEOLOGICAL ESSAYS. ESSAYS ON SOME OF THE MODERN GUIDES OF ENGLISH THOUGHT IN MATTERS OF FAITH.

GOETHE'S MAXIMS AND REFLECTIONS. Translated by T. BAILEY SAUNDERS.

LETTERS OF EDWARD FITZGERALD. Edited by W. ALDIS WRIGHT. Two Vols.

LIFE OF SWIFT. By HENRY CRAIK, C.B. Two Vols.

MACMILLAN AND CO., LONDON.

www.ingramcontent.com/pod-product-compliance
Lightning Source LLC
Chambersburg PA
CBHW081215170426
43198CB00017B/2615